# Guardians of Peace

## The Civilian Joint Task Force in Countering Boko Haram in Borno State, Nigeria

**Seun Bamidele**

*University of Johannesburg, South Africa /
Federal University Oye-Ekiti, Nigeria*

Series in Politics

VERNON PRESS

www.vernonpress.com

*In the Americas:*
Vernon Press
1000 N West Street, Suite 1200,
Wilmington, Delaware 19801
United States

*In the rest of the world:*
Vernon Press
C/Sancti Espiritu 17,
Malaga, 29006
Spain

Series in Politics

Library of Congress Control Number: 2025930805

DOI: 10.54094/b-bfc22e8ab7

ISBN: 979-8-8819-0212-4

Also available: 979-8-8819-0210-0 [Hardback]; 979-8-8819-0211-7 [PDF, E-Book]

Cover design by Vernon Press.

Cover image by Seun Bamidele.

# DEDICATION

It is a privilege to dedicate this book to my mother, who taught me that poverty does not define me. I also dedicate this book to my wife, Titilayo Bamidele, and my son, Jesulayoayemi Bamidele. Both endured my frequent absences during the fieldwork conducted for this book and always helped me put things in perspective. Your name, Titilayo, will be woven into my heart forever.

To all the inhabitants of Borno State in Nigeria who are longing for security and the means of earning a peaceful living in a quarrelsome nation: May your prayers for peace be answered, and may you enjoy the fruits of a stable and integrated community after suffering so much.

# CONTENTS

# LIST OF FIGURES

# FOREWORD

Jonathan S. Maiangwa
*University of Maiduguri, Nigeria*

I count it as a mark of respect to write the foreword of this book, *Guardians of Peace: The Civilian Joint Task Force Countering Boko Haram in Borno State*. I am persuasively fascinated by the level of dedication and commitment as well as the originality demonstrated by the author, Dr Seun Bamidele, to assemble this book at a critical time when research in violence-prone areas is difficult to carry out. I have closely related and worked with the author, and I have no doubt about his judgement and skill. He is a distinguished academic with vast experience in teaching and research in the field of Peace and Conflict Studies. He has made valuable contributions to edited volumes of books and journals and has attracted several grants and scholarships, one of which was by Gerda Henkel Stiftung, Germany, under the Special Programme on Security, Society and the State. This book, essentially focused on the activities of the Civilian Joint Task Force (CJTF) in Borno State, will undoubtedly enhance understanding and provoke more thoughts in this field.

Borno State, fondly known as the "Home of Peace", is renowned for its cosmopolitan settlement with international borders with the Republic of Chad, Niger, and Cameroon and a national boundary between the Adamawa, Yobe, and Gombe states. It used to be one of the most serene places in Northern Nigeria; social relations among its inhabitants and communities were very cordial, and small-scale economic activities such as handcrafts, fabric dying, buying and selling, livestock, and cattle herding and marketing are trademarks of the state. Although Islam is regarded as the leading religion in the state, Christianity and some forms of traditional worship exist side by side. The major ethnic groups are Kanuri, Marghi, Babur/Bura, and Mandara, while people from other ethnicities from other parts of Nigeria are also found in the state. The Hausa language is the predominant medium of communication. Before now, the state was not known for religious uprisings or communal clashes like some states in Northern Nigeria. However, as an agrarian economy, unemployment, glaring poverty, out-of-school children as well as street urchins (*Almajirinci*), and hawking is high, and the National Bureau of Statistics designates the state as one of the poorest in northeastern Nigeria. This is in view of the fact that the largest employer in the state is the government, as most urban and semi-urban dwellers are either federal, state, or local government employees.

This is interesting, since the First Republic of Borno State has always been on the side of the opposition party against the national government. However, the All Peoples Congress (APC) won the 2015 general election at the national level, and Borno State coincidentally found itself on the same page as the ruling party. Since the country's return to civil democratic paths in 1999, party politics has become a major preoccupation of both the political class and the youth population, and the latter is often used as political thugs at election times. More worrisome of this development is that the political actors have seized the opportunity to take advantage of a high level of illiteracy, ignorance, and poverty in the state to promote their political ambition. It is, therefore, against this unpleasant circumstance that radical Islamists (Boko Haram) emerged in the state to engage in proselytisation and use violence as its tool of mobilisation against the political class to denounce anything "Western", including Western education.

After the poor military strategy against Boko Haram in 2013, some youths formed a group called "*Yan Kato da gora*" in the Hausa language (CJTF) and staged a protest against Boko Haram in Maiduguri that successfully pushed the group out of the city centre and into rural communities. It is within the context of this book, *Guardians of Peace: The Civilian Joint Task Force Countering Boko Haram in Borno State*, authored by Dr Seun Bamidele, one of the compendiums on the CJTF ever written captures attention. He conscientiously explores the dynamics and gradation that stimulated the evolution of the concept of insurgency-related peace as a line of thinking for countering insurgency in Borno State. He argues that insurgency-related peace is a collective effort made by locals to reject violence in their communities and promote the right to local governance. Dr Bamidele seeks to explain the inner workings of the CJTF in relation to its insurgency response, providing a panoramic overview of counterinsurgency strategies by the CJTF in Borno State.

This eleven-chapter book is carefully organised and coherent. As an empirical study, it relies on ethnographic design to provide firsthand information on the CJTF to enrich our knowledge and inform us about the group and its operations. The book is an evidence-based, probing study with pictorials of the CJTF and figures and graphs that clearly demonstrate the validity of claims. In addition, Dr Bamidele explores the gender dimension to illustrate how women can play a critical role in counterinsurgency. Another important discussion this book touched on is the promotion of collective action against insurgency, for which the author drew an inference from David Galula's theory of inclusivity on counterinsurgency that highlights the role of the civilian population and security agencies in defeating radical movements and ideology. I hereby recommend this book to a wider readership as instruction and learning material for members of the academia, security experts, lawyers, criminologists, postgraduate students in the fields of Political Science, Peace and Conflict Studies, Sociology and Anthropology, Migration Studies, and Defence and Strategic Studies, and, very importantly, government agencies, policy- and decision-makers, and international organisations.

*Jonathan S. Maiangwa PhD*
*Professor of Political Science and Counterterrorism*
*Department of Political Science*
*University of Maiduguri, Nigeria*

# FOREWORD

*University of Jos, Plateau State, Nigeria*

In a security landscape that is fractured and disrupted by a plethora of actors, it has indeed become critical to ask the right questions. In the last decades since Nigeria returned to civil rule in 1999, scholars of the state and security provisioning, while still interested in who should be providing security, have also become interested in who is actually providing security. The State, through its mandated institutions, is increasingly finding it challenging to maintain law and order and provide adequate security for citizens. This may be due to a lack of financial and technical resources or necessary equipment as a result of competing demands in other sectors, the absence of political will, and, in some cases, the contradictions inherent in the origins and structures of state security institutions. There are varied non-state security actors cooperating with the state in providing security and, in other cases, competing with the state. It is this frame of state-non-state cooperation and collaboration that Seun Bamidele has explored in this topical, enthralling offering.

Since 2009, the Nigerian government has been battling the Islamist insurgency orchestrated by the Jama'at Ahl-Sunna Lidda'awati wal Jihad, colloquially known as Boko Haram. The key factor that has underpinned the insurgency is the group's extreme interpretation of Islamic doctrine. Boko Haram conveniently mobilised support and, in some instances, demanded compulsory conscription by harnessing the notion that broader Islamic piety had been fundamentally undermined and thus needed to be fought for. Furthermore, the group's anti-establishment position was welcomed by frustrated young men who saw recruitment into the ranks as an opportunity to oppose the ruling class.

The government counter-insurgency strategy found a willing and timely ally in the aptly named Civilian Joint Task Force (CJTF). The Borno State government formally endorsed the CJTF in 2013 as a partner in counter-insurgency-related efforts. The book documents how the CJTF has been an effective partner to the military in combating Boko Haram's activities in the region. The specific counter-insurgency requirement demanded the need for innovative approaches to counter the persistent threat of Boko Haram. In *Guardians of Peace: The Civilian Joint Task Force in Countering Boko Haram in Borno State, Nigeria*, Dr. Seun Bamidele offers a compelling examination of how local communities, through the Civilian Joint Task Force (CJTF), have stepped up to confront this challenge. Drawing on comprehensive field research and insights from David Galula's counterinsurgency theory, Dr Bamidele presents a detailed analysis of the CJTF's critical contributions to restoring peace and security in Borno State. The book seeks to underscore the importance of local initiatives in combating insurgency.

The book does not overlook the challenges associated with the CJTF's operations. It thoughtfully addresses allegations of human rights abuses, operational weaknesses, and the need for formal integration into Nigeria's security framework. Through this balanced approach, the reader gains a nuanced understanding of the CJTF's successes, shortcomings, and its potential role in ensuring sustainable peace in a post-insurgency era. Bamidele's analysis reminds us of the role local communities play in security provisioning, in this case, counter-insurgency-related peace efforts. This challenges the classical view of insurgency-related peace as the responsibility of the State or traditional security forces. The book also documents the lack of a systematic approach to integrating CJTF members into local communities and Nigerian security formations; this is emerging as an issue of formal and continued concern.

When we consider the bigger picture, the role that non-state security actors like the CJTF and others around the country are playing underscores the need to reassess the premise and focus of Security Sector Reform and Governance (SSRG) policy and strategy, a serious policy and strategy will need to incorporate the role of non-state security actors. Bamidele's major recommendation is for the legalisation and institutionalisation of the CJTF as a formal local security entity, working with the military. The book advocates for a holistic local security approach, emphasising community participation and the increased involvement of women. Dr. Bamidele highlights how these grassroots efforts complement conventional security strategies, challenging traditional approaches to counterinsurgency and advocating for a stronger partnership between local actors and state institutions.

While the book is rooted in the experiences of northeastern Nigeria, its relevance extends far beyond the region. Scholars, policymakers, and practitioners nationally, across the region, and, of course, internationally - will find the book valuable for understanding the interplay between local initiatives and national security efforts. At a time when addressing global security issues increasingly relies on community-driven initiatives, this book underscores the importance of recognizing and providing a national framework for the engagement and management of non-state security actors. It makes a significant contribution to the fields of community security, counterinsurgency, and peacebuilding, emphasizing the vital role of grassroots participation in resolving modern security crises.

Dr. Bamidele's extensive experience in conflict, security and development studies shines through in this work. His commitment to rigorous research and his deep connection to the subject matter make this book an essential resource for understanding the complex dynamics of hybrid counter-insurgency and peacebuilding. As the world faces evolving security threats, *Guardians of Peace* serves as a vital reminder of the power of community-led efforts in creating lasting solutions. It is therefore my pleasure to wholeheartedly recommend this book, and I am confident that it will spark meaningful conversations and inspire innovative strategies to address security challenges in Nigeria and beyond.

*Dr. Jimam T. Lar*
*University of Jos, Plateau State, Nigeria*

# PREFACE

This book seeks to provide a renewed understanding of insurgency-related peace by emphasising the significance of local insurgency-related peace initiatives. The term "insurgency-related peace" describes the collective efforts made by locals to reject violent insurgency, secure their rights to self-protection and local governance, and protect their lives. The book adopts a qualitative, ethnographic approach within the context of insurgency-related peace discourse and focuses on the Civilian Joint Task Force (CJTF), an insurgency-related peace group in Borno State, Nigeria. It aims to evaluate the potential of unconventional local insurgency-related peace measures and offer insights into how insurgency-related peace initiatives can be more successful in combatting Islamic extremism in Nigeria. By directing attention to the role of local community members in insurgency-related peace efforts, this book challenges the orthodox view of insurgency-related peace as the sole responsibility of the state or traditional security measures.

The rise of religious insurgency in the twenty-first century has led to the formation of several insurgency-related peace groups employing various strategies. The CJTF, also known as Durza Ka in the Kanuri language, has emerged as a major player in Borno State, Nigeria. It was formed as a response to the atrocities committed by the Boko Haram insurgency, starting as a call for volunteers in 2009 by locals. The group, now totalling over 26,000 men and women, has become a critical player in ending Boko Haram's reign of terror. The literature on this topic focuses on the challenges these insurgents pose to civilians and the insurgency-related peace efforts of the state, including military operations. Nevertheless, little is known about the CJTF specifically.

This book aims to bridge this gap and provide a qualitative, ethnographic analysis of the group, using David Galula's insurgency-related peace theory to examine its actions and contest the dualistic understanding of conventional vs unconventional local insurgency-related peace approaches. The goal is to establish the value of the CJTF insurgency-related peace group, position unconventional local insurgency-related peace movements as a viable complement to conventional methods and offer insights into how insurgency-related peace initiatives can effectively combat Islamic insurgency in Nigeria.

Boko Haram is one of the most notorious insurgent groups in Africa. It has caused the death of thousands of locals in Borno State since its activities began in 2009. The group's motivations are based on issues such as the implementation of the Salafi doctrine in the caliphate, claims of religious superiority, corruption among political leaders, and fear of religious domination. Thus, violent insurgency has devastated Borno State for more than 10 years, leaving visible impacts on itssociety with serious implications for insurgency-related peace, security, and development in the country.

In response to the actions of Boko Haram, locals in Borno State began organising meetings calling for armed resistance against the group's atrocities. Over time, their insurgency-related peace efforts have evolved into a well-organised group of at least 26,000 members, who regularly collaborate with the military in both urban and rural communities. They are armed with weapons such as dynamite, advanced firearms, cutlasses, and charms.

The Borno State government formally endorsed the CJTF in 2013 as a pragmatic insurgency-related peace strategy in response to the devastation caused by Boko Haram. However, despite joint insurgency-related peace efforts between the CJTF and the military, debates have arisen about their alliance, and there remains a deep-seated distrust between them. Moreover, there is limited knowledge about the CJTF as an organised insurgency-related peace group.

The CJTF has gained notoriety, being accused of acts of hooliganism, robbery, vandalism, rape, and thuggery. Despite these allegations, the CJTF remains armed and strong, growing in size. This is due to a prevailing atmosphere of suspicion and fear among locals, who believe that the CJTF is necessary for their protection both from one another and from Boko Haram attacks. The concern is that if the CJTF were to be disarmed and disbanded, the locals would be vulnerable to the insurgency-related peace efforts of the state, i.e., military operations. As a result, some see CJTF members as unsung heroes who are necessary for the survival of locals in the state.

The primary focus of the book is the problem of the security threat posed by Boko Haram extremism in Borno State, the limitations of the military in addressing the insurgency, and the history, character, and strategies of the local group, CJTF, which has risen against the insurgency. Moreover, the alliance between the military and CJTF raises important questions about the significance and role of a local, nontraditional movement not initially trained in military warfare and their involvement in insurgency-related peace efforts. Some view this as conflicting with the military's objectives, while others recognise the importance of local, community-led security architectures in addressing specific security challenges in an area. Many argue that local security groups are better equipped to identify the enemy, have better knowledgeof the terrain, and possess stronger intelligence-gathering abilities than the military, while scholars have focused mainly on the political, military, and law enforcement approaches implemented by the government. Nevertheless, the Nigerian military's choice to involve the CJTF in insurgency-related peace operations in Borno State has sparked new discussions on community self-defence and civilian-military cooperation.

Therefore, the book aims to examine the group's potential as an effective insurgency-related peace tool by applying David Galula's insurgency-related peace theory to analyse its actions and challenge the traditional dichotomy of conventional vs unconventional local insurgency-related peace.

# ACKNOWLEDGEMENTS

This book is the result of a long and inspiring research process, during which I have collected many experiences and met several people who helped and encouraged me to discover the richness and potentialities of the topic.

The research for this book was enabled by a generous grant from Gerda Henkel Stiftung, Germany, under the Special Programme on Security, Society and the State scholarship, which supported the fieldwork on which most of this book is based.

An ethnographer is a burdensome presence in the lives of study participants: As I need guidance to accomplish basic tasks in unfamiliar cultural settings, I ask tedious questions about why people are doing what they are doing, and I always watch and listen. In other words, as an ethnographer, I ask much of my study participants, and I am infinitely grateful to everyone in Maiduguri who generously gave me their time, energy, and perspectives. Since my degree, I am especially indebted to my host, Prof Jonathan Maiangwa. Particular thanks are also extended to Dr Olusegun Idowu, Mr Segun Omolayo, Dr Samuel Oyewole, and the late Mr Abubarkar Musa, who were extraordinarily patient and helpful throughout my fieldwork. They helped me make connections, talked to me about their lives, and even assisted me in navigating the opaque insurgency and conflict zones. I would also like to thank the CJTF, as an insurgency-related peace group, for providing me with logistical support and a base of operations. The members were central to the progress of my research. To all of you, *Na go de.*

I express my deepest gratitude to my mentors and colleagues, who provided both intellectual and moral support throughout this process. For guidance and comments on various versions of this work, I thank Prof Anthony Diala, Dr Bonnie Ayodele, Prof Azeez Olaniyan, Dr Samuel Oyewole, Prof Jim Lar, and Prof Kunle Ajayi. I would also like to thank the peer reviewers, whose constructive suggestions helped to strengthen this book. I also want to thank my colleagues for providing me with an intellectually stimulating and warmly collegial environment in which to write this manuscript.

Parts of Chapters 5 and 6 were previously published in two journal articles: "Securing through the failure to secure? Civilian Joint Task Force and Counter-Insurgency Operations in the North-Eastern Region of Nigeria", which appeared in the *Journal of African-Centered Solutions in Peace and Security*, Volume 4, Issue 1, and "Sweat is Invisible in the Rain': Civilian Joint Task Force and Counter-Insurgency in Borno State, Nigeria", which appeared in *Security and*

*Defence Quarterly*, Volume 31, Issue 4. Earlier versions of Chapters 4 and 6 were published in the following articles: "The Civilian Joint Task Force and the Struggle Against Insurgency in Borno State, Nigeria", in the *African Conflict and Peacebuilding Review*, Volume 7, Issue 2 as a briefing, and "Creating the Deserved Protection: Reflections on Civilian Joint Task Force (CJTF) Counter-Insurgency Operations in the North-Eastern Region of Nigeria" in the *Journal of Law, Society and Development*, Volume 4, Issue 1.

Many thanks go to the editorial service of Dr ML Klos, Mrs Jane Mqamelo and Ms Ingrid Kluyts, they shepherded this book project through completion. I have greatly appreciated their careful, timely management of all aspects of the editorial and production process.

I deeply appreciate my family, who spurred me on from fieldwork to a finished manuscript. To my spouse and partner in life, Titilayo Bamidele, it is hard to overstate what you did to make this book possible. From your long-distance moral support during my many months of fieldwork to your careful readings and thoughtful feedback on every single chapter at every single stage of its development to your sweetly uninhibited enthusiasm for this project, you saw it through with me from start to finish. Finally, to my parents, thank you for the love of learning and curiosity about the world you instilled in me all my life.

The author gratefully acknowledges the Gerda Henkel Foundation Duesseldorf for their invaluable support towards his research, which this book is based on.

# INTRODUCTION

The conflict between the Nigerian state and Boko Haram has been one of the most devastating insurgencies in recent African history. The Boko Haram insurgency, which began in the early 2000s, escalated significantly in 2009, causing widespread destruction, death, and displacement in northeastern Nigeria, particularly in Borno State. As the conflict raged, the Nigerian military struggled to contain the insurgency, and despite various military operations, Boko Haram continued its violent campaign, leading to questions about the effectiveness of traditional state security efforts in addressing the insurgency. However, a significant shift occurred when local communities, increasingly frustrated by the inability of the state to protect them, began to organize their own defence initiatives. One such initiative, the Civilian Joint Task Force (CJTF), emerged as a local militia that played a crucial role in complementing the state's security efforts and confronting the Boko Haram insurgents. This book seeks to explore the emergence, evolution, and impact of the CJTF and to examine its significance as an unconventional and grassroots-driven peace initiative in the face of a brutal insurgency.

This study is both timely and critical, as it explores a novel and often overlooked aspect of peacebuilding: the role of local civilian groups in counterinsurgency efforts. While most scholarship on insurgencies and counterinsurgency focuses on the military or state-led efforts to combat insurgent groups, this book shifts the focus to local civilian initiatives. The CJTF, a group initially formed out of desperation to defend local communities, has evolved into a formidable force that has become a vital partner in the fight against Boko Haram. Its contribution to local security in Borno State, particularly in terms of intelligence gathering, local knowledge, and community mobilization, challenges traditional approaches to counterinsurgency, which often exclude civilian actors or treat them as secondary to the military.

The book traces the history of the CJTF from its origins in 2009, when local volunteers began organizing in response to Boko Haram's increasing violence, to its eventual formal recognition by the Borno State government in 2013. During this time, the CJTF has grown from a loose network of vigilantes into a highly organized and structured militia of more than 26,000 men and women. It has played a central role in defending local communities, gathering intelligence, and providing critical support to the Nigerian military. The CJTF's growing role and influence in the fight against Boko Haram is emblematic of a broader shift in how insurgency-related peace is conceptualized and operationalized. The book contends that the CJTF's efforts represent a new model of peacebuilding that is based on the active involvement of local communities in securing their own peace and stability, rather than relying solely on top-down interventions from state forces.

At its core, this study presents a challenge to the prevailing view that insurgency-related peace is the sole responsibility of the state and its military. While the military's role is undeniably important, this book argues that it is not sufficient to combat insurgency and restore peace without the active participation of local communities. The CJTF provides a powerful example of how local groups can fill the gaps left by state security forces, offering a valuable complement to traditional counterinsurgency strategies. The book emphasizes the importance of integrating local initiatives into the broader peace process and security framework, arguing that such efforts are essential to achieving lasting peace in conflict zones.

The study also addresses the complexities and challenges that arise from civilian-led security initiatives like the CJTF. While the group has been widely recognized for its successes in curbing Boko Haram's activities, it has also faced criticism and controversy. The CJTF has been accused of committing human rights abuses, including extortion, arbitrary arrests, and violent reprisals against suspected insurgents. These issues have led to debates about the role of untrained civilians in security operations, with some arguing that the CJTF's actions may ultimately undermine peace and security rather than promote it. This book does not shy away from these criticisms but seeks to engage with them critically, exploring the delicate balance between the CJTF's positive contributions to local security and the potential risks posed by its unchecked actions.

Furthermore, the study considers the future of the CJTF and the challenges it will face in a post-insurgency Nigeria. As the conflict with Boko Haram winds down, there are growing concerns about what will become of the CJTF. Should it be disbanded, or can it be integrated into a more formalized and regulated security structure? The book offers recommendations for how the CJTF can be institutionalized and incorporated into the broader security framework of Borno State and Nigeria. By exploring the group's successes, challenges, and future prospects, the study provides valuable insights into how local militia groups can be effectively managed and integrated into long-term peace and security strategies.

## Contextualizing the Study

The significance of this book lies in its contribution to the ongoing debates on insurgency, counterinsurgency, and peacebuilding. Insurgencies and violent extremism are not isolated to Nigeria; they are global issues that affect many regions, from the Middle East to Southeast Asia, and sub-Saharan Africa to Central America. As the international community grapples with the challenge of combating insurgencies and violent extremism, the role of local communities in addressing these threats has become a focal point for scholars and policymakers alike. This book builds on existing scholarship in the fields of counterinsurgency, peace studies, and security studies by offering a nuanced examination of how local civilian groups can play a central role in addressing the challenges posed by insurgency.

In particular, the book draws on the work of scholars who have examined the importance of local knowledge and community participation in counterinsurgency efforts. Theories of counterinsurgency, such as those articulated by David Galula (1964), emphasize the need for a comprehensive strategy that incorporates both military and civilian elements. Galula's framework, which focuses on winning the hearts and minds of the local population, underscores the importance of local involvement in counterinsurgency operations. This book extends Galula's ideas by showing how local militias, like the CJTF, can actively contribute to the security and peacebuilding process. By focusing on the CJTF's evolution, operational strategies, and collaboration with the military, the book highlights how local actors can be integral to the success of counterinsurgency operations.

Moreover, the book engages with the literature on peacebuilding and post-conflict reconstruction, which often stresses the importance of community involvement in rebuilding societies torn apart by conflict. As the world increasingly recognizes that sustainable peace cannot be imposed from the outside, but must be built from within, this book makes an important contribution by demonstrating the value of local peace initiatives. The CJTF's success in Borno State provides a compelling case for why local groups should be considered central players in peacebuilding efforts.

### The Contribution of Bamidele's Research

Bamidele's research represents a significant contribution to the literature on local insurgency-related peace efforts, offering new insights into the role of civilian-led initiatives in countering Boko Haram and other insurgent groups. His work is particularly noteworthy for its focus on the CJTF, a local militia that has played an outsized role in securing peace in Borno State. By conducting original fieldwork and analyzing the CJTF's operations, Bamidele fills a critical gap in the existing scholarship on insurgency and peacebuilding. The book's findings challenge the prevailing narratives about the role of state security forces in counterinsurgency operations and offer a fresh perspective on the importance of community-driven peace efforts.

Bamidele's work also engages with broader theoretical and methodological debates in the field of conflict studies. By utilizing a case study approach, the book offers a detailed, grounded analysis of the CJTF, providing a rich understanding of how local groups can contribute to peace and security in complex conflict environments. The study is firmly rooted in the context of Borno State and the Nigerian experience, but its implications extend far beyond Nigeria, offering lessons for other regions facing similar security challenges. The book's emphasis on the integration of military and civilian efforts, and its exploration of the future of local security groups like the CJTF, offers valuable insights for policymakers, practitioners, and scholars working in conflict zones around the world.

## Structure of the Book

The book is structured to provide a comprehensive examination of the CJTF and its role in insurgency-related peace. Each chapter builds on the previous one, offering both a historical and theoretical analysis of the CJTF's emergence, development, and impact. Chapter 1 introduces the CJTF and its origins, setting the stage for the rest of the book. Chapters 2 and 3 provide a theoretical framework and review of relevant literature, highlighting the importance of local security initiatives in counterinsurgency. Chapters 4 through 7 provide a detailed analysis of the CJTF's operations, strategies, and collaboration with the military. Chapter 8 focuses on the operational skills of the CJTF and its contributions to intelligence gathering, while Chapter 9 evaluates the group's effectiveness and the challenges it faces. Chapter 10 addresses the broader challenges facing the CJTF, including legal issues, military training, and criticisms of its tactics. Finally, Chapter 11 concludes the book by offering recommendations for strengthening the CJTF's role in the future of Borno State's security landscape.

## Conclusion

This book offers an in-depth exploration of the CJTF's role in insurgency-related peace in Borno State, Nigeria. By focusing on the contributions of this local, civilian-led security group, it challenges conventional notions of counterinsurgency and peacebuilding. Through a detailed analysis of the CJTF's strategies, successes, and challenges, this work makes a significant contribution to the field of conflict resolution and peace studies. The book emphasizes the need for a more integrated approach to security, one that includes both military and civilian actors working together to combat insurgency and build sustainable peace. In doing so, it provides valuable lessons for policymakers, scholars, and practitioners working in conflict-affected regions around the world.

# CHAPTER ONE
# INTRODUCTION: CIVILIAN JOINT TASK FORCE'S INSURGENCY-RELATED PEACE OPERATIONS IN BORNO STATE

## Introduction

In contemporary Nigeria, where intercommunal wars are becoming less common, insurgent groups operating for social, economic, religious, political, or ethnic reasons are responsible for most new wars (Bamidele, 2020; Watson, 2023). One such group is Boko Haram, operating in northeast Nigeria. Since its formation in 2002, and particularly since 2009, Boko Haram (not originally named as such) has become increasingly violent, initially focusing its attention on the police and other authorities but eventually moving to attacks on churches, schools, newspaper offices, and other public spaces (Adesoji, 2010, 2011). It has caused numerous deaths among locals in Borno State since 2009 as part of its stated goal of establishing a "pure" Islamic state ruled by Sharia law. It advocates a return to the Salafi doctrine and way of life, views the Nigerian political system as irredeemably corrupt, and rejects what it views as religious domination by moderate Muslims (Adesoji, 2010, 2011; Bamidele, 2018b). Its violent insurgency has devastated Borno State for over a decade, leaving a visible impact on its society with serious implications for local security and national development.

In a country as conflict-ridden as Nigeria, it is not unusual for local people to form counterinsurgency groups to defend their communities. One such group is the CJTF, known as "Yan Kato da Gora" in the Hausa language, which is located in Borno State. The CJTF has emerged as a child of necessity, forced into existence by the incessant and spontaneous atrocities of Boko Haram.

Much of the literature on the topic of insurgency focuses on the challenges posed by insurgents to locals and formal military operations (Nagl, 2002; Skjelderup & Ainashe, 2023). This study focuses on counterinsurgency, particularly the CJTF, which has become a necessary feature of daily life in Borno State. Since 2011, the CJTF's rudimentary insurgent peace operations have evolved into an organised and active group of at least 26,000 members who regularly collaborate with the military in both urban and rural areas. They are now armed with dynamite, guns, cutlasses, and "charms" (Idris et al., 2014; Hassan, 2015; International Crisis Group, 2017). Of particular interest is the way in which this once informal cluster of disaffected youth has metamorphosed into an established insurgency-related peace operation, recognised and, indeed, relied upon by the national army of Nigeria in Borno State. In 2013, the CJTF was initially established as a youth vanguard programme and later evolved into a pragmatic insurgency-related peace strategy (Bamidele, 2017, 2020, 2023; Agbiboa, 2018; Agbiboa, 2020; Owonikoko & Onuoha, 2019).

However, despite the joint operations between the CJTF and the military, there remains deep-seated distrust between the two groups, and the CJTF has gained notoriety for accusations of hooliganism, robbery, vandalism, rape, and thuggery (Bamidele, 2020). Nonetheless, the group has remained strong, and even in the face of its purported criminal activities, locals still want them around for protection, owing to a prevailing atmosphere of suspicion and fear of Boko Haram.

It is evident from the functional role of the CJTF that they provide local security, and residents are concerned that they would be left unprotected if the CJTF ceased to exist. Since the group is effective, its members are widely considered heroes who are essential to the survival of local communities in Borno State. This book takes the stance that local security architecture, currently separate from the national army and police, forms an essential and practical bulwark against Boko Haram's efforts.

However, the alliance between the CJTF and the military is not universally accepted. Debate rages constantly, and fundamental questions have been asked about the value and role of an unconventional, nontraditional, and localised civilian movement that was initially untrained in combatant warfare. The CJTF's participation in insurgency-related peace operations is regarded by some as antithetical to the overall objectives of the military (Hassan, 2015).

On the other side of the debate is the recognition of a locally led security architecture in managing the situational security challenges of immediate localities (Bamidele, 2017a, 2018a, 2018b; Idris et al., 2014). Many point out that local security groups are better placed to identify the enemy, with superior knowledge of the terrain and more effective intelligence-gathering capabilities than the military. In addition, supporters raise the issue that groups such as the CJTF are not uncommon in strife-torn regions and have become a necessity for otherwise defenceless communities in the face of a radical, ideologically driven insurgency group such as Boko Haram, against whom conventional military tactics may be ill-suited. Thus far, it would appear that scholarly attention has been predominantly directed at the military approaches adopted by the government (Hassan, 2015; Bamidele, 2018b). Little attention has been paid to the nature, operational style, and value of counterinsurgency groups such as the CJTF.

Debate about the group's existence was heightened when, at some point in 2016, the decision was taken to incorporate some members of the CJTF into the Nigerian army. This began with the commissioning of 250 members in 2016, a further 103 in 2018, and a further 400 in November 2020 (ICIR Nigeria, 2016). The men and women, all from Borno State, were trained, kitted, deployed, and paid as members of the army (ICIR Nigeria, 2016). Sociopolitical groups such as Afenifere, the Middle Belt Forum, and the Pan Niger Delta Forum have accused the government of "regionalising" the army and violating its federal nature. The Middle Belt Forum said that if the army wanted to recruit CJTF members into its fold, it should also bring in similar outfits in other parts of the country, so that there would be equity of representation in the army. In essence, the government was being accused of what it has long been accused of: upholding factionalism and promoting certain groups over others.

The incorporation of some CJTF members into the army has not, however, eclipsed the CJTF, which continues to operate as a separate group, acting independently of the army and occasionally in collaboration with it. This has allowed a fluid and somewhat indefinable situation to prevail in which the CJTF can act with impunity, unofficially recognised by the authorities and answerable to none. The development has opened new avenues of thinking about local self- security and tactical civilian–military alliances. It has not attracted great interest among security experts, which has left a gap in insurgency and peace literature.

Galula's (1964) insurgency-related peace theory contests the conventional understanding of military approaches to security and shows that an unconventional, locally based security component can play an essential adjunct role to conventional military operations. The current research sought to determine how the unconventional component has fared in peacekeeping in Borno State in light of many strongly held, opposing views on its existence.

The field-based study asked the following research questions:

- What factors necessitated the emergence of the CJTF as a peace-security measure?
- What is the role of the CJTF?
- How does the CJTF fit into the military's operational structure?
- What are the challenges associated with the CJTF's involvement in peace operations in Borno State?
- What policies could inform future insurgency-related peace activities by the CJTF and other similar groups?

## Notes on the research methodology used

A qualitative, exploratory, and single-case study design was used to analyse the drivers of local insurgency-related peace operations in northeast Nigeria. A case study, by definition, is a comprehensive, empirical investigation that analyses contemporary phenomena in a real-life environment in depth. It is especially beneficial when the borders between phenomena and their context are unclear (Yin, 2014). The case study design, with its emphasis on the real-world context, is appropriate for data gathering in insurgency-related contexts, where an overreliance on derived data (Bromley, 1986, p. 23) may not yield the same wealth and depth of information as a case study.

A single-case study design was used to collect extensive, in-depth data from numerous sources ina specific place about a specific group, with data gleaned from local security actors (the CJTF) and government security actors (the military) in Borno State. According to Creswell (2013), a single case study can be more helpful than one that seeks insight from multiple examples. At the same time, case studies may be vulnerable to selection bias, indeterminacy issues, and low external validity. Attempts were made to deal with these possible weaknesses through the employment of a focused logic of case selection firmly based on the research questions, aims, and objectives.

A qualitative research design was appropriate for the research because, although the topic did not lend itself to statistical testing, it could be qualitatively analysed, which would lead to theory development (George & Bennett, 2005). The qualitative research design also avoided "conceptual stretching" (Sartori, 1984), which is a problem frequently associated with statistical and largecomparative studies that subject quite dissimilar cases to a one-size-fits-all analytical framework. Furthermore, by allowing the identification and analysis of indicators that best embody the underlying theoretical principles, a qualitative research design may allow for high levels of internal validation.

The design was explanatory in nature, since the study sought to understand the inner workings of the CJTF in relation to its insurgency response. In addition to interviews with members of the CJTF and the army, data was gathered from secondary sources such as official records, reports, and unpublished documents, along with all the literature on insurgency and counterinsurgency in Nigeria.

The empirical research was conducted in Borno State, northeast Nigeria, which is home to four major ethnic groups – the Kanuri, Marghi, Babur/Bura, and Mandara. Minor ethnic groups also populate Borno State, but the Kanuri group and language are dominant. Religiously, approximately 85% of the state's population is Muslim, while smaller minorities of Christians and adherents of traditional religions each constitute around 7%, with the latter groups primarily concentrated in the south (Pew Research Center, 2015; U.S. Department of State, 2022). The state has three senatorial districts: Borno Central Senatorial District (comprising Maiduguri, Ngala, Kala-Balge, Mafa, Konduga, Bama, Jere, and Dikwa); Borno South Senatorial District (comprising Askira/Uba, Biu, Bayo, Chibok, Damboa, Gwoza, and Hawul); and Borno North Senatorial District (comprising Marte, Magumeri, Kukawa, Kaga, Guzamala, Gubio, and Abadam).

Three data collection methods were used to gather data from members of the population of Borno State in the three senatorial districts: semi-structured interviews, focus group discussions, and observation. Data was also collected through the analysis of documents at the study site.

Sixty semi-structured interviews were conducted with three groups of actors: local people, CJTF members, and the military. The first group comprised Borno State residents who were either knowledgeable about the topic or had played important roles in the pre-insurgency and insurgency-related peace operation periods. This group consisted of members of the public, traditional rulers, chiefs, elders, youths, government officials responsible for policy formulation at the local level, and members of nongovernment organisations working in various localities in Borno State. The second group comprised CJTF members and three leaders: the CJTF chairperson and two heads of intelligence. The interviews were conducted at command sites, including the CJTF headquarters in Maiduguri. The third group consisted of members of the military who had worked in Borno since the Boko Haram insurgency began. Field commanders were included in the military interviews.

Semi-structured interviews with these individuals guarded against bias, because they provided a flexible and open-ended approach to data collection, which allowed for diverse perspectives to be heard and prevented interviews from becoming too tightly controlled. Semi-structured interviews involved the use of a predesigned set of questions, so that all participants were asked the same core questions, which minimised the risk of interviewer bias (Corbin & Strauss, 2008). They also allowed for flexibility, since the researcher could adapt and add questions according to interviewees' responses. This allowed for interviews to be structured around the interviewees' ideas and prevented the researchers' own preconceptions, expectations, assumptions, and biases from intruding into responses. In addition, semi-structured interviews encouraged open and honest communication from the interviewees, who could express themselves in their own words (Creswell, 2007, 2013).

The interviewees were identified through purposive sampling. Out of 60 interviewees, 20 were locals, 20 were CJTF members, and 20 were military personnel. The interviews took place from May to November 2022. On average, each interview lasted between 60 and 90 minutes and covered a broad range of issues, depending on the respondent's experience or area of expertise.

Interviews are one-on-one, qualitative, in-depth discussions in which the researcher assumes the position of an investigator. This suggests that the researcher asks questions, directs the dynamics of the discussion, and converses with a single person at a time. In a focus group discussion, the researcher assumes the role of facilitator or moderator, adopting a peripheral rather than a central position (Nyumba et al., 2018). Five focus group discussions took place with local people and CJTF members who had lived for five or more years in localities affected by the Boko Haram insurgency. All were in towns in the three senatorial districts where the CJTF has bases.

Data was also collected through observation. The researcher observed the behaviour of the interviewees and focus group participants, noting their nonverbal cues, such as body language, gestures, tone of voice, facial expressions, and degree of confidence in what they were saying (Gray, 2009). Nonverbal cues can be extremely helpful in revealing conviction, uncertainty, or internal conflict.

In addition, published and unpublished documents were studied, sourced from the Centre for Human Resources Development and the Centre for Trans-Saharan Studies, Borno State. Local security reports, memoranda, minutes of meetings, and other authoritative documents were obtained from sector command centres in various localities in Borno State.

### Ethical considerations

Ethical considerations are a fundamental factor in any study, particularly when the study involves military or counterinsurgency operations where security is vulnerable, and, of course, in any study involving people. The researcher adhered to all relevant ethical requirements in gathering information to avoid causing harm or jeopardising operations, as described below.

Before commencing the interviews, focus group discussions, and observation sessions, the researcher asked interviewees to read a description of the study and give their signed, written consent to participate. Interviewees also consented to the use of an audio recording device and camera. They were informed that, should they feel uncomfortable or insecure, they were free to exit the interviews and discussions at any time.

Confidentiality is key in interviews and focus group discussions. Since there was a high chance that participants would be discussing sensitive information, all were assured that whatever they revealed would be used for research purposes only, and that their identities would remain confidential both throughout the research process and in the final report. The objectives of the study were clearly explained both in writing and verbally, along with details of how data would be gathered, stored, and analysed, and how the findings would be used. Participants' names were not used at any stage, either during or after interviews.

## Outline of the book

Chapter One, "Introduction", contextualises the study, explaining the CJTF's origins and role. It presents the study's objectives, methodological approach, and ethical considerations. It establishes the necessary background knowledge on the topic, showing how Boko Haram members' lethal activities have rendered the military incapable of moderating or stemming the sect's insurrectional acts. This provides the rationale for the rise of the CJTF, a growing group of civilians now approved by the government to keep the state free of insurgents.

The diversity of opinions on the CJTF's contribution to peace in Borno State gave rise to this study, which is, to the best of the researcher's knowledge, one of the few that closely investigates a counterinsurgency group in Nigeria.

Chapter Two, "Key concepts", explains the key concepts of the research. An understanding of the notions of security, insurgency, local insurgency, insurgency-related peace, counterinsurgency, and epistemic/transversal locals creates a fitting foundation for an investigation into how these concepts play out in Borno State, Nigeria. Most research demonstrates that the meanings of these terms depend on their context and the perceptions of whoever is using them. They might well be misconstrued if they are not understood in light of the research questions, aims, and objectives.

Chapter Three, "Theoretical and empirical approaches to insurgency-related peace", explains what theory and empirical literature have to say on the concept of insurgency-related peace. It describes the top-down approach to insurgency-related peace, whereby the state's military operations exclude local security efforts and thus fail to harness a valuable source of local knowledge, experience, and expertise. This is contrasted with the bottom-up approach in which the state actively incorporates local security initiatives into its counterinsurgency efforts. This approach has never been fully adopted, as it requires deep collaboration between the military and local people, which may go against conventional military thinking and practice. Indications are that there is an uneasy state of co-existence between the Nigerian National Army and the CJTF, in which the latter is recognised and relied upon but with varying levels of trust and success. This chapter also discusses local security strategies and experiences in establishing peace in the state.

Chapter Four, "Boko Haram and local security challenges in Borno State", explains the foundations of Boko Haram as a sect and the trajectory of its actions. It also examines the Nigerian federal government's unsuccessful efforts to quell the insurgency. The chapter shows that the military's collaboration with the CJTF has been limited to certain areas.

Chapter Five, "State security architecture and insurgency-related peace in Borno State", focuses on Borno State's security architecture, examining its military capabilities, challenges, and strategies for counterinsurgency. The state's security architecture is, of course, largely shaped by laws and policies that cover diverse responses to insurgency, so that, in theory, the state benefits from a coherent set of guidelines for action. The chapter evaluates the legislative provisions and the degree to which the state's security forces implement them. Lastly, the effectiveness of collaboration between the state's security forces and the CJTF is discussed.

Chapter Six, "The history of the CJTF in Borno State", explores the evolution of the CJTF, investigating the factors responsible for its birth and role in establishing insurgency-related peace in the state. The group is examined under the following subheadings: The origins of the CJTF, CJTF activities in Borno State, and the formation of the CJTF.

Chapter Seven, "Organisational structure and operational strategies of the CJTF", investigates the group's working system – its skills, intelligence, and information management, and how effectively it has adapted to the military's operational framework. The chapter describes the measures taken by the CJTF to supplement military operations in Borno State, such as monitoring internally displaced persons (IDPs), evacuating besieged villages, and staffing posts or stations in most towns. It goes on to discuss the military's perceptions of the CJTF. Whereas low-ranking officers interviewed in the study admitted that the CJTF made valuable contributions to stability in the region, high-ranking officers contested the effectiveness of the army's joint operations with the CJTF. Ultimately, the chapter validates the CJTF's pivotal role in securing peace in Borno State.

Chapter Eight, "CJTF's interventionism and insurgency-related peace in Borno State", investigates how the CJTF has intervened in the military's response to Boko Haram attacks in Borno State. In addition, it examines how the group has incorporated the military's insurgency-related peace strategy into its activities. The CJTF's interventionist role is evaluated in light of its successes and failures.

Chapter Nine, "Assessment of the CJTF's effectiveness", discusses the implications of the CJTF's insurgency-related peace operations, based on Galula's (1964) five attributes for measuring the effectiveness of local security initiatives in establishing insurgency-related peace. These attributes are grounded in the capacity of local security groups to draw on the resources provided by the state.

Chapter Ten, "Challenges to the CJTF's implementation of Nigeria's local security policy", explores the challenges faced by the CJTF in Nigeria. These challenges include the roles and functionality of local security institutions, the difficulties encountered as an unconventional, complementary combatant group working with an established military force, and the obstacles posed by the strategies they have employed.

Chapter Eleven, "Conclusion and recapturing", recaptures the findings and reflects further on the CJTF's efforts to promote insurgency-related peace and protect the local population. Conclusionsare based on all the significant areas covered by this study. The chapter concludes with recommendations and advocates a comprehensive and multifaceted approach to peace in local conflict-ridden areas such as Borno State, in which community intelligence gathering and participation are highly valued and incorporated into the national government's efforts.

# CHAPTER TWO
# KEY CONCEPTS

## Introduction

Certain concepts are fundamental to an understanding of the security challenges posed by Boko Haram and the responses of the CJTF. The military's operational and organisational challenges in the face of escalating insurgency have created fertile ground in which the CJTF has been able to take root and flourish. The group has finally won a measure of recognition from the Nigerian government, prompting debate in the country about the wisdom of engaging untrained civilians in counterinsurgency warfare. One of the concerns is that civilian involvement could jeopardise the role of the military. On the other hand, supporters view local community-led security efforts as a pragmatic response to an untenable situation that has destabilised communities for over a decade. Many believe that local security groups are better equipped to identify the enemy, know the terrain better, and have better human intelligence-gathering capabilities than the military.

Scholarly attention has predominantly been directed at political, military, and other law enforcement-related approaches (Abdullahi, 2015; Idu, 2019; Adeyeye, 2020; Onuoha et al., 2020). However, the military's decision to incorporate the CJTF in counterinsurgency operations has led to a new evaluation of security issues that support community self-defence and civilian-military synergies.

The term "insurgency-related peace" is used in this book to highlight a new understanding of peace in Africa as the result of a socio-spatial local counterinsurgency initiative or struggle. Insurgency-related peace involves the collective efforts of local communities to oppose violent local insurgencies and assert their right to protect their lives, occasionally against nonstate groups. In this empirical and theoretically informed analysis, the traditional, army-only approach to insurgency is challenged. The analysis directs scholarly attention to insurgency-related peace operations that involve locals who, in reality, have become crucial to maintaining peace in their localities.

The terms security, insurgency, local insurgency, insurgency-related peace, counterinsurgency, and epistemic/transversal locals continue to generate mixed reactions, depending on the perspective of the person using them. These concepts have been defined from various perspectives in scholarly works, making a critical review of the definitions necessary in this chapter.

## Security

The English word "security" originates from the Latin words "se-curus" and "se", meaning "without" and "curus", suggesting "uneasiness" (Mesjasz, 2004). Thus, the Latin word means liberation from uneasiness or a peaceful state of affairs with an absence of risks or threats.

The term "security" refers to a spectrum of conditions, ranging from the personal to the international. At the personal level, it refers to a feeling of physical and/or psychological safety, that is, freedom from physical threats and mental concerns. At the national level, and as used by politicians and the military, it generally refers to national safety attained by military strength. At the international level, it refers to the state attained by means of multipronged international peacekeeping efforts, which should contribute to amicable interstate relations and a reduction in threats.

Møller (2000) defines security in four ways: protection from physical damage, particularly killings; protection against attack or theft; protection from the possibility of future economic problems; and freedom from being vulnerable to a government's political or military takeover. Thus, the definition covers the full range of security levels: personal, community, national, and international.

Historically, on the international stage, national security has been viewed as a military matter, something that is maintained through the possibility of mutually assured destruction. In such a conception of security, the term becomes synonymous with power and the strategies used to attain it. Security is the desired outcome of an ideological struggle between the state and its enemies, which necessitates the defence of national sovereignty in terms of territory, citizens, and the state's system.

This position would occupy one end of a spectrum of definitions, ranging from "realist" military-based conceptions to more idealistic and multifaceted conceptions. Realism holds that security is tied to the state and can only be achieved through force or power; idealism posits that security can be achieved through collaboration and cooperation. The latter argues for a more inclusive approach to security that involves the participation of multiple actors, including civil society and nonstate actors.

Crawford and Hutchinson (2016) take this more nuanced and idealistic position, stating that security is a complex and multidimensional concept that arises from the interaction of many actors, each with their own values and identities. They argue that security can only be achieved through the recognition and promotion of these shared values and identities, which in turn can foster greater cooperation and collaboration among various actors.

Krause and Nye (1975) would appear to occupy the middle ground. They posit that security is a dynamic condition, not permanent but flexible, and subject to change according to context and time. To them, security is not an either/or proposition but rather a complex and multifaceted concept that requires a range of approaches and strategies to achieve.

Other scholars, occupying a range of positions on the spectrum, also offer valuable insights. Von Boemcken and Schetter (2016) state that security is the absence of severe threats to the basic elements of survival, recognising that acceptable levels of these elements will vary according to the context. To these authors, the crucial question to ask is, "Security for whom?"

Bamidele (2016) defines security as the absence of threat to nonheritable values – those that cannot be genetically passed on, such as identity, a nation's sovereignty, and people's well-being. The study later revised this definition due to the ambiguity of the term "absence", stating that security constitutes a low likelihood of harm to nonheritable standards.

Baldwin (1997) makes the valuable point that security cannot be achieved in isolation; actors without security will inevitably become a threat. Therefore, security must be pursued through cooperative and collaborative efforts and be sought by all parties in a given context.

Similarly, Otto and Ukpere (2012) argue for a positive conception of security, pointing out that it encompasses the presence of peace, which extends beyond the absence of crisis or threats and is built on equitable access to resources.

Oladeji and Folorunso (2006), too, contend that security extends beyond the physical protection of territory through military intervention and encompasses the provision of higher standards of living in areas such as health and economic, human, physical, environmental, and food security. They also state that, within the national system, security is linked to a low probability of attacks on a state's nonheritable values. They expand on the idea of nonheritable values, mentioning territorial integrity, political independence, cultural heritage, natural resources, economic stability, social cohesion, and human rights. Nonheritable values are crucial to a state's survival and must be protected and preserved from both external and internal threats. Oladeji and Folorunso (2006) state that a state's national security policies and strategies are often designed to safeguard its nonheritable values.

In its most general sense, security is understood as the absence or minimisation of threats to individuals or groups. Krause and Nye's (1975) conception of security, referred to earlier, as something dynamic and flexible, broadens one's understanding of the term  and accommodates all aspects of security referred to above. To Krause and Nye (1975), security is a construct shaped by an individual, group, or collective value system. It will adopt slightly different meanings depending on the context.

Krause and Nye's insight has implications for security policy and practice. By recognising that security is not a fixed concept, policymakers and practitioners can adopt a more nuanced and flexible approach to security that takes into account the evolving nature of threats and challenges. This could include a greater focus on preventive measures, based on an understanding of the root causes of conflict and instability, and possibly involve nonmilitary tools and strategies such as diplomacy and development assistance. This approach has the potential to lead to more effective and sustainable security outcomes than is possible with a narrower and more military-oriented definition. A definition that acknowledges the dynamism and multifaceted nature of security may be better aligned with the needs and aspirations of local communities.

It is worth noting that the concept of security extends beyond the protection of human life and property to encompass other entities, such as animal life, physical infrastructure, the natural environment, or an entire geographic region. Environmental security has not been extensively studied, in part, because it is unclear who or what is to be secured.

While security is not easily measured through quantitative methods, governments often allocate resources to ensure security, demonstrating its importance. National security requires comprehensive policies that protect citizens against all forms of threat, whether military or nonmilitary, foreign or domestic.

According to Oladeji and Folorunso (2006), Nigeria faces challenges in providing military protection, as it does not manufacture arms and ammunition and depends on other countries for such supplies. In addition, the country faces a high risk of harm to its nonheritable values, making it less secure. Oladeji and Folorunso (2006) highlight the complex nature of security and the need for a comprehensive approach that considers a broad range of factors to ensure the safety and protection of individuals, communities, and nations.

The concept of national security should not be viewed in isolation from individual, human security, which concerns whether or not conditions conducive to happiness are present in a society. Hendrickson and Karkoszka (2002), writing within the context of a nuclear age in which nuclear weapons threaten everyone's security, emphasise the importance of human security over nuclear security. Human security refers to protection from hunger, disease, repression, and other harmful disruptions. These authors state that the 1992 Report of the Palme Commission proposed the idea of "common security" amid the potential for global destruction. They contend that states can no longer pursue security at the expense of each other and that mutual security should be the goal of all nations. This is achievable only through collaborative efforts. Thus, security pertains to economic and political goals as well, not only military ones (Hendrickson & Karkoszka, 2002).

It is important that both theorists and practitioners understand the multiple and contested meanings of security as well as the implications of different conceptualisations. Ultimately, a more inclusive and holistic approach to security is needed, which recognises the diverse perspectives and experiences of different actors and communities and seeks to identify underlying causes of insecurity and conflict. Security cannot be achieved through individual efforts alone; rather, it is dependent on a system of interactions, collaborations, cooperation, and negotiations among various actors.

## Local security

Local communities are formed by evolutionary stages, and local security is often managed by groups that have agreed on standards and rules appropriate to the stage the community has reached. These will be relevant at the town or district level. The existence of local security strategies does not obviate the need for the state to play its role in maintaining local security (Community Tool Box, n.d.; Community Policing Consortium, 1994).

The concept of locality is abstract, multilayered, and complex, and the normative quality of local security may change if a locality expands its boundaries or its definition of security (Cilliers & Solomon, 1997; Netswera, 2023; Rahman et al., 2023; Agbiboa, 2021; Agbiboa, 2020). Therefore, describing localities based on local security goes beyond defining geographic boundaries. At times, it may require a dissolution of the idea of "local" and other identities that replicate unhelpful definitions of security.

The reasoning behind what constitutes security in any given locality is not predetermined. Local security may be seen as a function of integration, rather than local isolation, and often involves cooperation among groups (Sedra, 2010; Buzan & Wæver, 2003; Yusuf & Mohd, 2022). Whether or not this occurs depends on the identity adopted by people in a given location.

What emerges from the literature is that local security discourse is pragmatic; it is concerned with specific issues and precise solutions, as may be seen in the works of Al-Hindawi and Saffah (2019), Mokhoathi (2020), Baldwin (1997) and Rafliana et al. (2022). To make it easier to understand, security discourse focuses on who or what needs to be protected and why. While emphasising the importance of individual and local security, it is also essential to examine the reasons why a particular group needs protection (Baldwin, 1997).

There are two main perspectives on local security in the scholarly field. The first argues that the state should be responsible for providing security at all levels, since this establishes an intrinsic level of order in society that enables individuals to pursue their own interpretation of a good life (Levi-Faur, 2023; Khanyile, 2003; United Nations, 2012; Slaughter, 2017). This perspective asserts that the state can create a secure environment that fosters development and individual liberty.

The second perspective argues that local security should be based on the common norms, values, interests, and identities of a particular community, and the need to identify and minimise threats to that community (Global Partnership for the Prevention of Armed Conflict, 2019; Ulusoy, 2003; Anthony, 2024). This viewpoint proposes that local security may be achieved through both state intervention and local efforts. Achumba et al. (2013), Bello and Oyedele (2012), and Igbuzor (2011) believe that the state should only intervene if the locals are unable to secure their own environment.

The idea of outsiders as potential threats is a critical component of a local approach to security, especially in an integrated community situated in an area affected by conflict. In such circumstances, noting the presence of others who may pose a threat to the community is necessary for safety. Outsiders may well be a threat to the survival of the state as well (Pringle, 2010; Bryden et al., 2008). By identifying potential threats and taking the necessary measures to mitigate them, the community can maintain a sense of security and stability and prevent such threats from escalating to the national level. The state should, of course, be made aware of any threat and be kept abreast of developments, consulting closely with actors at the local level so that it is ready to step in as and when required. It should also make additional funding available to local authorities where threats do exist.

Some scholars maintain that the state has historically defined security solely in terms of its own survival (Wivel, 2019; Bryden et al., 2008; Korab-Karpowicz, 2023; Buzan et al., 1998). This approach suggests that the state only views security crises as threats when the survival of the state is threatened. This perspective is flawed, because it fails to recognise the importance of local security and its relationship to state security. Despite their different mechanisms and approaches, local and state security are closely intertwined and interdependent.

The concept of local security is comprehensive and requires an acknowledgement of several factors (Grimmick, 2023). These include the self, the threat, the actors chosen to deal with the threat, and the appropriate reaction. By adopting a narrow definition of security, the state may overlook the unique security challenges that local communities face (Weiner, 2006;

Boege et al., 2008). This can lead to inadequate and ineffective security policies that fail to address the root causes of security challenges.

In contrast, a more holistic approach to security would recognise the importance of local communities in promoting and maintaining security (Smith & Whelan, 2008; Terre des hommes Switzerland, 2024; Soomro et al., 2016). Local communities have a deep understanding of their own security needs and are often better positioned to identify and address threats. Thus, state security policies should incorporate local perspectives, and the state should engage with local communities to develop effective security strategies. By doing so, the state can create a more comprehensive and effective approach to security that prioritises the security needs of both the state and its citizens.

In Borno State, which requires a range of interactions, collaborations, and negotiations to maintain some measure of peace, security has sunk to an all-time low. It has become a highly complex topic demanding multiple considerations at both the local and regional levels. Ongoing insurgency has prompted a plethora of coping and safety mechanisms that vary according to the evolving tactics of the insurgents, which include ambush, rather than straightforward combat, and infiltration rather than outright aggression.

The insurgents have adopted a strategy that helps them consistently maintain high levels of funding, even though they are surrounded by instability, unrest, and ethnic conflict. In other words, despite their significant challenges, they have been successful. They are evidently well-organised and have a sophisticated operational system in place to achieve their goals.

### National security

At the national level, security mostly pertains to the management of national threats and is viewed as the pursuit of freedom from threats. Security requires the identification of both the threat and the referent object, with the threat constituting the possibility of harm to a valued referent object. National security concerns the dynamics and interrelationships between internal security, i.e., threats from within the country, and external security, i.e., threats emanating from transnational conditions.

Arnold Wolfers (1960) defines national security as "the absence of threats to acquired values, and, subjectively, the absence of fear that such values will be attacked" (Paleri, 2008: 52; Bot, 2023). Maier (1990, as cited in Romm, 1993) similarly defines the concept through the lens of national power, noting that national security is the capacity to control those domestic and foreign conditions that the public in a given community believes necessary for the enjoyment of its own self-determination or autonomy, prosperity, and well-being (cited in Paleri, 2008; Bot, 2023). Also highlighting the intertwining relationship between internal and external security within the context of national security, Moshe Keinan defines national security as

> ... the dynamics of a state's ability and readiness to deal effectively with external threats caused by rival states and rival organizations, and deal effectively with internal threats caused by parties inside the society, which put in risk the physical existence of the state's population, its identity, its values ant its vital interests (cited in Bot, 2023).[11]

Some authorities define national security in terms of demographic threats occasioned by epidemics, natural disasters, climate change, and other events causing severe environmental damage. These authors maintain that national security depends on the efficacy of the state in protecting its population from such threats and enacting swift and well-organised responses when disasters do occur – including the rehabilitation of communities after such events.

National security has two distinct components – internal security and external security. Maintaining *internal security* requires upholding and deploying national laws, strategies, policies, and state-level law enforcement agencies to maintain peace and law and order, and safeguard citizens from fear or threats to their values, livelihood, liberty, lives, and property within a country's territory. While several secondary law enforcement agencies may be statutorily empowered to advance the internal security interests of a nation, the police force (known as the police *service* in South Africa, suggesting an interesting shift in perspective not generally held by Nigerian authorities) is acknowledged as the lead agency for maintaining the internal security of a nation. In contrast, maintaining *external security* means preserving the nation's physical integrity and territory; maintaining its economic relations with the rest of the world on reasonable terms; preserving a country's nature, institutions, and governance from external disruption; and controlling its borders (Ibrahim & Bala, 2018; Bot, 2023; Ide, 2023). The primary responsibility for guaranteeing external security lies with a nation's army. Where other security agencies contribute, the military will, ideally, take command and direct all operational relationships.

### Insurgency

Insurgency is a battle or war initiated and sustained by belligerent organisations. Marginalisation, alienation, and inequality are seen as the root causes of insurgency and violence at all levels of society, including at the state, regional, national, and global levels. Insecurity arising from insurgency has resulted in the displacement or dislocation of people, the undermining of national

---

[1] Moshe Keinan is a renowned Israeli national security analyst and systems theorist.

sovereignty, and the depletion of national resources such as funds, technologies, and human skills (Internal Displacement Monitoring Centre, 2018; International Alert, 2016). Insurgencies may be national, such as when insurgents fight against national authorities, or global, such as when insurgents take up arms against the ruling class everywhere (Gurr, 1993; Malešević, 2010).

Insurgency has assumed a prominent place in development discourse (Piazza, 2007). Like security, it is a complex concept exhibiting diversity in terms of targets, character, strategies, and operations at local, regional, and global levels (Gurr, 1970; Kilcullen, 2009). There is also a great diversity of opinion among researchers, scholars, and security professionals on the means, causes, types, and modus operandi of insurgency (Kilcullen, 2009; Piazza, 2007). Moreover, the very idea of insurgency is debatable (Gurr, 1970). The response to insurgency involves the development of coping mechanisms and safety networks, as it is viewed as a network threat (Bapat & Bond, 2014).

According to John F. Kennedy, cited by Olanisakin (2016), an insurgency is a form of armed conflict that has ancient roots that have always been associated with warfare. In recent times, insurgencies have taken on new forms, including guerrilla tactics, subversion, and assassination (Gurr, 1970).

Insurgencies have evolved their tactics from straightforward combat to ambushes, and from aggression to infiltration, with the intention of eroding and exhausting the enemy rather than engaging them in open warfare (Gurr, 1970). It is a strategy shaped by the idea of "a battle of liberation", ironically adopted to undermine the freedom of ordinary citizens (Kilcullen, 2006). Insurgency preys on financial instability, ethnic conflicts, and political unrest, among other factors (Kilcullen, 2005; Mamman, 2020). Olonisakin (2016) sees insurgency as an extraordinary type of force, a new and entirely specific type of military action that operates under unique conditions and causes unique challenges for governments. It is critical for experts on insurgencies to understand the dynamics of battle.

Olonisakin (2016, p. 2) defines insurgency as "a savage subversion used to effect or avoid political control, as a venture to set up authority". This definition touches upon the idea of a social, political, and economic struggle, often against overbearing control by military forces. Essentially, an insurgency is a battle or war typified by asymmetry among belligerent organisations, where the insurgents may have been driven to desperate acts by the belligerence, in one form or another, of a stronger power. It may also be used to describe warfare among groups and various power blocs. Insurgents typically belong to vulnerable or smaller organisations than the forces they attack, with the authorities that combat their efforts constituting the more robust side of the battle. However, since the tactics of insurgents are often subtle, they may be difficult to counteract. Their arsenal includes manipulation and ideological indoctrination of a local populace and seeking to shift political energy away from the government towards themselves (Mamman, 2020; Kilcullen, 2010).

Insurgents generally resort to both armed, violent battles and social and ideological hostility in their warfare with the authorities. A powerful approach to curbing insurgency is to reduce the insurgent group's political performance and capacity to conduct its struggle (Gurr, 1970). It is important to study the various approaches followed to combat insurgency, drawing from numerous scholars' understandings of the meaning, targets, causes, types, and modus operandi of insurgency.

Counterinsurgency has a long history, dating back to the Greek and Roman empires, where frequent uprisings occurred in opposition to leaders (Mamman, 2020). Insurgency aims to overthrow the incumbent government and establish a new one with new social and political directives. Sheldon (2020) points out that insurgents employ various methods to instigate and propagate rebellion, including attacking religious and political institutions to subvert or weaken the state. Guerrilla fighters involved in insurgency tend to use specific types of weapons to defeat those in authority.

In contemporary times, insurgencies have evolved to include the ambush, infiltration, ideological indoctrination, and manipulation of local populations to erode and exhaust the enemy (Olonisakin, 2016). In their push to bring about revolution, subversion, and devastation, insurgents also make use of guerrilla warfare tactics (Gurr, 1970). It is important to note that uprisings seeking to effect changes in government are not all insurgency-based; such uprisings may include civil resistance by social movements that cannot be classified as insurgency (Britannica, 2023). Examples are Kwame Nkrumah's movement against the British authorities and colonial government in Ghana, the social change movement led by Martin Luther King Jr. against racial discrimination in the United States in the 1960s, and Mahatma Gandhi's political resistance against the British authorities in India (Martin Luther King, Jr. Research and Education Institute, n.d.; Nanda, 2012).

According to Evans and Newnham (1997), insurgencies can be divided into two broad categories: centripetal and centrifugal insurgencies. Centripetal insurgencies aim to convert orsubstitute modern-day authorities with what is beneficial to the insurgents and the people they represent. This type of insurgency was prevalent during the colonial era when authorities had the power to crush all opposition, leading insurgents to adopt diplomatic means of replacing governments. However, a centripetal insurgency can also be violent.

In contrast, centrifugal insurgencies aim to address the matter of a country's formation through secession from the mother state. They are often characterised by ethnic prejudice or jingoism.

Research by Evans and Newnham (1997) makes it clear that local populations may be involved in insurgency because of their ethnic-spiritual identity, sociopolitical loyalty, or the perception that they are being marginalised. Unconventional warfare, including guerrilla attacks and suicide bombings, is the main tactic of insurgency movements.

### Causes of insurgency

Some aspects of the causes of insurgency have been touched on above. Myint (2000) lists numerous causal factors, such as corruption, discrimination, tyranny, and abuse of power, the illegitimacy of the regime as a result of a coup d'état, inequality, injustice, a yearning for liberation and self-determination, poverty, the enormous reach of an army, the availability of small arms and light weapons (SALW), a disavowal of human rights, and fragile democracies. Dreher and Kreibaum (2016) add that insurgency can also be the result of greed.

Kilcullen (2005), too, notes that insurgency can stem from various sources, such as grievances resulting from economic, political, or social marginalisation. Hoffman (2011) argues that weak political systems are one of the fundamental causes of insurgency, regardless of its cultural, religious, or ethnic roots. In agreement, Muzan (2014) asserts that political division is the main factor behind insurgency, and that the denial of political freedoms can trigger conflicts. The lack of political freedom leads to feelings of marginalisation and alienation among the population, which can culminate in violence. A classic example prevails in the Niger Delta region of Nigeria, where the Ogoni people have been calling for better living conditions, and among the indigenous people of Biafra (IPOB) in southeast Nigeria. In most cases, authorities struggle to contain the insurgency, as it is often popular and widespread, a result of political marginalisation and exclusion (Paterson, 2023; Nwankpa, 2024).

Muzan (2014) cites class stratification as a motive for insurgency, noting that social class sensitivities can give rise to violent uprisings. Any community that has experienced a decline in its status may be the fomenting ground for insurgency. Marginalisation, alienation, and inequality have frequently led to insurgency and violence. This can occur at any stage or level of society, whether at the local, state, regional, national, or global level (Muzan, 2014). Muzan (2014) maintains that there is no state in Africa in which the lower class does not outnumber the upper or middle class; as a result, all African countries have a high potential for insurgency.

Muzan points out that all forms of discrimination against human beings and all forms of alienation from socioeconomic and political power can bring about insurgency. Discrimination or marginalisation may arise from social and economic factors, such as unemployment, corruption, and a shortage of adequate infrastructure and services. Most ethnic minorities in the geopolitical zones of Nigeria are plagued with social upheavals that amount to insurgency (Usman, 2015; Odusola et al., n.d.). Muzan (2014) posits that insurgents may draw strength from social miseries that have their origins in rifts within society. Insurgents may hire mercenaries to further their political ambitions (Muzan, 2014).

Galula's (1964) definition of insurgency is commonly used as an operating template to understand the various aspects of insurgency. Galula (1964) defines insurgency as  an extended armed conflict, methodically and properly ordered, which aims to attain particular, intermediate objectives and ultimately overthrow a government. Displacement occurs when people are forced to flee their homes as a result of insurgency, civil war, disasters, or a situation where the government or state authorities are either incapable, unwilling, or unable to protect them (Internal Displacement Monitoring Centre, 2019; UNHCR, 2019).

The high number of violent conflicts in Africa has resulted in extensive literature on internal IDPs (George & Adelaja, 2022; Joint Data Center on Forced Displacement, 2024). Insurgency and political conflicts arising from economic inequalities pose a significant threat to peace and security and consume resources that should be spent on health, housing, and education (Bellamy, 2020; Stewart, 2005). The seemingly endless cycle of violent uprisings and counterrevolutionary activities in Africa has displaced many men, women, and children who are tormented by long-lasting conflicts (Human Rights Watch, 2023).

At nearly any given time, about one-third of African nations are experiencing warfare, which is the main reason for the displacement of millions of people (Migration Data Portal, 2024). Deci and Ryan (2000) posit that conflict arises as a result of the "pursuit of incompatible dreams or pursuits by special agencies or individuals". This implies that all people and their social institutions have unique goals defined by their interests, and that these are in constant competition with other entities and their interests. As struggles over competing interests intensify, they absorb energy and resources, and economic activities tend to be neutralised, damaged, or eliminated (Onuoha et al., 2023). Haferkamp and Smelser (1992) and Simmel (2021) concur that conflict arises from the pursuit of competing goals, wherein individuals or groups attempt to outdo the competition or manoeuvre themselves into positions where they can realise certain objectives.

Britannica (2023) define insurgency as an organised movement to overthrow a constituted authority through subversion and armed conflict. This definition suggests that insurgents are not subtle but lethal, since they are determined to undermine the sovereignty of a country and seize resources. In addition, they employ illegal means that go beyond sociopolitical techniques to advance their cause (Mockaitis, 2011; Javed, 2010). As a form of war, an insurgency may take the form of protracted, asymmetric violence, the use of complicated terrains (mountains, marshes, jungles), psychological attacks, and political mobilisation to destabilise the locus of power in favour of the insurgents. These techniques are responsible for the failure of the Nigerian government to quell the Boko Haram insurgency (Okoli, 2019).

In the case of national insurgency, the main antagonists are the insurgents and the national authorities. The distinction between the government and the insurgents, in this case, may be described in terms of legitimacy, ideology, economic class, and identity, or it may be based on ethnicity, race, religion, or certain political factors (Fitzsimmons, 2008; Berard, 2018). In the case of "liberation" insurgency, the insurgents pit themselves against a ruling group. The ruling group is dubbed alien because of their identity. The preoccupation of liberation insurgents is to liberate a population from what they understand as imperialism (Mockaitis, 2011; Berard, 2018).

The consequences of insurgency may be seen in the vast number of killings and displacements across the globe, with Africa having the largest share, and Nigeria the largest share in Africa (Akubo & Okolo, 2019). A 2024 Global Terrorism Index claims that Nigeria has the highest number of people killed and displaced by insurgency (Center for Preventive Action, 2024). Most of the insurgencies are instigated by Boko Haram in northeast Nigeria and fuelled by the government's counterinsurgency attacks. States such as Borno, Yobe, Taraba, Gombe, Bauchi, and Adamawa have been at the receiving end of several insurgency attacks (Mudasiru et al., 2019; Akubo & Okolo, 2019).

Given the spate of Boko Haram insurgencies in Borno State, the sovereignty of this Nigerian state has been under severe threat. To cite an instance, Boko Haram insurgents managed to control 20 of the 27 local governments in Borno State at one point. At one point, Boko Haram insurgents managed to gain control over 20 of the 27 local government areas in Borno State. Their strategy for establishing control was multifaceted and involved both violent and coercive tactics. In many cases, Boko Haram did not directly replace local councillors with their own members; instead, they often employed a combination of intimidation, threats, and violence. Local councillors and officials who opposed or resisted the insurgents were frequently targeted, either through assassination or severe threats, to instil fear and enforce compliance. This strategy created an atmosphere where existing local governance structures were rendered either ineffective or nonfunctional.

The insurgents would often seize control of administrative offices and local government buildings, establishing their own governance structures in these areas. By controlling key locations and essential services, Boko Haram was able to exert significant influence over the local population. Their presence led to the widespread disruption of daily life, including the imposition of their own form of law and order, which included harsh penalties for those who did not conform to their rules. This level of control allowed them to further entrench their influence and suppress any potential resistance from local government officials or the general populace.

As of the most recent updates, Boko Haram no longer maintains control over the same number of local government areas in Borno State. Military operations and counterinsurgency efforts by Nigerian forces, alongside the efforts of local security groups and international support, have reclaimed several of these areas. However, the situation remains fluid, with ongoing security challenges and intermittent insurgent activities still impacting the region. The extent of Boko Haram's control fluctuates based on the current security dynamics and counterinsurgency operations. The attacks and counterattacks by state counterinsurgency operatives deployed in the area have caused many people to be killed or displaced from their homes, with those who can escape fleeing to internally displaced persons (IDP) camps (Buchanan-Clarke & Knoope, 2012; Brechenmacher, 2019).

## Local insurgency

Insurgency is almost always a locally generated violent uprising stemming from an experience of deprivation, alienation, or political marginalisation among a particular group.

Thus, local insurgency will often arise as a result of unaddressed grievances among a population who feel pushed beyond their limits in one respect or another. Misago (2019) and Khobragade (2010) argue that all forms of local insurgency, whether cultural, religious, or ethnic, arise because of a weak political system. Moreover, Muzan (2014) suggests that the predominant cause of local insurgency is political division. Thus, it is apparent that deprivation, especially curtailment of freedom due to political decisions, can lead to local insurgency.

A typical example of conditions that give rise to local insurgency is the festering, sordid conditions in which people in the Niger Delta live, which have provoked calls for improvements in the circumstances of the Ogoni people (Imobighe, n.d.). Another instance is the case of the Indigenous People of

Biafra (IPOB) in the south-eastern part of the country (Nwangwu, 2023). In most of these cases, authorities struggle to maintain the upper hand militarily (Crisis24, 2023).

Class stratification is a significant precursor to global insurgency, as social class sensitivities have the propensity to propel local uprisings (United Nations Development Programme, 2016). All forms of discrimination against human beings and alienation from socioeconomic and political power can bring about local insurgency. Discrimination or marginalisation may arise from social and economic factors, such as unemployment, corruption, and a shortage of adequate infrastructure and services (United Nations Development Programme, 2016; Seekings, 2003). Galula (1964) defines a local insurgency as a methodically and properly ordered, extended armed conflict that aims to attain particular intermediate objectives and ultimately overthrow a government.

The high number of local insurgencies in Africa has broadened the scope of literature on insurgency and combating insurgency in Africa (Johnson, n.d.). Local insurgency, triggered as it is by socioeconomic inequalities, is the bane of peace and security, absorbing resources that could better be deployed elsewhere (Paffenholz, 2021; Bøås & Dunn, 2017).

A prolonged state of crisis in Borno State as a result of local insurgency has resulted in what can be called "insurgent peace", which will be discussed in the next section.

### Insurgent peace

The term "insurgency-related peace" was coined by Macaspac (2020) to refer to a renewed understanding of peace in conditions where the dissatisfactions that gave rise to insurgency remain unaddressed. Insurgency-related peace is a peace that exists where the threat remains, which may be a necessary precursor to more lasting peace. This form of peace is attained through the socio-spatial efforts of local people who assert their right to self-protection and local governance within, and occasionally against, antistate groups such as Boko Haram. Zambernardi (2010) states that insurgency-related peace is the result of local initiatives and strategies to curtail local insurgents. It is ushered in by local people standing up collectively against violent local insurgency and asserting their right to security and local governance.

The conceptualisation of insurgency-related peace is challenging, given its ever-changing and migratory nature. This makes it unlimitable to a single definition. Insurgency-related peace is essential to the survival of any community afflicted by local insurgency. Macaspac (2020) states that insurgency-related peace refers to comprehensive local efforts and initiatives taken to defeat and contain local insurgency. It does not preclude efforts made to deal with root causes.

The concept of insurgency-related peace presupposes the presence of a weak state that is either incapable or unwilling to assert its authority and address insurgencies, whether through military means or by addressing their root causes. While local insurgencies challenge the existing order, insurgency-related peace initiatives aim to enhance state capacity and improve the status quo by addressing the underlying causes of the insurgencies. As Kitson (1971) notes, insurgency-related peace operations are not exclusively military operations, since local insurgencies are not primarily military, and military forces alone cannot provide a solution to the problem. Kitson (1971) argues that a whole-of-government approach is necessary to address the root causes of local insurgencies. He emphasises the importance of winning the "hearts and minds" of the local population and integrating civil and military efforts in counterinsurgency operations.

To comprehend the concept of insurgency-related peace, it is essential to consider the definitions provided by Galula (1964), Thompson (1967), Moore (2007), Petraeus (2010), and Macaspac (2020). According to these authors, insurgency-related peace can be defined as an integrated set of local security measures intended to end and prevent the recurrence of local armed violence or insurgencies, create and maintain stable societal structures, and resolve the underlying causes of local insurgency to establish and sustain the conditions necessary for lasting peace. In addition, it aims to guard against the causal factors of local insurgency (Galula, 1964; Moore, 2007; Petraeus, 2010; Thompson, 1967).

In establishing insurgency-related peace, attention is given to repelling attacks against the local population and limiting the scale and frequency of local insurgency. Importantly, effective insurgency-related peace activities transcend the provision of local security to include the maintenance of essential services, the preservation of a local administration, the restoration of state authority, the promotion of economic growth, and the encouragement of reconciliation (Galula, 1964). However, the role of the military should be limited to soldierly duties only (Galula, 1964); social responsibilities should be entrusted to locals.

To be effective, insurgency-related peace designs must encompass a combination of monetary, political, protective, and information components that strengthen a state's legitimacy, control, and authority while weakening local insurgents' ideological grip on the population (Galula, 1964; Petraeus, 2010; Moore, 2007). The model used must protect the local population from the atrocities of the local insurgents and attack the insurgency locally (Thompson, 1967). However, practical limitations make it impossible to implement all models simultaneously. Therefore, it is necessary to choose the most suitable model based on the specific context and circumstances of the insurgency and the local population (Zambernardi, 2010).

Achieving functional insurgency-related peace depends on distinguishing between innocent locals and local insurgents (the enemy) during combat. This necessitates the participation of locals as agents of local security, as they are best equipped to identify members of the local community and prevent collateral damage (Galula, 1964). A state can only secure the safety of its citizens with the support of the local population. Consequently, for optimal performance, a state must pursue only two aims and strategies: repelling attacks against the local population and preventing the incidence and frequency of local insurgency (Moore, 2007).

In line with Galula's (1964) stipulations, certain principles apply to the execution of insurgency-related peace. As has been made clear, an insurgency-related peace operation combines the efforts of both locals and the military, which simultaneously strive to annihilate every causal factor of local insurgency. Insurgency-related peace arises when a local insurgency group enters into a ceasefire or peace agreement with the government but continues to retain its objectives and armament. The primary aim of insurgency-related peace is to diminish violence and establish a framework for negotiations, while recognising that the fundamental issues that ignited the conflict remain unresolved. This contrasts with the more enduring peace that typically follows conventional warfare, which involves extensive combat between organised military forces or local factions, with the military intervening to restore stability (Petraeus, 2010).

Since insurgency-related peace requires the help of the local population, the route to attaining it may be long and convoluted. Both the military and local people need to take on specific, mutually agreed-on roles (Thompson, 1967). For this reason, state forces need to work on gaining the trust of the local population (Moore, 2013). The operation requires not only the elimination of insurgent elements but also the restoration of public services (Macaspac, 2020). In addition, local administration and state authority must be reestablished (Zambernardi, 2010), and economic growth and reconciliation encouraged (Galula, 1964).

Insurgency-related peace must be both adaptable and dynamic to effectively address local grievances while simultaneously combating insurgents, who are often local inhabitants themselves. To reconcile this approach, certain measures may need to be focused on the broader local population rather than solely on the insurgents. This strategy aims to strengthen the legitimacy and authority of the state, demonstrating its commitment to resolving underlying issues and defeating the insurgents. This approach is advocated by Thompson

(1967), Kitson (1971), and Kiras (2010) as a means of achieving state endorsement and improving the discharge of social responsibilities. However, the effectiveness of the locals is limited, and their efforts cannot fully compensate for the ineffectiveness of the accepted authority (Kitson, 1971; Kiras, 2010).

Moore (2007) describes insurgency-related peace as a cohesive set of local protective measures aimed at ending armed violence, preventing its reoccurrence, and creating and sustaining stable political and social structures. The extent and depth of collaboration between the military and the local population will determine the success of operations to combat local insurgency (Bundeswehr Center of Military History and Social Sciences, 2017).

The integration of local intelligence and actions with military efforts is essential for achieving insurgency-related peace. It aligns with Macaspac's (2020) view that insurgency-related peace heavily depends on local involvement. This approach emphasises the importance of collaboration, which is crucial for reinforcing insurgency-related peace efforts and leveraging the strengths and experience of military forces. Macaspac's (2020) strategy supports Galula's (1964) guidelines for implementing insurgency-related peace, as Galula's (1964) predominantly focuses on military and local actions. Local initiatives can augment the state's efforts to eliminate all structures and causal factors of local insurgency (Macaspac, 2020). Therefore, insurgent peace can be defined as multiple joint partnerships that combine local and military intelligence and action to eradicate local insurgency and effect lasting peace in disturbed localities, states, or regions (Galula, 1964).

Insurgency-related peace is typically more population-driven, focusing on locals securing a given population, than enemy-driven, where the focus is on a particular local insurgency group (Macaspac, 2020; Galula, 1964). While proponents of insurgency-related peace generally advocate the integration of both local and military resources, the achievement of lasting peace is heavily reliant on involving and empowering local actors to weaken and defeat local insurgency groups, while also enhancing the government's legitimacy in the eyes of local populations (Macaspac, 2020).

## Counterinsurgency

Counterinsurgency refers to comprehensive civilian and military efforts aimed at defeating insurgency and addressing underlying grievances (Rakoto & Rauchfuss, 2017). The United States Army Field Manual defines counterinsurgency as the "military, paramilitary, political, economic, psychological, and social moves made by a government to squash insurgency" (U.S. Department of State, 2009). A slightly more nuanced definition is provided by the United States Government Counterinsurgency Guide (2009 p. 1), which defines counterinsurgency as "comprehensive civilian-military efforts taken to simultaneously defeat and contain insurgency and address its root causes". This definition gives some recognition to the role of civilians, and both NATO and the US Counterinsurgency Guide mention the need to address root causes.

Taken together, these conceptualisations of counterinsurgency highlight its multifaceted nature. Skjelderup and Ainashe (2023) also mention the military, civilian, political, economic, psychological, and intelligence aspects of the phenomenon. The notion of counterinsurgency implies the existence of an insurgent problem arising in opposition to a functioning yet weak state. While insurgents always create problems with the prevailing order, counterinsurgents seek to strengthen order and circumvent internal problems (Kilcullen, 2010).

In addition, for a good understanding of counterinsurgency, it is pertinent to look at the definitions given by Moore (2007), Galula (1964), Petraeus (2010), and Thompson (1967). Their explanations of counterinsurgency may be summarised as an integrated set of political, economic, social, and security measures intended to end and prevent the recurrence of armed violence; to create and maintain stable political, economic, and social structures; and to resolve the underlying causes of insurgency, with the aim of establishing and sustaining the conditions necessary for lasting stability. Moore (2007) makes the point that governments need to guard against the causal factors of insurgency.

Thus, as with other concepts fundamental to understanding the situation in Borno State, Nigeria, counterinsurgency is clearly a complex and multifaceted phenomenon with strands that affect every aspect of military and civilian life. Meaningful counterinsurgency operations incorporate a mix of monetary, political, security, and information components that fortify a government's legitimacy, control, and authority while diminishing insurgents' stranglehold on the local population (Thompson, 1967; Moore, 2007; Galula, 1964; Petraeus, 2010). Galula (1964) states that counterinsurgency needs to attack the insurgents monetarily, socially, and politically (Galula, 1964).

Counterinsurgency operations also need to be mindful of the fact that defeat of the enemy at any cost is not the goal; there is also a need to keep local communities intact and functional. This will invariably mean close cooperation between counterinsurgency forces and local populations. Galula (1964, p. 7) sums this up as "it is better to entrust civilian tasks to civilians".

Zambernardi (2010) argues that "counterinsurgency is a strategy to curtail the insurgents while insurgency is a rebellion against a constituted authority when those taking part in the rebellion are not recognized as belligerents" (p. 18). The United States Department of State Counterinsurgency Guide (2009, p. 1) depicts insurgency as the organised use of subversion and violence to "seize, nullify or challenge political control of a region. As such, it is primarily a political struggle, in which both sides use armed force to create space for their political and economic influence and activities to be effective".

Zambernardi (2010) notes that counterinsurgency draws from three principal models: political, military, and monetary. The political model recognises the political aspects of the insurgents' cause and aims to address these by winning the hearts and minds of the local population. In essence, this means providing people with the basic services they need, taking care not to exclude political representation for any group, and promoting economic growth. The military model focuses on the use of force to defeat insurgents. It includes offensive operations to eliminate the insurgents' capacity to carry out attacks and defensive operations to protect the population from attacks. The monetary or economic model involves implementing programmes and initiatives that, like the political model, address the underlyingcauses of the insurgency, such as poverty, unemployment, and inequality. It aims to provide economic opportunities and incentives to the local population as a means of reducing support for the insurgents and increasing support for the government.

Zambernardi (2010) recommends that a standard technique for counterinsurgency is to select two of these models to avoid overstretching resources and losing focus. However, Zambernardi (2010) also notes that it is often difficult to distinguish between the local population and insurgents, which makes successful counterinsurgency challenging to achieve without some collateral damage. Insurgents dress like the local population, speak the same language, and may even share the same cultural and ethnic background.

In addition, insurgents may use intimidation tactics or violence to force the local population toprovide them with support, shelter, and supplies, making it difficult to identify who is truly sympathetic to their cause and who is being coerced. This creates a challenging situation for counterinsurgency forces as they must carefully identify and target the insurgents without causing harm to innocent civilians. Therefore, effective counterinsurgency requires a nuanced approach that integrates the three models while minimising harm to the local population.

According to Galula (1964), several key principles should guide the implementation of effective counterinsurgency strategies. A multifaceted approach is needed that combines the efforts of both the military and the local population to defeat an insurgency and eliminate its underlying causes. Unlike in traditional warfare, the strategies of local populations are typically the most dynamic and impactful components of counterinsurgency, with the militaryplaying a supporting role. As Galula (1964) states, counterinsurgency is a highly complex operation that requires the active involvement and support of the local population, with the military and local networks each playing a specific role in the fight against insurgents (Galula,1964).

Counterinsurgency systems must also be flexible and dynamic. Of necessity, much attention may need to be directed towards the local population rather than the insurgents in order to win their trust and support for military actions. Thompson (1967), Kitson (1971), and Kiras (2010) argue that this can be achieved through providing political support, improving administrative functions, and addressing grievances or injustices. However, while the local population can play an important role in counterinsurgency operations, they cannot completely compensate for the inefficiencies or flaws in the government or local administration.

Insurgent groups such as Boko Haram often carry out their activities under the guise of Islam, using behaviour, political rhetoric, and ideological justifications that link them to jihadist movements. These groups frequently target local populations through suicide bombings, turning innocent civilians into casualties of war (Robinson, 2021; Kaldor, 2012). Their goal is to implement an extreme and highly politicised version of Islam worldwide, which they claim is the purest and most authentic form of religion (Van Aarde, 2018).

Moore (2007) provides a comprehensive definition of counterinsurgency, conceptualising it as a combination of political, economic, social, and security measures aimed at ending and preventing armed violence, creating stable political, economic, and social structures, and addressing the underlying causes of insurgency to establish and sustain conditions necessary for lasting stability. This definition emphasises the need for a holistic approach to counterinsurgency operations.

Thompson (1967) is fairly unique among theorists in defining counterinsurgency as a government initiative that combats insurgency through military operations alone without the collaboration of other stakeholders. In contrast, Petraeus (2010) stresses the importance of using all available national power to protect the current government and eliminate all forms and causes of insurgency. Petraeus (2010) maintains that effective and lasting counterinsurgency strategies require community support, and that locals play a crucial role in protecting their own community and supporting the government's actions. Petraeus (2010) adds that the success of counterinsurgency depends on the state enabling local involvement in security operations. Kitson (1971), Nagl (2002), and Kilcullen (2010) concur with this, with Nagl (202) making the point that counterinsurgency should be more population-driven (focused on securing a given population or populations) than enemy-driven (focused on defeating a particular insurgency group).

Theorists on counterinsurgency, such as Kitson (1971) and Nagl (2002), stress the importance of integrating and synchronising the efforts of the local population and military forces for successful and efficient operations. In addition, a comprehensive approach aims to weaken and defeat the insurgents while maintaining community functionality. Kaldor (2012) adds that successful counterinsurgency also bolsters the government's credibility among the local population.

### Epistemic and transversal locals

The term "epistemic locals" refers to a group of people who share common knowledge or expertise in a particular field, such as the military or those in a particular industry (Mabon et al., 2019). The term "transversal local" refers to a group of people who are connected through social and economic networks, and who may have different areas of expertise or knowledge (Bueger, 2015).

Within the context of local security, both epistemic and transversal locals play an important role. For example, epistemic locals in the military have specialised knowledge and expertise in security and defence, while transversal locals in a particular community have connections to other communities or social networks that can support local security (Faleg, 2012). Both groups are needed, each having different perspectives and interests. This can lead to tensions and disagreements about the best approaches to use (Macaspac, 2019). Fundamentally, counterinsurgency should involve both categories of locals (Kalyvas, 2006).

In general, epistemic locals are deliberate in their contribution, advocating a functional social model that may be used in constituting groups, instituting power, and implementing credible tactics. The goal is to reduce civic and national concerns. In addition, they aim to contribute to the intelligence and uniformity of strategic plans to curb insurgency challenges (Kalyvas, 2006). Transversal locals focus on the links between various groups, bringing together facets of existing localities to entrench local security (Kalyvas, 2006). Experts advocate a blend of the epistemic and transversal models, insisting on the need for state support and appropriate, blended means of defending local populations from insurgents (Kalyvas, 2006; Nagl, 2002).

Kapatika (2022) proposes that epistemic locals make valuable contributions only under four crucial conditions: there need to be common normative views, common beliefs about a cause, a common approach to operations, and a precedent on which to base an assessment of local expertise. The formation of epistemic groups can contribute to the construction of logical intelligence in a specific area of expertise, allowing local people to agree on anticipated activities and the allocation of tasks. Epistemic groups also establish conventional attitudes about certain issues, creating deeply entrenched rationales for behaviour. Epistemic locals participate in and add significantly to the building of better strategies (Kapatika, 2022). This enables individuals to differentiate between appropriate and inappropriate public declarations, the channels through which declarations are authorised, and the best initiatives and strategies to adopt.

In any given locality, epistemic locals establish their own identity and interests, which may be distinct from the interests of the state in which they reside. Hence, the interests of both parties may clash. This may prompt the military to take certain actions that appear contrary to the interests and identities of the epistemic locals (Millar, 2018).

As has been established, transversal locals comprise social networks that cut across social groups and ethnic, cultural, and economic boundaries. The terms emphasise the interconnectedness and interdependence of different groups within a locality. Transversal local groups can be shaped by various physical, social, and cultural forces. According to Castells (1997), transversal locals play a crucial role in terms of collective identities, often giving rise to social movements. Castells (1997) argues that these social networks provide a basis for collective action and resistance against dominant power structures.

Local security is an essential aspect of the well-being of any community. In recent years, there has been growing interest in the concept of transversal local security, which involves the collaboration of different groups in the community to address security challenges. Established social networks can be especially valuable in protecting and strengthening a community. Usually operating independently of the state, they comprise various social groupings, including community leaders, religious groups, civil society organisations, and security agencies. The concept of transversal locals in local security is particularly relevant in situations where state security institutions are weak or ineffective. In such situations, community-based security initiatives become essential for addressing security challenges. However, if the state is not ready to cooperate or lacks the support of the locals, strong local networks will not suffice. The plans and objectives of a weak or unpopular state will be frustrated in any local security challenge (Millar, 2018).

## Conclusion

This chapter examined the concepts of security, insurgency, local insurgency, insurgent peace, counterinsurgency, and epistemic and transversal locals. It conceptualised security as the absence of uneasiness, risks, or threats to individuals or groups, and to their collective values. In Borno State, the vestiges of security have dwindled, making the restoration of security a complex and pressing matter at all levels of governance. Insurgency is the main cause of this insecurity, but, as has been established, the causes of insurgency may be traced, at least in part, to perceived weaknesses and injustices on the part of the state. Local insurgency, the type of insurgency that occurs at the community or regional level, is often driven by local grievances such as political exclusion, economic deprivation, and ethnic or religious differences. The consequences of insurgency include displacement, the undermining of national sovereignty and resources, and the diversion of funds, technology, and human resources.

The chapter has introduced the concept of insurgency-related peace, a type of peace that applies in localities where local people have collectively asserted themselves against violent local insurgency, and where the causes of the insurgency remain unaddressed – meaning that insurgency is an ever-present threat. Counterinsurgency is a dynamic and multidirectional concept that requires a combination of military, political, economic, psychological, financial, political, and security- and information-related factors to succeed.

# CHAPTER THREE
# THEORETICAL AND EMPIRICAL APPROACHES TO INSURGENT PEACE

## Introduction

Both theoretical and empirical approaches are needed to inform peace initiatives in nations and local communities. While the issue of security in Nigeria and across Africa has garnered significant scholarly attention, Nigeria is currently in the midst of its worst security crisis in living memory, and the gaps in knowledge have become all too apparent. The ongoing crisis caused by Boko Haram has, in fact, opened up new avenues for further study on insurgency- related peace.

Insurgency-related peace is a concept enabled by an alignment of military power and local or community contributions in areas affected by local insurgency. A local insurgency poses a significant threat to both state and nonstate groups and is carried out through conventional and unconventional methods. This has raised questions about the strategies employed by locals to counter insurgency, which may involve creative or unconventional methods. In this chapter, the various approaches to counterinsurgency are viewed through the lens of Galula's (1964) study on insurgency and Macaspac's (2020) insurgency-related peace theory. The general narrative of the CJTF aligns with insurgency-related peace theory.

The chapter's position is that achieving insurgency-related peace requires the adoption of unconventional warfare strategies. The CJTF strategy, as described by Bamidele (2017), is primarily grassroots, drawing strength from the support and intervention of locals. Like many scholars, Bamidele (2017) sees collaboration between locals and the military as a prerequisite for defeating insurgency at the local level. This collaborative effort is a viable bottom-up approach for insurgency-related peace operations in the twenty-first century, combining military force and local intelligence in a compelling partnership that has a chance of succeeding.

In Borno State, insurgency-related peace may be viewed as a top-down or bottom-up process. Initially, the top-down approach served as a valuable starting point for addressing local insurgency, but it has been recognised as insufficient on its own. It is generally acknowledged byactivists in Borno State that the top-down approach must be integrated with the bottom-up approach to effectively bring subordinate groups into the peace effort.

However, the bottom-up approach has been criticised for potentially promoting an independent agenda from that of the state (Bamidele, 2023; Owonikoko & Onuoha, 2019). Gana (2020) maintains that it can be effective when locals and the military are committed to working together.

This study advocates a combination of ethnographic-synchronic and thematic approaches to developing and establishing local security interventions. These should involve dynamic cooperation and pragmatic solutions to local security challenges (Wright, 2022; Agbiboa, 2018; Agbiboa, 2021; Agbiboa, 2020). An ethnographic-synchronic approach involves studying the social and cultural context of insurgency in Nigeria as it appears at any given time, so that security interventions may be tailored to suit current realities on the ground. This is essential to building relationships of trust and cooperation with local communities. A thematic approach, on the other hand, involves analysing the underlying themes and concepts that shape our understanding of insurgency and counterinsurgency, identifying key drivers of the insurgency, and developing nuanced strategies to address them. By combining these approaches, practical local security interventions can be established, dynamic cooperation can be developed, and working solutions can be found for local security challenges (Wright, 2022).

The involvement of local security measures in a bottom-up approach is essential for achieving security and insurgency-related peace in Nigeria. This approach recognises the importance of involving local communities in finding solutions to their own security challenges, and it seeks to build relationships of trust and cooperation between these communities and security forces (Bamidele, 2023). The bottom-up approach raises the chances that workable solutions will be found to an ongoing insurgency that always has multifaceted origins and, in addition, involves ongoing grievances on both sides. An approach that involves both state security agencies and local people creates a solid foundation for achieving security and insurgency-related peace in Nigeria.

### Understanding insurgent peace in Borno State

Various theoretical perspectives and fields of study offer insights into the interminable insurgency issues besieging Borno State. The analysis in this section is situated in Macaspac's (2020) and Galula's (1964) insurgency-related peace theories. The chapter highlights the centrality of local security in Borno State, recognising its pertinence to insurgency issues. Existing studies on insurgency-related peace reveal many interconnections between the military and locals in the fight against local insurgency are analysed (Gana, 2020; Bamidele, 2017; Brechenmacher, 2019).

Galula's (1964) insurgency-related peace theory offers vital insights that apply to CJTF's collaboration with the military. Galula's seminal work establishes that collaboration between the military and local people is key to achieving insurgency-related peace. The chapter aligns with this theory, maintaining that the military cannot overcome the challenges of insurgency without the support and collaboration of local communities. Kalyvas (2006) concurs that interventions by the locals are necessary for the defeat of local insurgency and the establishment of insurgency- related peace.

In conventional warfare, the chances of overcoming an enemy are assessed on the basis of the strength of the military, the number of divisions, the position of the enemy and the availability of resources. However, in unconventional warfare, as in Borno State, strength must necessarily be measured by the existence of support from locals at the grassroots level. Accordingly, Borno State gains an advantage when the influence of the military is strongly backed by the locals (Agbiboa, 2021).

The chapter views that a resurgence of energy is needed in insurgent peace operations, and that locals need to be empowered to assume a more dynamic role in combating the crisis of persistent local insurgency. An expanded role would allow locals to make joint decisions with the military concerning local security issues, and to play some part in implementing them. Planning and implementation by locals would benefit the entire country by enhancing the military's response to the Boko Haram insurgency (Ibrahim & Bala, 2018).

By involving locals who have the skills to combat insurgency, state authorities would gain greater control over insurgents and effectively multiply their efforts. This approach allows for the integration of local values into military and insurgency-related peace operations, ultimately providing locals with access to military capabilities not typically available to locals during sporadic incidents of insurgency. Moreover, the involvement of locals would instil a sense of ownership in the peace effort and encourage their commitment to the success of any insurgency- related peace operation (Kalyvas, 2006; Allen, 2023).

The theoretical foundation of this approach is increasingly relevant as both scholars and role-players recognise the military's current inability to defeat local insurgencies. The military should examine its modus operandi and consider far greater collaboration with locals who possess superior information about their localities and are stakeholders in establishing insurgency-related peace. Moreover, the changing nature of local insurgencies, where nonuniformed contenders live among locals, poses a significant challenge to military recognition of insurgents, indicating that conventional approaches are no longer effective (Kilcullen, 2009).

Operatives working on insurgency-related peace should adopt a holistic, locally driven, population-centred, system-of-systems approach to ensure peace and security. The system-of- systems approach recognises that complex systems are composed of interconnected sets of smaller, individual systems that operate together to create certain conditions. In military operations, a system-of-systems approach might involve coordinating the efforts of different units, agencies, and partners to achieve a common objective. This approach is useful in situations where the complexity of the system renders traditional methods inadequate. It acknowledges the value of local support in defeating insurgents and contributing to state security efforts for long-term success (Kilcullen, 2009).

The system-of-systems approach also recognises that the military is just one part of the solution, with other factors, such as political processes, also playing a significant role. Local initiatives are vital, even as the military maintains control over the state and secures lawful assistance (Kilcullen, 2009). Locals can provide valuable support in areas where military efforts alone fall short.

Intelligence gathering and sharing is another key aspect of the ideal insurgency-related peace approach, as it provides in-depth knowledge of the adversary and enhances the effectiveness of military operations (Kilcullen, 2009). With the specific goal of targeting, finding, and confronting the enemy, adequate intelligence is essential and best accessed by the locals (Akubo & Okolo, 2019). Overall, the insurgency-related peace approach represents a significant departure from earlier thinking on counterinsurgency and a recognition of the critical role played by locals in defeating insurgencies.

In this joint approach, there is a need for all role-players to keep in mind the end goal of resolving the issues that gave rise to local insurgency in the first place. In any joint approach to managing and resolving local insurgencies, it is crucial for all involved parties to maintain a clear focus on the ultimate goal: addressing and resolving the root causes that initially led to the insurgency. This involves recognising that the insurgency is often a symptom of deeper, unresolved issues within the community or state, such as socioeconomic disparities, political disenfranchisement, or cultural grievances. By concentrating on these underlying problems, stakeholders can develop more effective and sustainable strategies to address the conflict comprehensively rather than merely managing its symptoms.

To effectively address these root causes, collaboration between local actors and external entities must be guided by a shared understanding of the issues at hand. This requires open communication, mutual respect, and a commitment to integrating diverse perspectives and expertise. Local communities, with their firsthand knowledge and experiences, can provide invaluable insights into the grievances that fuel insurgencies, while external actors, such as governmental and international organisations, can offer resources, technical support, and broader strategic frameworks. The synergy between these different players is essential for crafting solutions that are both contextually relevant and practical.

The joint approach should emphasise the importance of building long-term resilience and stability within the affected regions. This means not only implementing immediate measures to quell violence but also investing in initiatives that promote social cohesion, economic development, and good governance. By focusing on these broader objectives, all role-players can contribute to creating an environment where the conditions that foster insurgency are systematically addressed and mitigated. This holistic perspective ensures that efforts to resolve the insurgency are sustainable and contribute to lasting peace and stability. Essentially, the successful elimination of all forms of local guerrilla fighting demands that insurgency-related peace be regarded as the product of a unique and fundamental partnership between the military and locals, which will sustain the locals in the fight (International Crisis Group, 2017).

The CJTF insurgency-related peace operation is a strategic and workable approach, because it is local, agile, and flexible; however, it requires planning and cooperation with the military ahead of particular offensive and defensive operations (Gana, 2020). Insurgency-related peace initiatives must prioritise the achievement of both the locals' and the military's objectives during emergencies by leveraging their respective strengths and combining their collective efforts (Mamman, 2020). This allows for continual adjustments to be made to operational strategies by both groups to best suit the unique circumstances of the locality (Njuafac & Katman, 2023).

It is notable that studies pay little attention to specific instances of military and local collaboration in counterinsurgency, especially in Africa. Specifically, the literature reveals that many studies on military operations in Borno State have failed to address the tactics and origins of local security groups such as the CJTF, as also noted by Muhammad and Salleh (2024).

To close this gap in the literature, this chapter explores the operational effectiveness or otherwise of the CJTF and the challenges posed by its initiation into Nigeria's insurgency-related peace operations (Dietrich, 2015). Rather than viewing insurgency-related peace solely as the responsibility of the military, the chapter acknowledges the local initiative of the CJTF as an essential element of a comprehensive approach to insurgency-related peace, which supplements the strength and strategy of military operations.

**Insurgency-related peace: Combining top-down and bottom-up approaches**

A combination of the top-down and bottom-up approaches to insurgency-related peace has been recognised as an effective strategy. Scholars such as Hassan (2015) and Bamidele (2017) are proponents of this strategy, with each slightly emphasising one or the other approach. However, regardless of where the emphasis lies, the goal of this chapter is to assess the combination of both approaches and the ways in which the combination affects communities. The combined approach involves the deployment of local security tactics, the empowerment of locals, the development of strong partnerships, especially with the military, and improvements in the qualityof life and prosperity of the locals.

The combined approach means that the government works with the locals to reduce killings, instability, and the destruction of property. Therefore, it is essential to understand these two approaches in some detail.

**Insurgency-related peace: The top-down approach**

Pérouse de Montclos (2014, 2020), Onuoha et al. (2021), and Osumah (2013) maintain that with the top-down approach to counterinsurgency, the initiator and primary insurgency-related peace group is the state, working through its security agencies. With this approach, the military holds the primary responsibility for establishing and maintaining peace in local communities. However, there might be discord within the military, with various military personnel having different perspectives on how to approach local insurgency. This can lead to conflicting interests within the same body (Onuoha et al., 2021). For example, some military officials may prioritise a more aggressive approach to insurgency, relying heavily on force and military intervention to suppress perceived threats to security, while others may advocate a more diplomatic approach, seeking to negotiate with local insurgent groups and address the root causes of conflict through social and political reforms (Onuoha & Ugwueze, 2020).

These differing perspectives can create challenges for the top-down approach, as conflicting interests lead to a lack of cohesion and coordination in the state's efforts. Moreover, if military officials do not consider the desires and needs of local communities, their approach to insurgency-related peace will probably not address the underlying causes of conflict (Onuoha & Ugwueze, 2020).

The top-down approach may make use of local perspectives and knowledge to ensure that strategies are tailored to the needs and desires of the community (Onuoha & Ugwueze, 2020). However, the reins of power remain firmly in the hands of the state. State agencies risk overlooking the primary goal of fulfilling the locals' desire for lasting peace. The top-down approach needs to consider the conditions that gave rise to dissatisfaction and, where possible, negotiate with insurgent groups as part of the peace process (Osumah, 2013). Although proponents of the top-down approach support the idea of state security agencies as the key insurgency-related peace group, most acknowledge the need to involve the locals in some way, since they know the locality and can play the role of undercover intelligence agents (Onuoha et al., 2021).

Thus, even with the top-down approach, the state (military) may incorporate local groups into local security and allow their particular local initiatives to play a role. This approach still maintains the military's dominance of the insurgency-related peace initiatives, and the locals might still have to battle with the state to demonstrate their knowledge of what is beneficial for their security (Onuoha & Ugwueze, 2020; Onuoha et al., 2021; Osumah, 2013).

Raffoul (2019) concurs that the top-down approach to local insurgency is typically driven by state actors who hold most of the power and resources. This approach tends to prioritise the state's interests over those of the local community, which can create a sense of distrust and exploitation. For example, in some cases, the state may impose security measures on local communities without proper consultation or consent, such as setting up military checkpoints or conducting raids on suspected insurgents (Ackah-Arthur, 2023). These measures can disrupt the daily lives of locals and even lead to human rights abuses, such as wrongful arrests or extrajudicial killings (Aydinli, 2018). Thus, the implementation of a top-down insurgency-related peace approach can be unfair to the locals because of the abuse of human rights, the rigidity of the approach (Forde et al., 2021), and the forcing of solutions on locals, who may well end up being victims of local insurgency-related peace (Muzan, 2014).

The state may also exploit the resources of local communities, such as their land or other natural resources, in the name of protecting them from insurgents (Rincón Barajas et al., 2024). This can lead to resentment and resistance from locals, who may feel that their resources are being taken without their consent or fair compensation.

Overall, the top-down approach risks creating a power imbalance between the state and local communities, which can lead to active obstruction on the part of locals. To address this, the state needs simply to become more sensitive and aware of the effects of its actions on communities. To gain the necessary awareness, it should consult with local community structures, taking care to ensure that the groups and structures they meet with are recognised in the community and have community support. This will ensure that state agencies incorporate the perspectives and needs of local people in the establishment of insurgency-related peace, and that their voices are heard throughout the process (Kalyvas, 2006).

Historically, in Nigeria, the use of the army and other state-mandated groups to enforce citizen compliance has long been the norm (Mudasiru et al., 2019). Thus, the top-down insurgency-related peace approach has either quelled or attempted to quell most local uprisings. The top-down approach tends to disregard local groups and is likely to comprise only state-mandated groups (Muzan, 2014).

Bamidele (2023) notes that the top-down insurgency-related peace approach gives the military a sense of being effective and in control. However, the approach invariably results in insurgency- related peace plans that do not consider the sociocultural and environmental circumstances that shape communities in different geographical areas. Strategies worked on in isolation from the locals risk being ill-suited for resolving the root causes of local insurgency or ensuring lasting peace. In fact, they can exacerbate the situation. For example, a state-mandated insurgency-related peace group operating in a rural area may propose a peace plan that focuses on land reform to address the economic grievances of the local population. However, if the local population relies on other forms of livelihood, such as fishing, land reform would not be an effective solution. Therefore, the chapter argues for a bottom-up approach, which involves the locals in plans concerning them and considers their unique circumstances. The bottom-up insurgency-related peace approach has proven to be more effective, objective, and feasible than the top-down approach (Mac Ginty & Richmond, 2013; Mac Ginty, 2015b; Galula, 1964).

### Insurgent peace: The bottom-up approach

The bottom-up approach, involving local partnership arrangements between state agencies and local community structures, encourages local communities to participate actively in and support insurgency-related peace efforts in their respective localities. This approach is tailored to align with locals' initiatives, desires, and plans, as well as various sociocultural factors. (Idris et al., 2014). Idris et al. (2014) and Bamidele (2018) acknowledge that insurgency-related peace arrangements may change long-existing ways of life.

The bottom-up approach to insurgency-related peace requires skilful handling so that local people do not become confused or form unrealistic expectations. If communication is not clear and frequent and state agencies lack patience and persistence, local people may misunderstand or circulate contradictory messages, and end up obstructing the process. The bottom-up insurgency-related peace approach needs to be locally focused, demonstrating trust in local endeavours to implement security measures against insurgency in their localities. Such insurgency-relatedpeace operations can be moderately large-scale.

The bottom-up insurgency-related peace approach succeeds precisely where the top-down insurgency-related peace approach disappoints because it makes use of local people's ideas, giving them the freedom to devise insurgency-related peace initiatives in response to large-scale local security exigencies (Onapajo & Ozden, 2020). Local groups frame their views on local protection based on their specific circumstances and understanding of their locality, enabling them to carry out physical combat operations (Idris et al., 2014).

Bottom-up proponents are criticised for overvaluing the level of local independence from the state, as this insurgency-related peace strategy would not work without the resources and institutional structures provided by the state through the military (Idris et al., 2014). The criticism draws attention to the area of resource management. Bamidele (2020) states that effective resource management is a critical factor in the success of the insurgency-related peace process, and Bamidele (2020) adds that the availability of resources can greatly affect the abilityof both locals and military forces to combat insurgency and create sustainable peace. However, resources alone cannot guarantee the success of a bottom-up insurgency-related peace process (Dixon, 2009), which should be followed in conditions that denote a partnership.

The level of partnership, however, may vary. Bamidele (2018) distinguishes between "uninvolved involvement" and "dynamic involvement". Uninvolved involvement means allowing locals to take necessary action on their own, with consultative cooperation, material support, and limited cooperation on the part of the military (Idris et al., 2014). Dynamic involvement occurs when locals are fully integrated into the peace process (Ruppel & Leib, 2022). It is crucial to consider the level of partnership desired by both parties in the design of effective insurgency-related peace processes.

The bottom-up process implies involving the locals at different levels, with the specific end goal of overcoming the local insurgency, either straightforwardly or through certain bodies representing local interests. In addition, the bottom-up process involves respecting the views and sociocultural diversity of the locals while ensuring the achievement and sustainability of insurgency-related peace (Idris et al., 2014) through the effective mobilisation of those involved.

Numerous studies have been conducted on the bottom-up insurgency-related peace approach, including those by Galula (1964), Hassan (2015), Idris et al. (2014), Bamidele (2017, pp. 18 & 20), and Paffenholz (2015). As established, the approach is based on the idea of local partnerships that encourage locals to take the lead and shape plans around their own capabilities, sustaining power and sociocultural priorities (Hassan, 2015). However, as stated earlier, this approach must be handled sensitively to avoid confusing the locals and causing significant obstruction and disappointment with the process. Collaborative local and military operations are considered advantageous and tend to elicit a more dynamic and cooperative response to local insurgency than operations that involve the military only (Idris et al., 2014).

The distribution of responsibilities in the bottom-up approach involves allowing the locals to assume some operational responsibilities, such as intelligence gathering (Galula, 1964). It is also critical to distinguish between different groups living in a locality and have preoperation discussions with each to sharpen their appreciation of what the insurgency-related peace process will entail (Paffenholz, 2015). Such operations may involve local rulers and their cabinets, sundry working and nonworking groups, local politicians, and youth and women's groups (Idris et al., 2014).

The adoption of the bottom-up approach entails several key stages: planning, intelligence gathering, execution, and monitoring (Hassan, 2015). Each stage of the process can incorporate locals based on their skills, experience, and knowledge. Ideally, local leaders should select and deploy qualified individuals to ensure the operation's success and minimise casualties. However, it is crucial to ensure that the approach genuinely reflects a bottom-up strategy, where locals have a significant role in designing and implementing the action plans, rather than merely being utilised by the state. To prevent dissatisfaction and potential obstruction, state agencies should also be responsible for covering the costs associated with involving locals in the insurgency peace process. This inclusive approach helps to engage all community members effectively, promoting a more comprehensive and cooperative effort towards achieving peace.

### Approaches to local security

The concept of "local" is imperative in insurgency-related peace, cropping up frequently in the discourse (Bellamy & Williams, 2011; Kindersley & Rolandsen, 2019b; Macaspac, 2019; Mac Ginty & Richmond, 2013; Philipsen, 2022). However, there is no agreed-upon definition of the term "local"; it is assumed to refer to the inhabitants of a particular area. From a social point of view, "local" refers to a group of people who share a history and value system that define their collective character. However, the term can also refer to a cluster of people composed of two or more population groups who acknowledge and rise above their differences in their social, ethnic, economic, political, and spiritual lives in order to live harmoniously and achieve common goals.

An analysis of the works by Bellamy and Williams (2011), Kindersley and Rolandsen (2019a), Macaspac (2019), Mac Ginty and Richmond (2013), and Philipsen (2022) identifies three primary interpretations of the term "local". The first interpretation refers to a geographically defined area, the second highlights social interactions and networks within a community, and the third emphasises sociopolitical responsibility as essential for collective action and reconciliation among group members. Consequently, a comprehensive definition of "local" within the context of insurgency-related peace should incorporate the social connections within a community and the ways in which their collaborative efforts address local security challenges. The lack of consensus on the meaning of "local" has been highlighted in previous works; for example, Mac Ginty (2010, 2015) and Paffenholz (2015) emphasise the need to investigate sources of disparity within a populace to ensure efficient security, while Bellamy and Williams (2011) view locals as an exceptional, homogeneous whole. Mac Ginty and Richmond (2013) note that the prerequisite for locals to exist in direct connection with one another makes it more difficult to establish the nature of transitional groups of people.

It is important to consider the categories of collaboration when defining "local" within a given context. Collaboration is recognised in the idea of "conceptualising local", as defined by Mac Ginty and Richmond (2013). Their idea of conceptualising local suggests the existence of strong bonds of feeling and values among people in a given location. However, the idea of local identity may be regularly reconstructed and questioned, with political locals often arising from social interactions that are influenced by common values, interests, logic, language, identity, and beliefs.

The idea of values, interests, identity, and belief crops up frequently in the literature when the term "local" is discussed (Bräuchler & Naucke, 2024). These elements offer an understanding of social formation as a process that traverses several stages of abstraction (Karbo, 2012). Norms play a critical role in the security of locals, so that the development and maintenance of norms is essential (Chandler, 2018). These norms may be expressed through partnership rules that recognise legitimate members of a group and legitimate forms of participation (Bramble & Paffenholz, 2021).

A geographic meaning of local should not be seen as the only legitimate form of "local"; the term may include members of institutions that are heavily invested in a community. Thus, there is a need to understand the complex processes of social formation that constitute the term "locals".

Social interaction emerges from connections formed under prevailing ideologies (Russo, 2022). These interactions can span various temporal and spatial contexts, ranging from direct face-to-face exchanges to more mediated forms such as text messages. The complexity of social formation is characterised by its multilevel, continuous, and occasionally contradictory nature. To further this understanding, two key concepts are proposed. First, the idea of "continuity in discontinuity", which suggests that phases of social continuity and discontinuity are present in all social interactions. Local values, norms, interests, and identities are subject to change due to discontinuities and disruptions, driven by ongoing changes and unpredictability. This notion is supported by Bramble and Paffenholz (2021), who assert that local groups undergo various stages of social formation, each influenced by these continuous shifts.

The second concept addresses the fluidity of identity within local contexts. A local exists at the intersection of different stages of social conceptualisation, making it challenging to define a fixed identity for any individual within this framework. The term "local" encompasses simultaneous social processes, which may either persist or shift across different stages of formation. As the scope of formation broadens, the term increasingly reflects continuity amid change, leading to a cross-level formation of social identities. Consequently, the notion of "local" is continually represented, reproduced, reinterpreted, established, and recognised at a conceptual level, adapting to the evolving social landscape.

Many social formation theories attempt to resolve contradictions by favouring one particular phase, but this approach may not adequately address the complexities involved. A more effective strategy is to engage with these contradictions, as understanding apparent illogicalities is crucial for studying social transformation. The term "local" is meaningful within a framework of social formation characterised by relationships of indefinite expansion. Therefore, conceptualisations of "local" should integrate the notion of continuity-in-discontinuity and consider how local identities both shape and are shaped by abstract concepts. Locals engage in processes that embed abstract ideas into local practices, which, in turn, help to rejuvenate these abstract ideas. This dynamic interaction contributes to the understanding of how local identities evolve over time (Bräuchler & Naucke, 2024). The term "local" encompasses a range of entities, including individuals, groups, subgroups, and institutions, that share common time, space, and resources in pursuit of mutual concerns. It also refers to individuals who live in close proximity to one another and share overlapping identities, interests, needs, qualities, and capabilities. This shared context creates a collective environment where interactions and relationships are shaped by these commonalities.

The concept of "local" becomes deeply ingrained in individual identities through socialisation processes. As abstract notions about what it means to be "local" are internalised, these ideas undergo reinterpretation and transformation influenced by personal experiences and linguistic nuances.

The notion of functional cooperation is crucial for understanding how locals act as conduits for social interaction and change. Within this context, unspoken rules play a significant role. These unwritten rules guide individuals on how to engage appropriately, perform tasks, and understand their fundamental rights and responsibilities. Leonardsson and Rudd (2015) and Mac Ginty (2011) highlight that social responsibility norms can vary. In loosely structured local security arrangements, social responsibilities are often defined by legal rights, such as the entitlement to strategise against insurgency or refrain from such actions (Wolff, 2022). Conversely, in more structured local security frameworks, groups within the locality have the right to seek support if they face aggression from other groups.

## The role of social responsibility in constituting the "local"

The concept of social responsibility plays an important role in tightly constituted local groups. Social responsibility refers to the idea that individuals and groups are obligated to act in the best interests of the group. In tightly constituted or highly integrated local groups, community members have a shared responsibility to ensure the safety and well-being of their neighbours and the community. When community members assume this responsibility and work together to create a safe and secure environment, they gain certain rights, such as the right to invest in the development of their community and participate in important discussions on security. In addition, in integrated local communities, the local population has the right to participate in all affairs of the locality. However, in such communities, there are usually no clear rules on participation.

Scholars in various disciplines, including peacebuilding, security, and peacekeeping, have discussed the role of local communities in promoting social responsibility and civic engagement (Giddens, 1990). Participation in local affairs is considered essential for democratic governance (Putnam, 2000). In addition, it has been shown that highly integrated localities provide a sense of community and belonging that ultimately boosts social capital and well-being (Kawachi & Berkman, 2001).

In Nigeria, there is general agreement among the states that decisions are made in consultation with traditional leaders, who are legally constituted and recognised as part of the state apparatus. This implies that social responsibility can be taken on by both national and local leadership. Thus, the idea that only the state has statutory responsibility for solving local problems is illogical. However, a problem arises in that the state has a social responsibility to recognise the rights of locals, yet there is no consensus on the extent of these responsibilities. In other words, there is a lack of agreement on whether the state should take a more active role in promoting responsibility among local communities or whether it is sufficient for it simply to acknowledge its role in keeping the community functional and safe.

### The role of mutually accepted norms, rules, and unity

Bamidele (2017a&b, 2018) contends that establishing norms about interventions and responsibility for local security serves as a foundation for planning, which in itself binds the state and locals together. However, this perspective is not universally accepted, and debate persists about the extent of the state's responsibility to local communities in Nigeria. Moreover, the notion that locals who provide local security have responsibilities on a par with those of the state is problematic. Nonetheless, locals have both a right and responsibility to protect community integrity and mobilise themselves to provide local security when necessary. In this endeavour, rules play a critical role. Rules distinguish legitimate local participants from illegitimate participants and ensure mutual respect among actors.

Bamidele (2017a&b) contends that social responsibility at the local level varies depending on the level of involvement. Individuals involved in local security roles are typically informed of their responsibilities through formal orientation or training processes. The clarity of these responsibilities can depend on whether local security groups are loosely organised or formally structured. In loosely constituted groups, roles may be less defined and evolve over time, while in highly integrated groups, responsibilities are usually clearly outlined from the outset.

Local security has a significant impact on local groups, often contributing to the norms and values that guide members' behaviours and actions. This system of norms and values is occasionally referred to as the logic of appropriateness (Bamidele, 2018). It defines what is considered acceptable and appropriate behaviour within the group, and what is not. The logic of appropriateness acts as a constraint on the behaviour of members by regulating their actions and decisions. Furthermore, local security issues also foster meaningful collaboration, cooperation, and partnership within and outside the locality. By working together to ensure local security, members of the locality can build trust and mutual respect among themselves. This trust and collaboration can extend beyond the locality to other groups and organisations, leading to broader partnerships and networks in a region. These partnerships are important for addressing wider security challenges, helping to improve the overall security situation of a region (Bamidele, 2016, 2017a&b).

Four essential attributes of a locality enhance local security. These are moral unity, wholeness, a sense of identity, and involvement. Moral unity refers to a shared sense of values and ethics among locals, which is crucial for nourishing cooperation and collaboration in local security efforts. Wholeness refers to the integration of different groups within the locality into a cohesive whole, which enhances the effectiveness of local security efforts (Bamidele, 2016, 2017a&b). A sense of identity refers to a sense of belonging to the locality, which fosters a sense of responsibility and ownership over local security efforts. Involvement is also critical, as threats cannot be successfully eliminated without the support and participation of locals.

### The role of local level

In addition, as has been shown, a locality is not fixed but continually rearticulated, meaning that it is subject to change over time. The recognition of a locality is based on functional cooperation within the community in which established norms, and practices guide how different groups work together. In-group ways to create, track, and pursue local security may require specific strategies or tactics that are best managed by certain groups (Bamidele, 2016, 2017a&b). In these endeavours, both epistemic and transversal groups will play a role, based on their shared knowledge or cross-cutting identities, respectively (Bamidele, 2016, 2017a&b).

### Cooperation between state and local

Owing to the high prevalence of insurgency groups in Nigeria, much scholarly work on the topic emanates from this country. Bamidele (2019), Ordu and Nnam (2017), Idris et al. (2014), and Hassan (2015), among others, have written extensively on the local level of securing communities in the face of near-continuous attack in one form or another. Local security is an issue that no African government can afford to treat lightly, because, as indicated by Leonardsson and Rudd (2015) and Mac Ginty and Richmond (2013), local security is at the heart of human safety, development, and peacebuilding.

The Nigerian Yoruba proverb *Ehinkunle l'ota wa, inu ile l'aseni ngbe* translates to "Our enemies are outside the gate, while those who will harm us live inside the house". This suggests that adversaries live and even flourish in the midst of local communities, and they are best handled by locals. If the state neglects its responsibilities, locals will inevitably compensate for its negligence. Thus, the security efforts of locals should function alongside state security, and if locals and government agents worked together, local security and insurgent peace – and even long-term peace – might well be within reach. For this, the state's local security efforts need to be more visible and accountable (Kitson, 1971). The state that has its citizens' best interests at heart will encourage collaboration between state security institutions and local communities (Mitchell & Hancock, 2012).

Locals involved in security measures should be viewed as collaborators rather than passive bystanders in the advancement of security. When a more active role is assumed by locals, the state becomes more of a peace-builder and decision-maker regarding beneficial actions that will enhance people's quality of life. At the same time, it would neither be feasible for the army to set goals for the community in the expectation that the community will develop and implement these plans, nor can either party expect the other to carry out plans it has not been party to in relation to local security.

Many authors concur with this point. Omeni (2017), Onuoha and Ugwueze (2020), and Olivius and Hedström (2021) all state that the state military and locals should work together to develop and implement plans for local security and insurgency-related peace operations. In the absence of effective planning and regulation, local security and insurgency-related peace operations would be a hazardous missile launched on an imprecise target – bound to go astray.

At the same time, caution needs to be exercised in terms of the devolution of power and authority. The complete democratisation or decentralisation of local security is not ideal, since such an approach would weaken the rule of law in localities already suffering from the lawlessness of local insurgency. Therefore, local security must be established by law-abiding locals who recognise the legitimacy of state security agents. Rather than seeing state and local responsibilities as separate, they should be perceived as interdependent.

While all evidence points to the idea that state and local efforts should be combined to secure insurgency-related peace, there is a need to acknowledge that this collaboration may come at a high cost (Olivius & Hedström, 2021). Limited budget allocations by the state and prevailing economic challenges could create resistance to the integration of locals into local security operations (Olonisakin, 2015). The financial costs of collaboration between state and local initiatives in local security operations would be high due to the need to train and equip locals (Onuoha & Ugwueze, 2020). In addition, integrating locals into state security forces would require investments in infrastructure, such as communication networks, transportation systems, and new administrative processes (Omeni, 2017). There would also be a need to provide compensation and benefits to locals who participate in security operations, in the form of hazard pay or insurance coverage (Osumah, 2013). Finally, there would be costs associated with the procurement and maintenance of new equipment.

There would also be social costs, including tensions that will invariably arise between locals and state security forces, as well as possible mistrust among community members of those who collaborate with the state. There may also be political costs, as some local elites may oppose collaboration owing to their vested interests in existing power structures (Onuoha et al., 2021).

Nevertheless, locals' collaboration with the military is advantageous in the long run because the benefits far outweigh the costs. Funding issues should not be a basis for its rejection.

Bamidele (2018) maintains that including locals in local security efforts has proved to be a cost- effective use of state resources. The deployment of community members who are already familiar with an area and its residents obviates the need for expensive external security measures (Bamidele, 2018). By investing in community security initiatives and involving locals in local security, the state can make optimal use of its resources, using funds to empower community members who are willing to take an active role in ensuring the safety of their own neighbourhoods.

Investing in community security initiatives has long-term benefits, such as improved relationships between law enforcement and community members, increased trust and cooperation, and a stronger sense of ownership and investment in the safety of the area. These benefits can ultimately lead to more sustainable and effective security outcomes as well as greater social cohesion and a sense of community well-being (Kelling & Moore, 1988; Rosenbaum & Lurigio, 1994). Thus, by building partnerships with local communities and involving them in the security process, the state can leverage its resources in a way that is both cost-effective and socially beneficial.

Coquilhat (2008) concurs, stating that involving locals in local security efforts can effectively bridge the gap between the state and the community in both rural and urban areas. Moreover, the use of local enquiry committees can assist in satisfying locals' expectations regarding the responsibilities of the military.

Stringham and Forney (2017) point out that eliminating all forms of substandard practice in local security can be a lengthy and tedious process, and that the ethics of local security are problematic and difficult to execute. Nonetheless, these authors maintain that the goal should be to transfer certain operations to locals as a way of partnering with them. They also state that local security should be viewed as a supportive measure rather than an alternative to all other required forms of security.

Arguments against local involvement in local security are often related to execution, public participation, monetary involvement, and the quantification of achievable outcomes. Some authors view the push to involve locals in local security as having ulterior motives, suggesting that the move springs from a place of political opportunism, in that proponents may want to influence the state politically (Kelling & Moore, 1988; Rosenbaum & Lurigio, 1994). However, as has been shown, many scholars support the inclusion of locals in local security measures, emphasising its advantages, such as improved relationships between law enforcement and community members, increased trust and cooperation, and a stronger sense of ownership and investment in the safety of an area (Kelling & Moore, 1988; Rosenbaum & Lurigio, 1994).

Despite the many arguments raised for and against local security, none have suggested a functional solution that could help resolve the challenges of local insurgency.

## Conclusion

Local security is required for sustaining human life, for the stability of a region, and for protecting physical infrastructure. A balanced approach is needed to ensure security in all three domains. Local security should put people in a position where they have a chance to attain peace and happiness, and it should ensure the safety of physical resources.

Insurgency-related peace emphasises the importance of local communities working together to achieve security, rather than relying solely on the state and its military. Local security includes access to food, health facilities, a sound economy, a hygienic environment, freedom from repression, and, in the case of Borno State, adequate arms and ammunition, because the insurgency in that region is ongoing and severe.

The state needs a thorough understanding of local values, identity, and culture and the social and economic forces that shape any community for which it seeks to provide security. It should take a collaborative approach and be prepared to listen before it engages in any actions – and on an ongoing basis, given the rapidly changing nature of insurgency.

In Borno State, northeast Nigeria, the CJTF has arisen as a neighbourhood cooperative effort to support military-led operations against Boko Haram. The chapter considers the CJTF in terms of David Galula's (1064) theory of insurgency-related peace, which supports the idea of combining local community-based security efforts with military power. The chapter takes the position that neither of these forces should dominate. The CJTF's indigenous knowledge and easy access to information have made it an effective counterinsurgency force, enabling members to capture many Boko Haram insurgents and sympathisers and thereby contribute to insurgency-related peace. The CJTF's collaboration with the military since 2013 has multiplied its effectiveness in recovering some communities from Boko Haram insurgents. The CJTF has received arms and military training from the Nigerian army, and they have worked on many counterinsurgency operations in many areas, such as Gwoza and other communities.

The weaknesses of the CJTF are mostly technical, operational, and institutional, and they are not particular to this local group. The group lacks training, organisation, financing, and the logistical assistance of the military, yet, despite these disadvantages, it has restored relative peace to Borno State, where the humanitarian situation has improved.

Evidence of this is the fact that, since the formation of the CJTF, Boko Haram rebels have lost many parts of Borno State that they once controlled. This suggests that the group should be integrated more fully into the army's efforts to keep peace in the region; that it should no longer be co-opted on an ad hoc basis but be recognised, equipped, and consulted. For this, flexibility would be required, since what works in one place might not work in another. The CJTF has enormous potential to supplement army efforts by being responsible for defensive operations, maintaining the infrastructure of local security, and gathering intelligence. The group should not be used in offensive operations other than to serve as leads to Boko Haram strongholds.

# CHAPTER FOUR
# BOKO HARAM AND LOCAL SECURITY CHALLENGES IN BORNO STATE

## Introduction

Although Boko Haram is just one of several militant groups operating in the region, the current underlying political, social, and economic factors have propelled the group's dominance in Borno State and elsewhere. The literature traces Boko Haram to the 1990s when its members, all members of Alhaji Muhammadu Ndimi Mosque in Maiduguri, Borno State, began to coalesce over a shared rejection of Western education (Walker, 2012).

The group held the Islamic establishment to be irredeemably corrupt and advocated a return to Sharia law and the transformation of Nigeria into a Sharia state. Sharia is a set of religious principles and guidelines that govern various aspects of a Muslim's life, including their conduct, social interactions, and legal affairs. In a Sharia state, the judicial system and all economic policies are based on Islamic law (Esposito, 2011; Hashemi, 2015; Kamali, 2008).

In 2002, a radical and violent splinter group of the original group that convened at Alhaji Muhammadu Ndimi Mosque in Maiduguri migrated to Kanama village in Yobe State under the leadership of Mohammed Ali. They began calling themselves the Association of the People of the Sunna for Proselytisation and Armed Struggle, later Boko Haram (B.A., personal communication, 10 July 2022).

During their time in Kanama village, the group clashed with the police over fishing rights to a dam, ultimately overpowering the police and taking their weapons. This led to a siege of the local mosque by the police and the death of their leader at the time, Mohammed Ali (Walker, 2012). Ali's death precipitated the group's return to Maiduguri, where they established their own mosque and lived relatively peacefully for some years, attracting people from all over the country and neighbouring states with their offers of free food and shelter.

Walker (2012) states that, according to observers, the group constructed a "state within a state", with its own "cabinet, its own religious police, and a large farm". Rumours abounded about the source of their funding; some said they received funds from Salafist contacts in Saudi Arabia, while others suggested they were supported by wealthy northern Nigerians.

According to Walker (2012), the group became increasingly violent, running into further clashes with the police. These led to attacks that were initially confined to government institutions but later included violent attacks against civilians as part of its goal of establishing an Islamic state. Their growing violence and insistence on the establishment of Sharia law prompted the declaration of a state of emergency in three northeastern states in 2009: Borno, Yobe, and Adamawa. The government began a severe crackdown on the group, catapulting the group into violent reprisals and a more violent overall strategy. Scholars such as Nsirim, Clement-Abraham, and Ajie (2024) have observed that the government's adoption of a coercive, rather than lawful, approach initially fuelled the group's aggression.

## Boko Haram's ideology

The word "boko" is a Kanuri word that means "fake" (Adesoji, 2010). The word was used to refer to a mythical "false lady" (*amaryar boko*) who rode on a stallion intended for a genuine lady in a parade, escorting her to her new home (Adesoji, 2010, 2011). Unfortunately, the word "boko" became associated with Western education among Kanuri-speaking people in West Africa, and there has never been any attempt to dissociate it from Western education other thanto use the word *ilimin zamani*, which means more or less the same thing (Adesoji, 2010). The word was also used in reference to schools, i.e., *makarantar boko* ("fake school"), now applied to refer to all Western education or Western schools (Bamidele, 2017). "Boko haram" can be translated as "Western education is forbidden" (Bamidele, 2017).

The Boko Haram insurgents appear to have derived their name and ideology from the Kanuri tradition, which has long been opposed to Western education and its effects. The group views anything official emanating from Western education as a symbol of evil. Adesoji (2011) concurs with Agbiboa (2021) that their initial targets were government establishments, and that they began to use violence as a means to acquire territories by force to establish Sharia states that they could govern. Mainstream Islam considers the teachings of Mohammed Yusuf, the group's most influential leader, to be erroneous (Onuoha, 2010; Osumah, 2013).

Boko Haram insurgents, for their part, view the government as a hindrance to the propagation of their religious beliefs, which is why they initially targeted Nigerian security forces that represent the administration (Mamman, 2020; International Crisis Group, 2014).

The group's religious belief system draws from Salafi thought, which holds that Muslims should live according to the standards and examples set by the Prophet Muhammad and his first three adherent sages, the "devout ancestors" (*al-salaf al-ṣāliḥ*). Salafis emphasise the "restoration" of Islamic doctrine to its "unadulterated frame" (B.A., personal communication, 2 July 2022). However, Salafi thought in the mid- twentieth century exhibited a solid innovator streak, encouraging constructive change and the acquisition of logical and mechanical knowledge (B.A., personal communication, 2 July 2022). Ironically, the Boko Haram belief system that condemns mainstream education and common administrative processes is, in fact, inconsistent with Salafi doctrine. Members themselves have mastered technology, becoming adept at bomb-making and relying heavily on cell phones and the internet. It appears that as long as technology helps further their religious and political battles, they are willing to use it (Islamic religious leader, M. A., personal communication, 13 August 2022).

It is worth noting that Nigerian society has a long history of Muslim dissatisfaction with Western mores and education, and breakaway groups have long advocated a return to an earlier, purer form of Islam. One such group is Ulama, many of whose members belong to the Izala Society, known for its opposition to what it sees as un-Islamic practices that have crept into Nigerian Islam. Long before the state began cracking down on Boko Haram, the Izala Society had been critical of Boko Haram's ideology, which it viewed as a perversion of Islamic teachings. Moreover, the Borno State government was aware of the danger posed by Boko Haram well before they took decisive action against the group (B.A., personal communication, 23 July 2022). Ideologically, the group represented a breakaway from existing reformist Salafi and Wahhabi groups in Northern Nigeria, which had constantly challenged the Tijaniyya and Qadiriyya groups since the late 1970s.

After the government had killed the group's first leader, it made no substantial attempt to put an end to the group, or, at the very least, to prevent its doctrines from spreading. Thus, instead of resolving the threat posed by the insurgency group at an early stage using lawful means, it chose the option of doing little for several years and then using overwhelming coercive power in July 2009. In that month, more than 1,000 individuals were murdered by Boko Haram in Borno State in Nigeria, especially in Maiduguri, the state capital, as a result of the government's aggressive action through military operations (B.A., personal communication, 10 July 2022). There were also many casualties in Gwoza, Malamfatori (community member, personal communication, 10 July 2022). The insurgency intensified in late 2010 with the emergence of another leader, Abubakar Shekau. At this stage, the name Boko Haram had become a cover for extensive criminal actions that amounted to thuggery. They engaged in several bank heists and prison breaks, and the political assassinations that occurred in various parts of Borno during the 2011 elections were also blamed on the insurgents (community member, personal communication, 3 August 2022).

The question often asked is whether Boko Haram is a distinct or undefined group. The group is decentralised but has retained a level of coordination through the Shura Council, the consultative body of the Islamic Movement in Nigeria (IMN), which is separate from the Nigerian government (Islamic religious leader, 2022). At the same time, the group's support base now extends beyond its initial ideological core (community member, personal communication, 27 July 2022). According to a source (2017a), the group seeks out individuals willing to engage in violent acts to advance their agenda. They target impressionable individuals vulnerable to their propaganda as well as those prone to violence. Additionally, they often coerce schools and entire communities to join their ranks, thereby expanding their support base and enhancing their operational capacity (personal communication, 14 July 2022). ECOMOG members and hooligans in the service of the former Borno State Governor, Ali Modu Sheriff, are influential in the insurgency group (B.A., personal communication, 9 July 2022).

Boko Haram targets not only ordinary citizens but also the northern political, religious, and traditional elite, as evidenced by their attempts to assassinate the Shehu of Borno (International Crisis Group, 2014). Ironically, the government initially accused the religious and political elite of Borno State of sponsoring the insurgents, as most of the violence has taken place in that state (Higazi, 2013). The accusation extended to Senator Mohammed Ali Ndume, former Senator of Borno South Senatorial District, who was detained by the military for allegedly sponsoring the Boko Haram insurgency. However, many Christians in Gwoza and Chibok, in Southern Borno, believed that Ndume was an innocent victim of a political plot (International Crisis Group, 2014).

In this regard, the narrative is that he was framed by Ali Modu Sheriff, who had supported an opposing candidate named Asabe Vilita for the Borno South senatorial seat, on the platform of the All-Nigeria People's Party (the ruling party in Borno) in 2011. He was unhappy that Ndume, who had decamped to the ruling People's Democratic Party (PDP), had won the election. Sheriff himself contested the Borno Central Senatorial seat and was defeated by another PDP candidate, Ahmed Zanna (B.A., personal communication, 3 July 2022). In other words, he was disgruntled. Instead of exposing what he perceived as Mohammed Ali Ndume's support of the insurgents, he attempted to accuse him of having done so. This suggests that his actions were an attempt to discredit his political rival rather than a genuine attempt to expose those providing political support for the insurgents.

Borno State is the main locus of Boko Haram's brutality, although attacks have been carried out in other parts of Nigeria. When attacks occur, it is not always easy to know who perpetrated them, and the tendency has been to associate all such acts with Boko Haram, often without verification. The tendency to blame the group is fuelled by the fact that they are constantly on the move, assaulting vital targets wherever they can. They conceal weapons in their kaftans and carry explosives in soft drink bottles (B.A., personal communication, 4 August 2022). In Borno State, they are known to attack jails, police, and military headquarters where they believe fellow members are being held, often burning these institutions to the ground, seizing any weapons and ammunition they find, and killing police officers (CJTF Unpublished Report, 2021).

From 2009 to 2021, over 100,000 locals died due to the Boko Haram insurgency in Borno State (CJTF Unpublished Report, 2022), and 2.9 million people in Borno, Adamawa, and Yobe were displaced (CJTF Unpublished Report, 2022). The concentration of violence in Borno has ripple effects throughout the region. Adamawa State, for example, has experienced a significant influx of displaced persons from neighbouring Borno State since the insurgency began (B.A., personal communication, 4 August 2022). While some of those fleeing violence find shelter with host families in other states, the majority end up in IDP camps. In these settings, they are highly vulnerable, often suffering violence, abuse, and exploitation. Women and girls are particularly vulnerable, often subject to sexual and gender-based violence, abduction, forced marriage, and exploitation by Boko Haram and other armed groups (B.A., personal communication, 4 August 2022). The situation in the northeast remains fragile, with ongoing violence and insecurity making it difficult for humanitarian organisations to aid those in need.

Figures 4.1 and 4.2 below clearly show that while Boko Haram is active all over the country, Borno State suffers the bulk of it. Figure 4.1 tracks the number of conflict incidents in Nigeria (shown in blue) and the number of incidents in Borno State (shown in orange) between 2009 and 2021.

**Figure 4.1**: Borno State's share of Boko Haram conflict incidents in Nigeria (2009–2021).

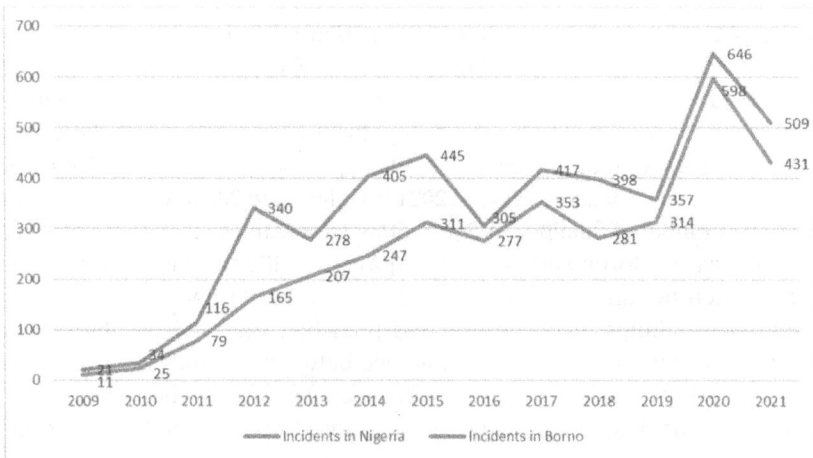

*Source*: Author.

As the graphic shows, violent conflict has risen steadily since 2009, decreasing slightly in 2016 before sharply increasing in 2019 and peaking in 2020. The trajectory of violence in the country is closely followed by that of Borno State, which takes the lion's share of incidents.

Figure 4.2 shows a similarly close correspondence between fatalities caused by Boko Haram in the country and in Borno State for the same period.

**Figure 4.2**: Borno State's share of fatalities caused by Boko Haram insurgency in Nigeria (2009–2021).

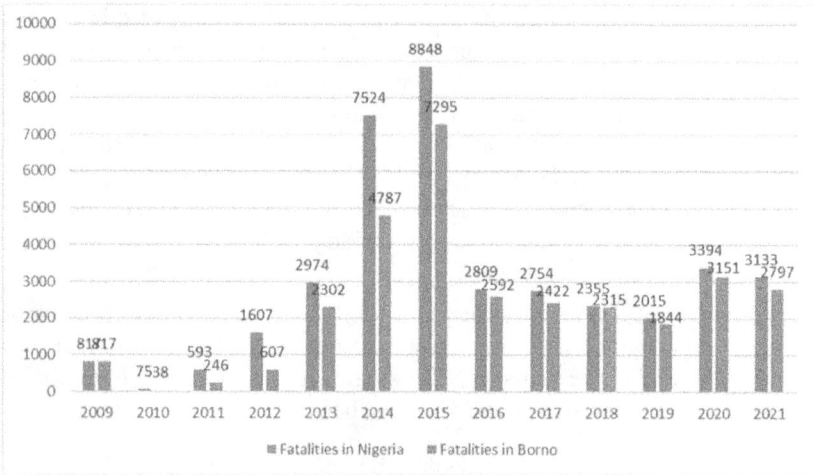

*Source*: Author.

Figure 4.2 shows that Borno State has experienced a disproportionately high number of fatalities in relation to the rest of Nigeria. This number has increased less steadily than the number of violent incidents, but there is nevertheless an upward trajectory, except for 2010 and 2011, when there were fewer incidents than in 2009. Fatalities peaked in 2015 but decreased significantly in 2016 and slightly in 2021 (in relation to 2020). The graph shows that the number of fatalities in Borno State closely tracks that of the country. In most cases, Borno suffered the majority of killings. The exceptions are 2010, when no killings occurred in Borno, and 2011 and 2012, when the number of killings in Borno was less than half the total number in the country. In 2014 and 2015, the difference between fatalities in Borno State and the rest of the country was more pronounced than in other years, but for the most part, killings in Borno account for almost all the killings in the country.

The security of its citizens is the foremost responsibility of the state. When the state fails to fulfil this duty, either through neglect or wilful action, local groups such as the CJTF will step in. However, this does not absolve the government of its responsibility to protect the population by securing the state (Bamidele, 2017b).

### Confusion surrounding the CJTF's role in perpetuating violence

In Borno State, the CJTF insurgency-related peace group has been identified as a contributing factor to the ongoing insurgency crisis (International Crisis Group, 2018). The International Crisis Group (2018) reports that the group has been accused of attacking both civilians and security forces. Some local communities have been accused of supporting or harbouring members of the group, leading to suspicions and increased scrutiny from government forces (HRW, 2019). However, the exact nature and extent of the group's involvement in the insurgency remains a matter of debate (International Crisis Group, 2018). The motivations behind the CJTF group's attacks against civilians and security forces are not entirely clear and may vary according to the specific circumstances. It has been suggested that the CJTF may be seeking power and control over the local population or may want to sow chaos and confusion to weaken both the state and insurgent groups operating in the region (S.M., personal communication, 13 August 2022). In addition, there may be internal divisions within the group that lead some members to engage in more violent or extreme tactics (S.M., personal communication, 13 August 2022).

It is worth noting that the situation in Borno State is highly complex, and understanding the motivations and actions of the various groups involved in the insurgency requires a context- specific approach. Factors such as historical grievances, political and ideological differences, and the desire to retaliate after state violence all play a role, as do internal conflicts within groups.

In the midst of this confusion about the CJTF, the state has implemented policies aimed at identifying members of Boko Haram and those who protect them (S.M., personal communication, 13 August 2022). These policies form part of the government's broader effort to combat the insurgency, maintain security in the region, and demonstrate a strong response to a perceived threat.

There are concerns, however, that these policies and the way in which they are implemented could have unintended consequences, such as reinforcing tensions between the government and affected communities (U.A., personal communication, 20 August 2022). To address the insurgency, the government needs to balance its security efforts with respect for human rights and a commitment to working collaboratively with local communities to achieve lasting peace (M.B., personal communication, 19 August 2022).

David Galula's theory of insurgency-related peace, contained in his influential 1964 book, *Counterinsurgency Warfare: Theory and Practice*, provides a foundation for understanding the challenges governments face in responding to insurgency threats. Other scholars, such as Kilcullen (2006), Kiras (2010), Mac Ginty (2018), and Moore (2007), have built upon Galula's work to further explore insurgency and insurgency-related peace strategies. Within the context of insurgency-related peace in Nigeria, the theory should have been used to frame collaborative operations by the military and CJTF. Had this been done, it is possible that these entities could have more effectively countered the Boko Haram insurgency.

The CJTF claims that it was formed to protect the community, but from the perspective of local communities, their actions are characterised more by human rights abuses than by legitimate insurgency-related peace measures. Their abuses are said to include arbitrary arrests, detention at the CJTF headquarters, and extortion. Their insurgency-related peace operations mainly target suspected Boko Haram sympathisers rather than Boko Haram itself; in the process, they have abused innocent locals. In the past, despite commendations by some locals, members of the CJTF were not recognised by the military. One reason for this may be that the government had no real means of vetting CJTF members (Kilcullen, 2006). In addition, lingering mistrust between the military and CJTF may have been exacerbated by claims that the group included individuals who had previously fought on behalf of Boko Haram or other insurgent groups (Moore, 2007). This mistrust would have made it difficult for the military to work effectively with CJTF members, even though they claimed to be supportive of the government's efforts to counter-insurgency (Mac Ginty, 2018).

An uneasy relationship between the Nigerian state military and the local CJTF group prevails to this day. Human Rights Watch (2019) says the group has been accused of crimes such as poaching and the illegal possession of arms, among other unlawful acts.

## Citizens' coping strategies in the face of insurgency

In the midst of insurgency, citizens may adopt various coping strategies. The most obvious physical life-sustaining one is to avoid all forms of violence by fleeing from one locality to another. Most locals in Borno State affected by insurgency have taken this option (D.U., personal communication, 17 August 2022). Another avoidance tactic is remaining informed through the circulation of information so that residents may be aware of planned attacks and take the necessary steps to avoid them (A.I., personal communication, 23 August 2022).

Others take a more proactive approach, engaging in negotiation, cutting deals, or paying money for security. Some engage the services of local armed groups, such as the CJTF and hunters' groups, to maintain access to their farmland.

In most cases, people remain silent and acquiesce to demands for loyalty. As instability increases and maintaining a livelihood becomes impossible, those with few resources may be forced to eat fewer meals until security is restored. Those with fewer choices are especially vulnerable, having to choose between the best of bad options or between short-term gains and longer-term losses.

The strategies to ensure the physical safety of humans and livestock have been necessitated by the urge to secure the environment. These include citizens' perceptions of the severity of the threat and their own capacities to act (Leonardsson & Rudd, 2015). In the Mafa district of Borno State, where livestock is central to livelihoods, and in Gwazo, Ngala and Maiduguri, where farmlands are under attack, locals invariably choose to move from their farms in the interest of security, which directly affects their livelihoods.

## Positive and negative outcomes of citizens' strategies

Some security strategies ensure the physical safety of humans and livestock, and may even ensure the continuation of livelihoods, education, health, and basic services. However, not all local security strategies are successful or achieve positive results, as many studies of local security indicate. For example, the CJTF's insurgent peace strategy of destroying properties to deter Boko Haram from using them as a base is an entirely negative outcome.

Locals who flee from insurgency may find that while they secure life, they lose all else. Fleeing exposes them to hunger, the division of families, the loss of all possessions, and even death in a different locality. The security strategy of fleeing the region harms the human dignity of the victims, who may resort to begging for assistance. Displaced persons undergo massive changes in lifestyle, which may affect their identity and cause lasting psychological damage.

Some coping strategies are negative in themselves. These include child and early marriages to reduce household or family expenditure during times of insurgency, or the sending away of family members to work as housemaids for an income (M.S., personal communication, 21 August 2022). These security strategies provide short-term gains at a high human cost.

The most effective strategy would be for the government to employ the services of a local insurgency-related peace group that is equipped, trained, and disciplined. Research conducted by the Borno State government reveals the positive effects of the CJTF's local security endeavours when it works in collaboration with the military rather than on its own (M.M., personal communication, 9 August 2022).

In Bama, a local government area 60 km southeast of Maiduguri, the capital city of Borno State, citizens have devised coping strategies that work in the short term. In visiting the area, the researcher found that women, rather than men, would take produce to market, since men were being targeted for attack. The strategy may have saved lives but is far from ideal, exposing women to danger and abuse. This highlights the pervasive and harmful nature of patriarchal attitudes, which in this case foster gender-based violence, or the constant threat thereof. Gender-based violence affects all members of a community, regardless of their gender (security expert, personal communication, 17 September 2022).

In Konduga, site visits revealed that displaced people had established connections in the new locale and were able to earn a livelihood. In addition, locals had engaged hunters known as *banga* to provide security. This strategy appeared to be working (U.A., personal communication, 12 August 2022).

In other cases, local security outcomes are mixed. Bamidele (2020) states that local security, ensured through collaboration between the military and CJTF, has had positive outcomes, while Onapajo and Ozden (2020) state that the use of other local security groups has had mixed results, since they tend to be formed along tribal and ethnic lines. In addition, although many locals in Borno State see the CJTF as the eyes and ears of their localities (A.A., personal communication, 29 August 2022), some see its members as collaborators and spies and not as sources of security.

Locals may distrust leaders of local security who are not from their area, regarding them as ineffective (D.U., personal communication, 11 August 2022). In addition, within contexts of insurgency, local security strategies may force people to form alliances or collaborate with one group of combatants to provide security against another. These alliances expose locals to harm, as they become targets for retaliation by the opposing group. Furthermore, locals may overestimate the effectiveness of their security strategies, leading to a false sense of security, which may put them in danger. Forced displacement can limit locals' access to local security networks and knowledge and, consequently, their ability to mitigate local threats effectively (Bamidele, 2021).

These observations highlight the complexity of attempting to devise local security strategies in insurgency situations and the need to carefully consider their potential consequences.

## Local groups as both security and predatory agents

Local security agents can be individuals or groups within a community who take responsibility for maintaining security in their area. They can include police officers, neighbourhood watch groups, or even armed militias (U.U., personal communication, 27 August 2022). However, during an insurgency, locals may serve as both protectors / active agents of security and perpetrators of harm. They may initially act as protectors but, over time, may turn into predatory agents who exploit their power and engage in harmful behaviour (Z.U., personal communication, 24 August 2022). This underscores the complex and multifaceted roles that locals play in insurgency situations, where they can simultaneously be victims, witnesses, survivors, protectors, and enablers of harm during the Boko Haram insurgency (M.B., personal communication, 26 August 2022). As a result, local security interventions that rely on locals as security agents can become problematic, as those initially seen as protectors may later be discovered to be predatory agents. They may end up engaging in violent actions against those whom they were supposed to be protecting (U.A., personal communication, 23 July 2022). This highlights the complex and dynamic nature of local security strategies, which can have unintended consequences and may perpetuate cycles of violence and harm in local communities.

It is important to recognise that locals may play multiple roles and have conflicting interests, which complicate efforts to establish effective security strategies. This means that state- implemented and local security interventions must consider the nuances of the local context to be effective.

In the presence of strangers in a location, local security agents may become particularly vigilant and active in their efforts to protect their community. They may work to gather information about these strangers, monitor their activities, and identify any potential threats they may pose (B.A., personal communication, 18 July 2022). They will monitor the movement of people in and out of their community and identify any suspect activities. This information can be crucial for identifying and preventing potential attacks by terrorist groups such as Boko Haram.

However, the presence of strangers can also create ambiguity and uncertainty when it comes to identifying potential threats. Local security agents must be careful not to target innocent individuals based solely on their status as outsiders. They must balance their responsibilities as protectors of their community with the need to respect the rights and dignity of all individuals, regardless of their background or status.

In a series of case studies, this chapter considered the security contributions of locals through the CJTF in Borno State. Owing to the CJTF's local connections, familiarity with the language and contextual knowledge, they often enjoy greater legitimacy and a better understanding of local insurgency dynamics than the military; they are also more adept at identifying and tracking Boko Haram local insurgents than the military (CJTF Unpublished Report, 2022). Therefore, the CJTF serves as a valuable intermediary between locals and the state.

The CJTF, whose members represent multiple ethnicities and religions, was formed in response to Boko Haram's local insurgency under the control of Abubakar Shekau and the government's inability to contain it – coupled with their abusive military operations, which often harmed as many civilians as insurgents. Military operations often amounted to spates of extrajudicial killings, torture, and unlawful detentions, all carried out under the pretext of fighting insurgency. These abuses were criticised by human rights organisations and led to concerns about the legitimacy of the government's efforts.

The CJTF enjoyed a great deal of local support when it was first formed. Many locals joined to secure themselves (B.M., personal communication, 16 August 2022), and other locals continue to serve as spies for both the military and CJTF. As the group itself states, they have evolved from defending the locals to harassing and attacking Boko Haram insurgents and killing suspected collaborators, working alongside the military to identify and contain the insurgency (CJTF Unpublished Report, 2022). However, its popularity has waned in the wake of accusations that it has committed atrocities against locals (U.M., personal communication, 18 August 2022).

The 2022 CJTF report explains the effects of insurgency on the evolution of the defence group; they protect and secure locals but treat those who become supporters of Boko Haram as collaborators. Similar dynamics were observed in Mali and South Sudan when victims of forced displacement became supporters of the groups that threatened them (whether voluntarily or by force), while groups such as the CJTF were attempting to protect them (CJTF Unpublished Report, 2022). Thus, in another study, the chapter identified a dualism at work in local defence groups. They claim to be decreasing violent insurgency on behalf of the government by collaborating with locals to identify insurgents, but they also turn against them when they do not collaborate or when the CJTF suspects them of assisting Boko Haram. The earlier study described the complex relationship that exists between groups such as the CJTF and locals, with the counterinsurgents often exploiting the uncertainty that prevails and engaging in opportunistic behaviour (Bamidele, 2020).

It appears that locals are deeply divided on the CJTF. It is important to recognise that while locals contribute to countering local insurgency by countering rumours and disseminating information, they can also incite or perpetuate local insurgency through their affiliations (A.U., personal communication, 13 August 2022). Their reliance on groups such as the CJTF is a double-edged sword. On the one hand, the CJTF provides locals with the means to block Boko Haram local insurgency activities, thereby reducing incidents of violence against civilians (A.A., personal communication, 23 August 2022). On the other hand, the group may be encouraging violence, since some individuals believe that their own violent acts will be supported by the CJTF, which is seen as a respected, powerful protector, who will defend their actions. It is essential to recognise both the positive and negative aspects of the CJTF to avoid idealising their actions.

## The context of local threats

Effective local security at any level requires a nuanced and thorough understanding of the context of local threats. This understanding should include a determination of the risks, vulnerabilities, opportunities, and challenges of proposed interventions. The context of the threat to locals includes the nature of their households and families, which humanitarian agencies and the state (military) need to understand, especially in terms of traditional, sociocultural values, roles, and beliefs. The context of a local threat will help to define it and identify existing coping strategies, which have local security implications. There will often be a need for protection against suicide bombers.

It has been observed, however, that analyses of local security contexts can be so mired in detail that the bigger picture becomes obscured. The search for understanding of a local context must not inadvertently overlook broader trends and threats to locals. Therefore, paradoxically, an understanding of the dangers and coping strategies of locals may be marred by an excessive focus on the CJTF.

Bamidele (2023) points out that many of the threats locals face cut across cultural and national boundaries. Bombings, torture, assault, and genocide pose threats to citizens that are not unique to a particular place or period, even though their specific manifestations may differ.

To help locals survive and cope with uncertainty and threats in their communities, it is important for them to hold onto a sense of normality. Faith and prayer can provide support by imparting a sense of meaning to people's suffering. It also imparts a sense of meaning to the violence itself. The causal link between religion and insurgency among locals in Borno State has been documented (Bamidele, 2018). A religious understanding of insurgency can make locals feel more secure, especially when they compare the hardships they are facing with the results of secular humanism. Their religious beliefs, in other words, give meaning to violence, on whichever side it is perpetrated.

Unfortunately, a deep religious faith can both help people cope with insecurity and perpetuate discrimination, a founding condition for violence against certain religious groups. For example, Christians in some areas of Borno State face discrimination and blame from Islamic-dominated communities. In addition, in many areas affected by the Boko Haram insurgency, religious beliefs are used to justify violence. What is clear is that an effective insurgency-related peace measure cannot ignore religious faith, which must be understood as part of the composition of a people, especially in Africa.

## Extended security networks

Studies on insurgency-related peace in Nigeria show that a plethora of local security groups exist, including diffuse security networks, formal agencies, and small local security groups (U., A, personal communication, 31 August 2022). Households and security networks play a critical role during the insurgency, providing resources, psychosocial assistance, and support to victims and nonvictims. In addition, family members and the remittances they send to victims of insurgency help victims remain in their communities and deal with the circumstances they face when violence ends (M., personal communication, 13 July 2022).

Local leaders in Borno State earn legitimacy by defending the interests of families in their area, while the initiatives they implement may enhance the status of locals. In some localities, the CJTF has supported peace and development, promoting local livelihoods and ensuring the continued provision of social security and basic amenities such as education, healthcare and shelter (B.A., personal communication, 14 July 2022). Local people will often reduce tensions by sheltering both strangers and relatives fleeing violent insurgency. They provide assistance and support and act as responders amid the violence of Boko Haram (B.A., personal communication, 14 July 2022).

The findings of this chapter show that the CJTF in Bama played a crucial role in creating a sense of tranquillity, providing security for lives and livelihoods, and ensuring the continuity of cultural practices (Bamidele, 2018). They were also responsible for determining the status of displaced persons, providing psychosocial and moral support, and advocating for the interests of the locals. The CJTF repeatedly stressed the importance of psychological sources of security in addition to physical security (S.M., personal communication, 19 July 2022).

In many situations in Borno State, members of the CJTF have provided shelter to victims of the Boko Haram insurgency. For example, during the attacks of 2020, when Maiduguri was the siteof horrific suicide bombings, the CJTF hid locals in different locations in Gwazo, saving many lives.

However, locals' behaviour towards local threats varies and can lead to both positive and negative security outcomes (Bamidele, 2017). In some cases, local leaders, including the CJTF, have involved external security networks to secure a fragile peace, which can have negative consequences. In Borno State, locals built a security network that included the military (Muzan, 2014) but found that the partnership damaged their credibility as leaders (Bamidele, 2023). In addition, the involvement of external actors can undermine the autonomy and agency of local communities, who may feel disempowered in their own security affairs.

Local security networks can also increase destruction and violence in conflict zones. Communities that network with and rely on military support, for example, have experienced more rather that fewer indiscriminate attacks on civilians, leading to the loss of innocent lives and property. State forces evidently do not discriminate when they open fire or conduct raids, and they are seemingly cavalier about collateral damage. These attacks create resentment and anger towards the government and military forces, which have fuelled support for militant groups such as Boko Haram. Therefore, one can easily conclude that the military's response to insurgency has contributed to the escalation of violent attacks by Boko Haram. Their heavy- handed attacks include aerial bombardments and mass arrests, exacerbating the humanitarian crisis in the region.

Thus, while external security networks may be necessary in some cases, it is important to recognise the potential negative consequences of such involvement and prioritise the autonomy and agency of local communities in their own security affairs. It is crucial to adopt a more nuanced and collaborative approach that recognises the importance of local knowledge and participation in ensuring sustainable and effective security measures.

## Factors that increase locals' ability to resist violence

A number of factors enhance a given community's ability to counter violence, remain cohesive, and resist being drawn into internal conflicts. The first is strong leadership. Studies on local security emphasise the importance of strong leaders in determining the ability of local people to negotiate effectively with state security agencies such as the military. Leaders need to accurately reflect the desires of the populace, state a clear position, and work as collaborators with the military, holding them to account when necessary. A study conducted in Borno State concluded that locals affected by the Boko Haram insurgency were better able to negotiate and confront local threats when they had strong relations with the military during operations (Omeni, 2017). This is effected through their leaders.

Leaders need to be closely connected with the population, drawing them into all plans made for their protection. It is widely recognised that engaging and involving locals in the formulation of security strategies is crucial for ensuring their sustainability, avoiding unintentional harm, and contributing to locals' sense of agency (Bamidele, 2018).

The ability to hold leaders to account is also crucial. Based on interviews with CJTF leaders in 2022, two understandings of locally based security may be identified: one that recognises external security agencies and their responsibility to lead locals, and another that holds that local security entails locals securing themselves. Both strategies emphasise the accountability of leaders, whether they are local or government. Accountability is particularly important in situations where locals lack knowledge about their legal rights, which hinders their ability to hold leaders to account for violations and harm. An analysis of CJTF-based security in Borno State revealed that the group engaged and empowered locals to hold leaders to account.

The way that locals behave can have a significant impact on the level of violence in a given area. For example, in Borno State, it has been observed that locals became aware of increasing polarisation in the state and attempted to counter it in various ways, which helped to discourage violence (H.U., personal communication, 28 September 2022). The locals asserted their values regarding security, livelihoods, and the value of human life, and their commitment to these values helped to prevent them from being drawn into violence. By standing up for what they believed in and refusing to be swayed by extremist ideologies, these individuals helped to create an atmosphere of peace and stability in their communities.

Locals' adherence to authority figures has also played a role in their resistance to violence. When people are obedient to authority figures, they are more likely to adhere to the values and norms of their society and promote peace and stability than when they are individualistic and rebellious. Local authorities and religious leaders usually discourage violence, and the population's obedience to these leaders can reinforce these norms. Therefore, obedience to authority can serve as a protective factor against participation in violence. Leaders make people aware of the danger of accepting unfamiliar interpretations of their religion and develop immunity to the allure of such interpretations. As a result, they are less likely to be swayed by extremist ideologies and are more resistant to being recruited by violent groups. This highlights the importance of promoting a culture of respect for authority and a sense of community cohesion in countering violent extremism.

Research conducted for this chapter furthermore shows that, despite the CJTF's multiethnic composition, people of all ethnicities in Borno State generally support and trust them to protect communities. This spirit of cooperation has helped to curb abuse. Although some acts of predation have occurred, they are less frequent than in other groups studied, owing to the deterrent effects of local disciplinary procedures and shaming by locals when dissenters were found (B.U., personal communication, 20 July 2022).

Multiple analyses have identified community cohesion as central to local security. Internal cohesion promotes the development of collective strategies, helping locals to achieve autonomy and continue with effective decision-making on security measures without outside influence.

It is clear that strong social bonds help to insulate locals from the physical and psychological harm of insurgency. The discussion has underscored the importance of engagement, participation, and strong local leadership in achieving positive local security outcomes.

## Conclusion

Security activities in Borno State tend to follow a standard pattern. They lack a strategic focus and appear to be formulated in a piecemeal way, without an overall plan. The approach appears to be one-dimensional, lacking recognition of the many factors that promote peace and the many contributions that could be made by different security groups, including the CJTF. There is also a lack of knowledge about why local groups engage or do not engage in peace efforts. Despite the increasing prevalence of Boko Haram insurgency, surprisingly few works focus on local security, apart from frameworks that speak to the threats and categories of locals. These are important but do not specifically indicate strategies for local security. Furthermore, most scholarly works discuss security within a defined local area. In Borno State, security groups must often diffuse violence in several localities simultaneously. This means that there is a need for an overarching plan that can be adapted, within certain boundaries, to specific locations.

The chapter has discussed the role of networks and affinity groups in maintaining peace. Any discussion on local security should involve an examination of the impact of such groups and networks in the complex interactions between security groups in the insurgency environment. A comprehensive understanding of their impact on local dynamics would inform more effective and sustainable local security initiatives. Affinity groups can be formed around a shared desire to protect the community from threats. They may include individuals from various backgrounds, such as religious leaders, community elders, and local business owners, who come together to take collective action to safeguard their community.

Patronage ties, on the other hand, refer to social relationships based on the exchange of favours or benefits. These ties can either promote or work against peace. Within the context of local security, patronage ties can be formed between security groups and local leaders, who provide support or resources in exchange for protection or assistance in achieving their objectives. These ties can influence the behaviour of security groups, as they may be incentivised to prioritise the interests of those who provide them with support or resources. However, patronage ties can also lead to corruption and the abuse of power, as security groups may use their position to extract additional benefits and resources from those who depend on their protection.

The diversity of groups involved in local security and the range of strategies they employ need to be understood by any group seeking to promote peace in the region. As has been pointed out numerous times, locals must be involved in the formulation and implementation of security plans for any hope of sustainability. Furthermore, the discussion has revealed the need to avoid homogenous categorisations and instead move towards further deconstruction and analysis of local security initiatives. A better understanding of the points of intersection between different groups and approaches will help to weave them together into a comprehensive plan for peace in insurgency situations. There is a great need to avoid the development of parallel security measures by disparate groups, with each pulling in different directions.

It is also important to avoid characterising local security groups as inherently good, as human beings are fallible and local security groups are as flawed as any other. Their one advantage is that locals know their area geographically, culturally, economically, and socially. They are, therefore essential to the peace process but not the only players. What is needed is an inclusive, comprehensive, collaborative, and flexible approach comprising an overall plan that is adaptable within the boundaries of certain guiding principles, so that it works within unique local contexts.

In moving forward, government agencies responsible for security, military, and law enforcement agencies, local security groups, civil society organisations, and international partners need to work collaboratively and adopt a context-specific approach to local security to protect communities facing threats such as the Boko Haram insurgency.

# CHAPTER FIVE
# THE STATE SECURITY ARCHITECTURE IN BORNO STATE, NIGERIA

## Introduction

Domestic security is generally understood as encompassing the protection of values, critical human and infrastructural assets, territorial integrity, and the lives and property of people in a country. The principles underlying domestic security are drawn from Thomas Hobbes's social contract theory, which states that a social contract exists in relations between rulers and the ruled that defines the rights and responsibilities of each. In an ideal security architecture, domestic security is driven by the citizens and the state's law enforcement agencies, with the people holding the primacy.

This chapter explores the internal security question in Nigeria from the perspective of the state, which has the statutory obligation to protect its citizens. As stated in Sec. 14(b) of the 1999 Constitution, "The security and welfare of the people shall be the primary purpose of government" (Federal Republic of Nigeria, 1999).

While the state holds the primary responsibility for protecting its people, it does so only with the people's permission and in a way that accords with their values and needs. Any internal security architecture that is not driven by the concept of citizen consent and partnership is a negation of Thomas Hobbes's social contract model, which should underlie all relations between the state and people in a democratic state. Without an underlying recognition of this partnership model, the state security architecture is bound to fail.

The current seemingly intractable internal security challenges in Nigeria are a direct consequence of the alienation of the civilian populace from the state, the absence of an internal security policy framework, and a poor understanding of the requirements and dynamics of internal security management on the part of strategic actors. These should include legislators, policymakers, and political actors, whose informed collaboration could engender a revitalisation of current approaches.

In addition, crime significantly contributes to the ongoing cycle of violence and reprisals in Borno State. The failure of security leaders to fully understand and address the impact of pervasive corruption impedes peace efforts. This corruption, which permeates various levels of authority, allows terrorist groups to maintain their influence and disrupt stability. It is crucial to identify and expose the specific actors involved in this corruption, including whether it pertains to Boko Haram members, leaders within the CJTF, or local and state politicians. Such clarity is essential for devising effective strategies to counteract the negative effects of corruption on peace and security.

To address these issues, there is an urgent need for a new approach to insurgent peacebuilding that is rooted in community involvement. This citizen-based peace architecture would prioritise transparency and accountability, ensuring that local populations have a role in shaping and overseeing security measures. By engaging the community in the peace process and addressing corruption head-on, it is possible to create a more effective and sustainable framework for achieving lasting stability in Borno State.

Ensuring local security is central to the survival and proper functioning of Nigeria's states. The essence of security at the state level is the protection of local interests and values, which overlap in all states despite the multiethnic and multireligious nature of Nigerian society. Most local populations in Nigeria understand the security of their region as a state responsibility, expressed through military operations (B.A., personal communication, 17 September 2022). To understand the context in which the state enacts its responsibilities, it is important to be familiar with the historical context, characterised as it was (and is) by ambiguities in the wording of policies and strategies, inefficient coordination between agencies, and inconsistent levels of readiness to face threats.

Addressing ambiguities would strengthen the foundations of security and better equip all role-players to understand their roles and deal with current and future challenges. Effective security measures encompass all critical assets, both tangible and intangible, and recognise the broad range of local threats. Assets may be related to local interests, sources of power, or a variety of valuable resources. Ultimately, the security of a state is synonymous with the security of the people who live within it. Prioritising local security can build a stronger state security foundation.

Prioritising local security also creates the necessary foundation for a stronger and more resilient society (Choi, 2016; Chen, 2018). Local security measures can include community policing initiatives, infrastructure protection, enhancement of emergency response capabilities, and public awareness and education on security issues (Buzan, 1991). Not all threats pertain to the military. Natural disasters constitute a security threat as well and need to be adequately prepared for, particularly in light of climate change. It is important to establish effective communication channels between government agencies, law enforcement, social service organisations, and local communities to ensure a coordinated and integrated approach to security (Feng, 2019).

In today's interconnected world, cybersecurity has become a critical component of state security. With the increasing reliance on technology and the internet, cyber threats can pose a significant risk to national security and public safety. Therefore, it is important to develop a comprehensive cybersecurity strategy that addresses the unique challenges and vulnerabilities of a state's digital infrastructure.

## State and local security

The interdependence between state and local security cannot be ignored, as they are closely linked (Bamidele, 2020). For a state to thrive, it must prioritise the security of local communities within its jurisdiction. This requires a coordinated effort between state and local security agencies. However, the security of the state is occasionally attained at the expense of local security, leading to incompatible and oversimplified policies that do not effectively address local security concerns. Therefore, it is crucial to establish a balance between state and local security. An effective and secure state is essential for the existence of local security, not only at the economic, social, and political levels but also at the psychological level in certain situations (Gillespie, 2017). Conversely, the security and proper functioning of life and livelihoods at the state level are essential to national security.

Thus, to ensure security in Nigeria, both the federal and state governments must take measures to protect the locals from all forms of insurgency, by political, economic, social, and military means. Effective local security measures involve isolating local threats, mobilising local resources to boost collaboration, implementing local security and emergency readiness actions, and enacting anti-coercion legislation (Peters, 2007). Other measures include strengthening local infrastructure, maintaining intelligence services, guarding classified information, and protecting the state from local insurgency attacks.

In Nigeria, the main focus of local security measures is, of necessity, protection against local insurgency. While local insurgency can originate from the local population, it is not the only possible source of such threats. In some cases, external actors, such as foreign extremist groups, may illicitly enter a locality to carry out acts of insurgency. Whether local or foreign in origin, insurgency must be preempted and met with measures that have been worked out and agreed upon in advance.

The focus on external threats does not preclude plans and actions that enhance the quality of life for locals. Poor living conditions will always constitute a security threat, since dissatisfied citizens are easy prey for radical ideologues seeking to foment violence. Thus, security measures must include ensuring the supply of food, water, healthcare, education, and economic opportunities. By addressing these factors, the government can work towards preventing or reducing the likelihood of local insurgency by addressing the underlying causes of discontent and unrest.

The ever-present danger with security measures is the possibility that their implementation will encroach upon the human rights of citizens. Thus, Nye (2017) states that there is a constant need to balance security with respect for human rights.

The maintenance of local security as a key responsibility of both the state and the local population is well recognised in Nigeria. It is understood that while the national government holds the overarching responsibility, individual states play an important role in managing internal threats. Nonetheless, in exceptional cases of severe disorder, Sec. 217 (2)(c) of the Constitution states that the military can be deployed to suppress insurrection and act in aid of civil authority. Relying on this provision, the President, Commander-in-Chief of the Armed Forces of Nigeria, has deployed the military to complement the people's efforts in serious internal security challenges, which have reached magnitudes that are beyond the operational capacity of the people.

However, a situation prevails in Nigeria where security responsibilities are not well defined when it comes to the role of the state and the people. The entire area is fraught with ambiguity. In the complex Nigerian security system, the original focus was on freedom from local insurgency through military action. The concept has now expanded to incorporate various forms of nonmilitary security in Nigeria.

### State security and the law

The law plays a critical role in ensuring the security of a population. According to a security expert (personal communication, 20 July 2022), the law is a system of rules created and enforced by social and state institutions to regulate behaviour among a country's citizens. In Nigeria, the National Security Act 19 of 1986 governs the security of the local population and identifies the protection agencies responsible for conducting the necessary aspects of security and related matters. These include the state security service, military intelligence divisions (army, navy, and air force), defence intelligence agencies, and the national intelligence agency (Federal Republic of Nigeria, 1986). The purpose of the Act is to clearly allocate state powers to various state agencies and ensure the proper management of security in the country.

In terms of local security, the responsibilities of the military include detecting local crimes associated with threats against the state, safeguarding classified documents and secrets related to local security threats, and performing social responsibilities occasionally assigned to them by the state or chief of defence. According to Sec. 1 of the Constitution, the state is responsible for appointing a state security coordinator, while Sec. 5(1) regulates the composition, membership, and appointment of the Council for State Security (Federal Republic of Nigeria, 1999).

The Terrorism (Prevention) Act of 2011 establishes a legal framework for combatting insurgency in Nigeria. It defines terrorism, creates a National Counter-Terrorism Centre, and establishes an Anti-Terrorism Fund (Federal Republic of Nigeria, 2011). Sec. 15 of the Terrorism (Prevention) Act of 2011 states that, with the approval of the Attorney General of the Federation and the coordinator of state security, any enforcement agency may apply to a judge for an interception of communications warrant to prevent acts of insurgency. The Terrorism (Prevention) (Amendment) Act of 2013 expands the scope of offences that constitute insurgency and provides for the designation of certain persons, groups, and entities as terrorists, as well as the freezing of their assets (Federal Republic of Nigeria, 2013).

Sec. 1(3) of the Terrorism (Prevention) (Amendment) Act of 2013 designates the National Counter-Terrorism Centre as the coordinating body for all security and intelligence agencies involved in the prevention and detection of insurgency in Nigeria. In addition, Sec. 2(6) of the Act empowers the military to initiate, develop, and run specific training programmes for its officers and other agencies responsible for securing, detaining, investigating, eliminating, and prosecuting local insurgency activities in the state. Among its provisions, the Act mandates the creation and regular updating of a database or record-keeping system to track the activities of local groups and individuals that may pose a threat to the security of the state. This database helps the military and other security agencies to monitor the movements and actions of potential insurgents and take necessary actions to prevent attacks and neutralise threats. Importantly, the Act also assigns to the military the social responsibility of monitoring and supervising the activities of all local groups, such as the CJTF.

Nigeria, like any other country, must prioritise the strengthening of local security measures to safeguard its citizens and prevent threats and attacks (National Security Strategy, 2014). However, while some local security measures may prove effective, others may have unintended consequences that harm the stability of local communities. Therefore, the Nigerian state must adopt a strategic and comprehensive approach to local security that carefully balances the effectiveness of security measures with their impact on local communities.

Within this context, the federal government needs to work closely with state governments to identify and prioritise local security threats that require urgent attention. Only after a local threat has been identified and evaluated should the federal government deploy its local security measures to address insurgency. This approach would ensure that the security measures deployed are targeted, effective, and sensitive to the needs and concerns of local communities (National Security Strategy, 2014).

## The National Security Strategy

In 2014, former President Goodluck Jonathan indirectly launched a local security strategy with the introduction of the National Security Strategy (NSS). The NSS aims to provide a holistic and coordinated response to the locally generated insurgency in Nigeria (security expert, personal communication, 10 July 2022). The strategy involves identifying local insurgency challenges and assigning roles to both the Nigerian state and locals to address them.

The strategy states that the government should establish a robust intelligence-gathering mechanism that involves the participation of various stakeholders, including local community leaders, civil society organisations, and security agencies (National Security Strategy, 2014). In addition, the government should invest in community-based policing strategies that prioritise community engagement and partnership in ensuring local security (National Security Strategy, 2014; Nigeria Police Trust Fund Act, 2019). Security measures should be backed by adequate funding, training, and resources to ensure their effectiveness. The strategy recognises that the state should provide regular and transparent feedback to local communities on the outcomes of its local security measures. This would enhance trust and cooperation between the government and local communities, leading to better intelligence gathering and more effective security measures (National Security Strategy, 2014).

While the National Security Strategy looks good on paper, it appears to be too vague to hold government security agents to account regarding their modus operandi. It requires state forces to consult with locals but does not specify whether local counterinsurgency groups are to be drawn into planning, strategising, implementing, monitoring, and evaluating local security measures; it makes no mention of equipping or training such groups, nor of financial recompense to locals providing essential services to the military. This leaves the relationship between the state and local groups ambiguous and open to interpretation. In reality, the state can claim to have consulted with locals on the basis of very little evidence.

## The need for a revised security architecture

Since 1960, Nigeria's local security apparatus has focused primarily on addressing internal upheavals, particularly those driven by religious and ethnic conflicts.

Initially, the government's strategy relied heavily on a robust military response to insurgency. However, this approach proved inadequate due to its failure to incorporate local initiatives into the security framework. Critics highlighted that the strong military stance lacked coordination with grassroots efforts, resulting in insufficient funding and limited effectiveness. Despite these efforts, conflicts and violence not only persisted but also often escalated, prompting calls for more comprehensive and context-sensitive solutions.

In response, the state shifted to a model that emphasised greater involvement of local communities in security matters. This approach aimed to empower local actors by transferring significant aspects of security responsibilities to them and expanding local security mechanisms over time. However, the model has encountered several challenges. Issues such as inadequate training, lack of resources, and insufficient integration with broader security strategies have undermined its effectiveness. Local security groups often struggle with limited support and coordination, which hampers their ability to effectively address complex security threats. Furthermore, the fragmentation of responsibilities and varying levels of commitment among local actors have created inconsistencies in security operations, leading to a lack of cohesion and undermining the overall impact of the model. Consequently, while local involvement was intended to enhance security, these persistent challenges have limited the model's success in achieving lasting peace and stability.

The problem is that, while the NSS recognises the role of locals, their role is not mandated; Nigerian state laws still mandate only the military to deal with local insurgency. The role of local counterinsurgency groups is not clearly stipulated, and the provisions of the various Acts may not be implemented as intended. It is worth noting that consultation and collaboration exist on a sliding scale; the state can engage in very little of it while still claiming to have fulfilled the stipulations of the NSS. The state also takes no responsibility for equipping, training, and reimbursing local security groups such as the CJTF.

In effect, state agencies continue to dominate counterinsurgency efforts, occasionally collaborating with local groups but appearing to be under no obligation to do so. Local groups are often ignored. For example, contrary to the stipulations of various Acts, local groups that coordinate intelligence are excluded from the training exercises of Borno State security groups. The state is effectively sidelining a valuable human resource in the form of thousands of willing, able-bodied, and trainable young people who could contribute substantially to security in their area, thus taking some of the burden off the state. Although Sec. 37 of the Terrorism Prevention Act of 2011 contains the necessary provisions, it is simply not sufficiently robust to ensure that the military makes an effort to include locals in security planning and actions against local insurgency (Federal Government of Nigeria 2011).

The approach cannot be said to be working; the continuous acts of insurrection and ongoing instability, particularly in the northeast, are clear evidence of this. Reliance on the military alone is inadequate and lacks the impetus to stem the ravaging tide of local insurgency. There is a pressing need for the Nigerian state to recognise the significance of local communities in local security and invest in community-based policing strategies that prioritise community engagement and partnership. The state should, indeed, establish a robust intelligence-gathering mechanism, as the NSS states; this should involve various stakeholders, including local community leaders, civil society organisations, and security agencies. As mentioned in Chapter One, the state has co-opted some members of the CJTF into the army but has not recognised the CJTF formally, in the sense that it does not train, equip, and reimburse local security groups such as the CJTF. By adopting a more balanced and strategic approach to local security, Nigeria could enhance its security and protect its citizens from local threats and attacks.

In addition, some of the legal mandates are not ideal. For example, although a national intelligence centre was established in the country, this ought to have been replicated in all six geopolitical zones in the country, which would have fostered an improvement in local intelligence gathering and sharing (legal officer, personal communication, 10 July 2022). Moreover, much of the funds budgeted for local security is embezzled and siphoned into private bank accounts (security expert, personal communication, 13 June 2022).

The allocation of funds for security forces in Nigeria, including the army, air force, navy, Department of State Security, National Intelligence Agency, Defence Intelligence Agency, National Security and Civil Defence Corps, Nigerian Immigration Service, and Nigerian Prisons Service, is significant. Despite this, the financial resources dedicated to security measures are deemed insufficient, given the persistent insurgency by Boko Haram since 2009 (security expert, personal communication, 17 June 2022). The inadequacy of these funds undermines efforts to effectively address and mitigate the extensive domestic security challenges faced by the country.

Scholarly literature underscores that the exclusion of local actors, such as the CJTF, from security operations can be both a legal and ethical issue. Researchers such as Bellamy and Williams (2011), Galula (1964), Kindersley and Rolandsen (2019), Mac Ginty and Richmond (2013), Macaspac (2019), Orchard (2014), Philipsen (2022), Rubin (2020), and Russo (2022) highlight that, in situations of local insurgency, it is not uncommon for governments to marginalise local participation. In Nigeria, Boko Haram has established control over several areas, enforcing peace through coercion and perceiving any local resistance as a threat to stability. Locals who oppose Boko Haram are often accused of colluding with the government or other external forces, which exacerbates conflict. This dynamic suggests that, in some instances, the government may tacitly support Boko Haram's control by excluding local security groups such as the CJTF from official operations, thereby perceiving this exclusion as a means to maintain overall stability.

## CJTF as a local security group

Limited information is available about the formation of the CJTF insurgency-related peace group and its active connection and operational association with the military in Borno State. However, studies indicate some collective causality and partnership between CJTF and military operations (Bamidele, 2020). According to the literature, locals have adopted many insurgency-related interventionist roles, forming auxiliary fighting groups and information-gathering networks to combat local insurgency operations (Olonisakin, 2016). However, a close analysis of the operational capability of the CJTF, and the extent of its collaboration with the military in Borno State, remains lacking.

Impressions of the CJTF coalesce around two main perspectives: On the one hand, local security mechanisms are regarded as unconventional, nontraditional, contradictory to the military's objectives, and hindering the military's efforts (Hassan, 2015). On the other hand, the involvement of locals such as the CJTF is regarded as an essential means of enhancing the local intelligence-gathering system based on these groups' knowledge of the terrain and the strategies of Boko Haram (Onapajo & Ozden, 2020; Idris et al., 2014).

Several scholars have attempted to explain the emergence of the CJTF in Borno State. Muzan (2014), Idris et al. (2014), and Bamidele (2017) have characterised the group as having an unconventional and nontraditional approach to insurgency-related peace. They suggest that locals view the CJTF's actions not only as essential to their safety and the restoration of order after attacks but as a means of legitimising local contributions to Nigeria's insurgency-related peace efforts.

Some scholars point out that the CJTF is a response to the failure of military insurgency-related peace operations. They argue that the military's approach to the conflict has been hindered by challenges such as a lack of resources, ineffective strategies, and the difficulties of trying to combat the influence of extremist ideologies. In addition, political factors such as corruption and state control are also seen as contributing to the failure of military operations. In response to these challenges, the CJTF emerged as a way for locals to take matters into their own hands and protect themselves from the insurgency. The CJTF is seen as a reaction to the severity of religious, ethnic, and political conflicts, aimed at preserving the lives and properties of locals in an unstable environment (Hassan, 2015).

Since mid-2013, the CJTF has been engaged in insurgency-related peace operations in an uneasy partnership with the military in Borno State. The primary objective has been to ensure the security of the lives and properties of the locals by allowing them to engage in both intelligence gathering and physical battles (International Crisis Group, 2018). However, despite their combined efforts to maintain peace in the region, scholars argue that their efforts have not been sufficient to ensure insurgency-related peace in the region. The state continues to be hampered by its own inadequacies and other factors, such as socioreligious pressure and political control, along with a lack of funding, training, and equipment (senior military officer, personal communication, 23 June 2022).

In certain instances, the state actively restricts local involvement in insurgency-related peace operations to preserve its own monopoly of control (senior military officer, personal communication, 26 June 2022). Conversely, there are situations where the state either tacitly endorses or overlooks the controversial and potentially harmful actions of the CJTF, including their use of violence and intimidation to achieve their objectives. This indicates that the CJTF's operations may extend beyond their role as a local security apparatus, occasionally contributing to injustices and human rights violations.

According to a senior researcher (personal communication, 5 September 2024), the emergence of local counterinsurgency groups such as the CJTF reflects fundamental weaknesses within the state's security framework. They argue that enhancing local security requires the establishment of structured, locally driven peace initiatives, or a bottom-up approach. In contrast to this view, the researcher posits that the CJTF already plays an active role in the insurgency-related peace process. This perspective diverges from the assessments of the International Crisis Group (2017), which regard the CJTF primarily as a reaction to military inadequacies. To fully understand the CJTF's impact, it is essential to adopt an ethnographic approach that considers local perceptions and cultural contexts. Analysing the CJTF's activities through a sociocultural lens can provide deeper insights into local attitudes towards the group and their effects on broader military operations.

The relationship between the CJTF and the military is intricate and multifaceted. While the CJTF has contributed to local security, it has also been implicated in human rights abuses. Consequently, it is crucial to evaluate the CJTF's activities from the perspectives of all stakeholders, recognising the group's need for improved training, discipline, and resources to become a more effective and respected local peacekeeping entity.

Hassan (2015) provides a systematic conceptualisation of the accomplishments of the CJTF. Hassan states that the group has achieved a kind of "synergistic interpenetration" through its coordinated efforts. The term "synergistic interpenetration" refers to the group's close coordination and collaboration with the military and other local security agents. In addition to participating in punishing and killing local insurgents, the CJTF has showcased its local capabilities by engaging in routine combined patrols and roadblocks with the military, which has led to the group being termed "local security" in Nigeria. Therefore, evaluations of insurgency-related peace and military operations in Borno State are viewed through this lens, with the CJTF often regarded as part of the establishment (Hassan, 2015).

However, in a discussion with a policy expert (personal communication, 28 September 2022), it was pointed out that the interplay between insurgency-related peace and military operations is a complex and multifaceted issue that requires a thorough understanding of the local context and perceptions. Ethnographic perceptions of the CJTF's activities provide valuable insights into the connections and disconnections between conventional, state-controlled means and unconventional, locally controlled means of maintaining security in Borno State. Many scholars have pointed out that the CJTF's effectiveness is not solely dependent on its partnership with the military but also on its ability to work with the local community and navigate the sociocultural dynamics of the region. The CJTF is often perceived as a more legitimate and trustworthy source of security than the military, owing to its local roots and community-driven approach.

By considering the CJTF's activities, one can gain a deeper understanding of how local security forces and insurgent groups interact with one another, as well as the various factors that shape their relationship. However, it is important to recognise that there are differences between the approaches taken by the military and local security forces in achieving peace and security. These differences stem from differences in their training, objectives, and resources.

## Conclusion

Clearly, the state security architecture and insurgency-related peace in Borno State, Nigeria, are complex issues that require a multifaceted approach. Local security forces, the military, and communities all play critical roles in maintaining peace and security in the region. The CJTF, as a local security force, has been essential in the fight against the Boko Haram insurgency, demonstrating its local capability in coordinating and collaborating with the military.

It is important to recognise that the dynamics between the military and local security forces, as well as their relationships with the community, are constantly evolving and require continuous evaluation. Such an evaluation is needed now, given the unstable and unclear nature of the relationship between state security forces and local counterinsurgency groups such as the CJTF.

In addition, it is quite clear that, in the long term, if the Nigerian government is truly interested in establishing peace in the country, it must address the underlying socioeconomic and political issues that contribute to the rise of insurgency. It is easy to assume that religious differences alone give rise to violent outbreaks in Nigeria, but a deeper examination of causes reveals that political issues (Walker, 2012), state corruption, poverty, and inequality create the conditions for dissatisfaction, which is often expressed along ethnic and religious lines. The state needs to work on boosting political inclusiveness and improving access to education and job opportunities – and do so with genuine intent.

Achieving insurgency-related peace in Borno State requires a comprehensive approach that considers a plethora of factors, both short and long-term.

# CHAPTER SIX
# THE HISTORY OF THE CIVILIAN JOINT TASK FORCE IN BORNO STATE

## Introduction

This chapter examines the factors leading to the formation of the CJTF and their role in insurgent peace operations and combatting the Boko Haram insurgency in Borno State. These factors include systemic and operational failures within the existing military framework. Systemic failures involve the misuse of substantial federal and state funding allocated to countering the Boko Haram insurgency. Despite significant financial investment, the impact on the frontlines is minimal, resulting in high casualty rates. In addition, innocent civilians find themselves in precarious situations: many face wrongful or arbitrary arrest, detention, conviction, and execution by the military, while also suffering from brutal violence inflicted by Boko Haram insurgents. These systemic issues undermine confidence and trust in the effectiveness of the military's antiterrorism campaign (B.H., personal communication, 16 August 2022). The operational failure was linked to the military's lack of adequate intelligence, which contributed to the victimisation of innocent civilians. However, the CJTF could provide the intelligence the military needed to combat the insurgents, who were skilfully camouflaged among the locals. The CJTF's intelligence gathering was linked to their knowledge of the locals and the community, allowing them to provide detailed profiles of the insurgents (U.M., personal communication, 17 August 2022).

The CJTF became a child of necessity due to the systemic and operational failures of the military. Moreover, by collaborating with the CJTF, the military was not only able to access intelligence but also participate with the group in the rehabilitation of IDP camps. The CJTF group, as a local community-based organisation, played an important role in supporting the rehabilitation of IDP camps in Borno State (B.A., personal communication, 13 July 2022). They worked closely with the military and other humanitarian organisations to aid and support the displaced persons in the camps. Their involvement helped to improve the living conditions and security of the IDPs and provided a sense of hope and stability in difficult and uncertain situations (B.A., personal communication, 13 July 2022). By working together with the military and other actors, they were able to provide critical support and assistance to those affected by the conflict and contribute to the overall efforts towards lasting peace and stability in the region. This collaboration has had a positive impact on the ongoing fight against the Boko Haram insurgency in Borno State (B.A., personal communication, 15 July 2022).

As mentioned above, the CJTF is an insurgent peace group that was originally formed without state support to resist the genocide orchestrated by Boko Haram insurgents. The group had to use traditional weapons, such as sticks, machetes, daggers, bows, and arrows, to attack and defend the locals. The group's tactics were inspired by the May 2013 heroics of Baba Lawan Jafar, who later became the chairman of the CJTF group. In June 2013, the locals responded to Jafar's local counterinsurgency initiative, which was adopted through a local referendum and christened "*Durza Ka*" (taken from the Kanuri language) (B.A., personal communication, 13 July 2022). The group's success in garnering support from the locals subsequently led to support from the government and military, which has resulted in their cordial relationship and operational success. The activities of the CJTF group complement the military operations.

Before the deployment of the CJTF, the military, state security service, and police, which constituted the allied force, adopted repressive approaches with brute force as the method of operation, killing, and capture of Boko Haram members. The complementary efforts of both the CJTF and military enforced the daily street patrols and house-to-house searches, which made insurgency peace effective. This prevented the notoriety and severity of the Boko Haram insurgency group. The CJTF group has a hierarchical structure that has become state-wide with two headquarters, one in Maiduguri Municipal Council (MMC) and one in Jere Local Government areas. Its leaders, termed "Babashehu Abdulganiu", come from these two areas and can be either male or female. Apart from collaborating with the military apparatuses, the group also collaborates with the *Yan Banga*, a group of hunters in cities, villages, and various communities.

The CJTF has advanced in its operational departments at the level of intelligence and rehabilitation of IDP camps and possible reintegration. Support from the government has been at the level of empowerment, establishing the Borno Youths Empowerment Scheme (BOYES) and monthly salary appropriation. The CJTF has received combined support from philanthropists and institutions for accommodation, empowerment schemes, and proficiency training support programmes (A.G., personal communication, 23 September 2022).

### Origin of the Civilian Joint Task Force

The origin of the CJTF can be traced to local self-defence activities against the Boko Haram insurgency in Borno State, Nigeria. In response to the insurgency, the federal government deployed the military, state security service, and police under a unified command. The military's counterinsurgency operations, which began under President Umar Yar'Adua's administration in 2009, were primarily repressive, relying heavily on brute force to kill and capture Boko Haram members (A., personal communication, 18 July 2022). Despite substantial federal and state funding aimed at combatting Boko Haram, very little of this funding appears to have reached the frontlines. As insecurity in Borno State escalated and reached its peak in 2013, locals found themselves caught between the insurgency of Boko Haram and the perceived incompetence of the military, resulting in the destruction of their livelihoods (U., personal communication, 17 July 2022). During an interview conducted in Maiduguri, Borno State, information was gathered about the events leading to the formation of the CJTF in May 2013. Baba Lawan Jafar, a trader from Maiduguri who later became the chairman of the CJTF, captured a Boko Haram member using only a stick (U., personal communication, 19 September 2022). This act of bravery inspired Modu Milo and other locals to join Jafar's initiative, leading them to engage in locally based counterinsurgency operations with whatever basic weapons they could access. Consequently, in June 2013, numerous locals armed with sticks, machetes, daggers, bows, and arrows united in Maiduguri to establish a local counterinsurgency initiative against Boko Haram.

This initiative involved daily street patrols and house-to-house searches, designed to complement the military's efforts, which were perceived as ineffective. The group, known as the CJTF in English and Yan kato da gora in Hausa, was established to function as an auxiliary military force in combatting Boko Haram's atrocities. An interview with a CJTF member revealed that the group evolved through various stages in response to changing Boko Haram attack strategies (H., personal communication, 21 June 2022). The member noted that Boko Haram had severely pressured the locals, compelling them to fight back and pledge to expose the enemy by swearing an oath on the Holy Qur'an. This determination to resist, coupled with frustration over the military's perceived inadequacies in addressing the ongoing attacks, led to the formation of the CJTF.

The CJTF distinguishes itself from other Islamic insurgency groups in Nigeria through its ethnic orientation and political stance. Primarily composed of Hausa and Kanuri members, the CJTF does not oppose the government or rival ethnic groups, setting it apart from other insurgent factions. The group's principal objective is to eradicate the Boko Haram insurgency in Borno State and neighbouring areas (B., personal communication, 15 July 2022).

In late 2013, when locals were caught in the conflict between the military and Boko Haram, the CJTF allied with the military in efforts against Boko Haram insurgents. Respondents indicated that the CJTF engaged in insurgent peace operations as a strategic measure to avoid suspicion of collusion with the insurgents by the government and military, which could have led to retaliation.

Before the formation of the CJTF, the situation in Borno State was dire. Innocent locals faced extreme violence from both Boko Haram insurgents and arbitrary actions by the military, including detention and execution. This high casualty rate and the severe threat from Boko Haram led many locals to shift their support from the military to the CJTF, albeit reluctantly (A., personal communication, 13 August 2022). As the CJTF's efforts in counterinsurgency complemented and enhanced the military's operations, community support for the group grew. One CJTF leader highlighted the group's positive impact, citing an incident where CJTF members successfully repelled armed insurgents attempting to rob a shop in the Babban Layi Business District of Maiduguri. The CJTF members not only overpowered the insurgents but also confiscated their weapons, detained them, and handed them over to the nearby military (B., personal communication, 13 July 2022). This success fostered significant community appreciation and endorsement, as well as military approval, which motivated continued CJTF intervention.

According to unpublished CJTF reports from 2021, the group's local insurgent peace operations extended to neighbouring communities in Maiduguri and beyond, leading to the capture of numerous Boko Haram insurgents. In addition, the CJTF's provision of language and intelligence support to the military has been widely recognised (B., personal communication, 13 July 2022). Prior to the CJTF's involvement, the military struggled with gathering critical intelligence due to a lack of local language skills and familiarity with the terrain (I., personal communication, 24 September 2022). This gap made it challenging for the military to distinguish between locals and insurgents during early operations (A., personal communication, 16 June 2022). The CJTF, with its members drawn from over 30 ethnic groups in Maiduguri, addressed this issue by providing essential language and intelligence support (M., personal communication, 13 July 2022). Their contributions have been instrumental in advancing peace in the insurgency-affected region (A., personal communication, 27 July 2022).

The CJTF has developed into a hierarchical organisation with branches established in all local government areas of Borno State, each headed by its own leader. According to one of the leaders of the CJTF, the group has expanded to over 2,000 members across the 27 local government areas (B.A., personal communication, 4 July 2022). The CJTF is currently organised into 10 command sectors, with two headquarters situated in the Maiduguri Municipality. Each sector comprises more than 50 members. The operational headquarters in Maiduguri are mobile and extend their activities beyond the city to rural communities and border areas to combat Boko Haram members (U., personal communication, 28 July 2022).

In the Jere Local Government Area, CJTF membership is relatively low, having recently increased to about 670 members, although the collection of biometric data for these members may not have been fully completed (J., personal communication, 30 July 2022). In areas such as Bagiau, Uwataku, and Giwa Kir Koma, no CJTF members are present; instead, local hunting groups known as Yan Banga, which are also recognised by the military, are utilised by indigenous locals. The CJTF collaborates closely with Yan Banga in their insurgency-related peace operations across various communities. Interviews reveal that many CJTF members have undergone formal military training and are recruited by the military. In addition, an intelligence-gathering unit within the CJTF provides crucial intelligence to the military (S., personal communication, 21 August 2022). Figure 6.1 illustrates a visit by the researcher to the CJTF Sector 8 headquarters, highlighting the organisation's operational scope.

**Figure 6.1**: Researcher with CJTF members at Command Sector 8.

Source: Author

**Figure 6.2**:  CJTF members at the parade.

*Source*: Author

To combat Boko Haram's increasing use of suicide bombers and hit-and-run attackers, the CJTF established a women's wing, composed of young Borno women (see Figure 6.2). Currently, the women's wing has a total of 231 members, assigned to various departments within the organisation, including the operational department, intelligence-gathering unit, rehabilitation training centres in IDP camps, and the welfare department (H., personal communication, 12 September 2022). Some members of the women's wing of the CJTF are deployed to various local communities across the state to fight against Boko Haram. Figure 6.2 below is a photo of a female member of the CJTF taken on Post Office Road, Maiduguri, Borno State, on 17 September 2022.

**Figure 6.3**: Member of the women's wing of the CJTF.

*Source*: Author

**Figure 6.4**: Member of the women's wing of the CJTF.

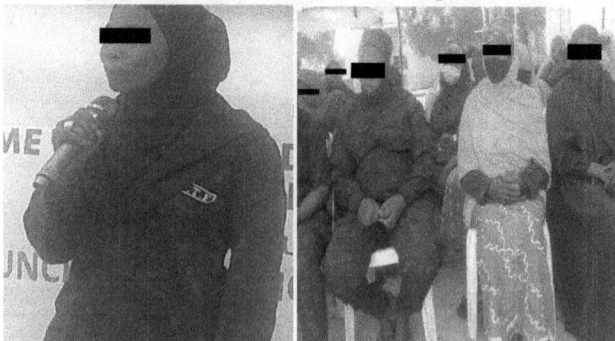

*Source*: Author.

Prior to the formation of the women's wing of the CJTF, Boko Haram insurgents exploited women by recruiting them as nonviolent operatives. These women were tasked with intelligence gathering, promoting radical ideologies, and, in some cases, abducted and forcibly converted to Islam within Boko Haram enclaves (Y., personal communication, 29 July 2022). The insurgents also used these women as suicide bombers to execute attacks (Y., personal communication, 29 July 2022).

The establishment of the CJTF women's wing significantly altered this dynamic. Female CJTF members now play a crucial role in community security. Their duties include conducting pat-downs of girls in churches, mosques, and other public venues, as well as patrolling cities and villages. Pat-downs involve a physical search of individuals to detect hidden items, such as weapons or explosives, by systematically feeling their clothing and body (A., personal communication, 27 August 2022). In addition, female CJTF members are involved in intelligence gathering and the arrest of suspected female Boko Haram insurgents or saboteurs. A prominent member of the CJTF, emphasised the importance of collaborative local efforts in safeguarding communities. Despite her family being located far from Maiduguri, in Chibok, she was driven to assist in preventing the spread of attacks to her home area, motivated by the diminishing strength of Boko Haram and her commitment to community protection (H., personal communication, 18 July 2022).

The selection of locals from hunter-families to lead the CJTF was a strategic decision based on their unique skills and knowledge of the local terrain. Hunters in the region possess specialised expertise in tracking and navigating difficult landscapes, which are crucial for detecting and tracking insurgents. These skills have proven valuable in gathering reliable intelligence on Boko Haram's planned attacks, significantly aiding in the prevention and thwarting of such operations (M.J., personal communication, 6 September 2022).

Since its formal acceptance by the Borno State government in 2013, the CJTF has received substantial support. The Borno State authorities, under Governor Kashim Shettima, provided over 60 vehicles, along with significant financial and logistical backing (A., personal communication, 10 August 2022). In addition to state support, the CJTF has benefitted from donations from local communities, leaders, and some politicians (A., personal communication, 12 July 2022). Many CJTF members have dedicated themselves full-time to the group's efforts, leaving their previous occupations to ensure community safety. The Borno Youths Empowerment Scheme (BOYES), established in collaboration with local governments, has also contributed to the CJTF's support, with members joining the task force. Initially, CJTF members received a monthly allowance of N15,000, which increased to N20,000 per month under the administration of Governor Prof Babagana Zulum starting in 2019. Additional welfare and capacity-building programmes have been implemented to further bolster the group's mission (B.A., personal communication, 4 July 2022).

Discussions with members of the CJTF reveal that the group has developed innovative strategies to support its operations and members. One such initiative is the establishment of a consolidated welfare treasury, where each member contributes N500.00 for emergency purposes. This scheme aims to create a financial safety net for unforeseen circumstances. In addition to internal contributions, the CJTF has secured substantial support from external partners and foundations committed to enhancing peace and security in Borno State.

For instance, the Dangote Group has provided 30 units of two-bedroom flats to CJTF members' families who lost their homes due to the insurgency. The Nigeria Institute of Management has integrated 50 CJTF members into its empowerment and training programmes. Furthermore, the International Committee of the Red Cross (ICRC) has trained 52 CJTF members in critical areas such as first aid and dead-body management, with these trained personnel now serving in various community support roles (A.A., personal communication, 18 June 2022). The United Nations Development Programme (UNDP) has also been a key partner, empowering approximately 4,000 CJTF and Borno State citizens through training in leadership, agriculture, trade, and education since 2014 (B., personal communication, 7 August 2022).

In addition, the Borno State government has contributed significantly by providing support, encouragement, and relief materials worth millions of Naira. This includes the allocation of 150 plots of land to the families of CJTF members who have died in service (Y., personal communication, 8 June 2022). Despite these substantial contributions, the CJTF continues to seek further support from Nigerians, corporate entities, international donors, and the federal government to sustain and expand their efforts in combating the Boko Haram insurgency.

### CJTF's activities in Borno State

The CJTF emerged as a response to the tragic experiences faced by the people of Borno State at the hands of Boko Haram insurgents and the Nigerian security apparatus. Unpublished CJTF reports (2021) indicated that innocent locals were being arrested and tortured by the military under the pretext that they were harbouring the insurgents. As a result, innocent locals were losing their lives daily due to Boko Haram attacks and the military's apprehension. In light of thissituation, the CJTF was formed to address the severe economic, social, political, and religious consequences suffered by the indigenous locals. An interview with a CJTF member revealed thatone of their primary functions was to identify and hand over members of Boko Haram among the locals to the military (M., personal communication, 19 September 2022). Their willingness to collaborate with the military was extraordinary, starting in the MMC and later expanding to other communities in the state.

The interviewee said that before becoming members of the CJTF, volunteers took an oath on both the Holy Qur'an and the Holy Bible against any form of betrayal, mistrust, sabotage, or leaking of information. They were also required to identify diligently, in different communities, insurgents who had inflicted untold hardships on the state in the name of false religious teachings. Muslim inductees took their oath before the Shehu of Bornu in his palace with the Holy Qur'an, while Christian members used the Bible. The terms and conditions of the oath encompass several important principles. First, members are required to uphold the integrity of the CJTF group by refraining from any acts of betrayal that may compromise the success of insurgent peace operations. Second, members are expected to demonstrate honesty towards both God and their fellow group members.

Another key tenet of the oath is the rejection of interpersonal animosity within the group and a commitment to overcoming any ethnic or religious differences in pursuit of a shared objective. Political interference is similarly discouraged, as the group seeks to remain focused on its core goals and objectives. Finally, members are expected to avoid any form of theft or discrimination, even in cases where the individual in question is not a member of their family, community, or personal circle (J., personal communication, 27 October 2022).

During the interview, it was disclosed that CJTF members took a solemn vow to make public, return, or surrender any recovered items or funds from the insurgency to the relevant authorities. The objective behind this was to demonstrate to both the locals and the government that the group's mission was solely dedicated to serving the community and facilitating its liberation from the persistent threat of Boko Haram's attacks. This measure was deemed necessary to establish trust and garner support from the government and locals alike and reassure them that the group's primary concern was the safety and security of the affected communities and the broader Borno State region. An interview conducted at the CJTF headquarters in Maiduguri added key details about the emergence of the group:

> *While the campaign against Boko Haram went on, hundreds of innocent young people ended up in detention camps of various security operatives in Maiduguri and other places. This was in addition to the arrest of actual suspects. Observers believe that this alleged brutality coming from the then military troops coupled with extreme hardship caused by the*

*declaration of state of emergency prompted inhabitants in Maiduguri to rise fearlessly against Boko Haram group members by cobbling together what would be known today as CJTF* (B., personal communication, 17 September 2022).

As mentioned earlier, the CJTF group was formed in response to the hardship and brutality caused by the Boko Haram attacks. The initial mobilisation for the group took place in the Hausari area of Maiduguri. In addition, as stated before, it was here that the group pledged to apprehend any insurgent who crossed the area en route to the Monday Market or Babban Layi to carry out acts of robbery, bombing, or shooting (S., personal communication, 8 October 2022). Baba Lawan Jafar, the chairman of the CJTF group in Borno State, impressed his friend Modu Milo by bravely chasing and capturing a Boko Haram member with only a stick, leading Milo to join the hunt (B.A., personal communication, 12 October 2022). While some viewed these locals as heroes, others regarded them as merely sounding the alarm and kept their distance to avoid attracting the wrath of Boko Haram insurgents. However, Jafar and Milo's survival for weeks encouraged dozens of young locals to join them, and they remained alive and healthy. The emergence of the local (civilian) militia dealt a significant blow to Boko Haram insurgents, who responded with reprisal attacks.

Following Jafar's courageous act, the insurgents staged a mock funeral procession and attacked Hausari using concealed weapons. They opened fire on residents, killing several people, including a 90-year-old woman and a nine-year-old girl (A., personal communication, 15 October 2022). However, the emergence of the civilian militia did not deter the CJTF from continuing their peace operations against Boko Haram. They extended their fight to eight emirate councils, namely Borno, Damboa, Dikwa, Biu, Askira, Gwoza, Shani, and Uba. However, they faced their own challenges, including ambushes by insurgents that resulted in casualties. Nevertheless, their efforts produced significant positive results, particularly in reducing Boko Haram's activities in Maiduguri. A community member also provided additional motivation for the CJTF's involvement in the fight against the Boko Haram insurgency (S., personal communication, 2 July 2022). This was hinged on an attempted robbery incident conducted by the vengeful Boko Haram insurgents, which was promptly thwarted. The account was described as follows:

*In late May last year, some gunmen came to a shop in Babban Layi business district with the intention to rob but were resisted. When we realized they had no ammo in their guns, we floored them and collected their guns, tied them up and handed them over to nearby soldiers. Later in the day, the soldiers came to thank us and urged us to continue doing what we're doing* (B.A., personal communication, 8 July 2022).

The success of the CJTF's operations led to their expansion to other areas in the state, resulting in the apprehension of hundreds of Boko Haram members. The military created a register for the locals, who had already organised themselves into command sectors similar to those in military circles. A schoolteacher in Maiduguri expressed gratitude for the CJTF's role in the community and wondered how life would have been without them (G., personal communication, 7 July 2022). He noted that Boko Haram attacks peaked between 2009 and 2013, with terrorists infiltrating local communities, killing civilians, and subsequently escaping undetected. The emergence of the CJTF's youth militia changed the tide by confronting the insurgents and ending their hit-and-run tactics. The success of their counter-reprisal inspired other locals to reject the violence. As a result, it would be challenging for the insurgents to return to Maiduguri and carry out their previous actions. Figures 6.3 and 6.4 below provide further evidence of the increasing conflict incidents and fatalities in the years to come, which the CJTF had to deal with.

**Figure 6.5**: Boko Haram and non-Boko Haram conflict incidences in Borno, 2009–2021.

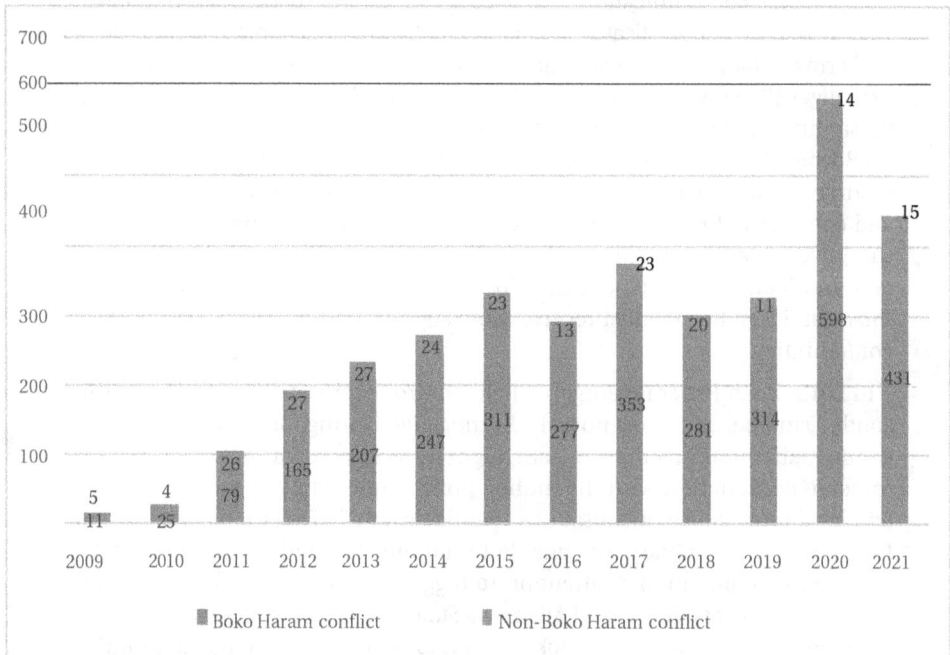

*Source:* Author.

**Figure 6.6**: Boko Haram and non-Boko Haram conflict fatalities in Borno, 2009–2021.

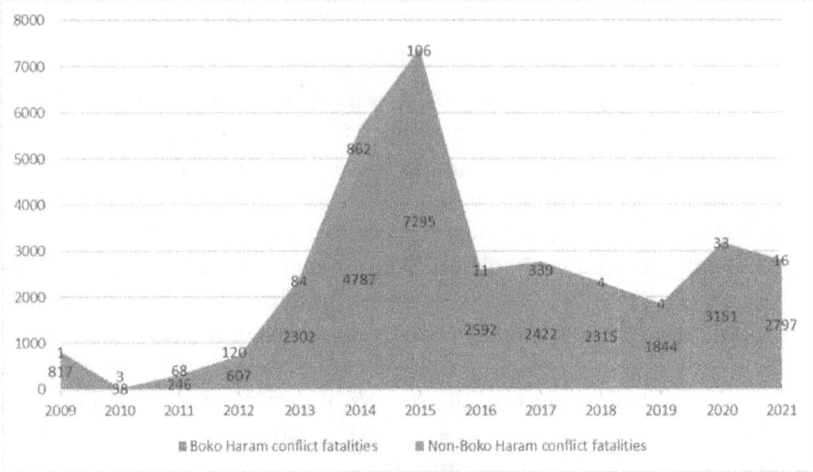

*Source*: Author

The military's increased insurgency-related peace operations in Borno State have successfully dislodged Boko Haram from previously conquered communities (M., personal communication, 5 June 2022). At the time of their takeover, Boko Haram acquired sophisticated weaponry, including substantial machine guns and arms obtained during assaults on military installations and through arms exchanges (B., personal communication, 8 August 2022). Despite the insurgents' versatility and mobility, the military's efforts have been primarily focused on Borno. However, the locals' main challenge is not just the brutality of the insurgency but also the disruption of farming, pastoral activities, trade, and commerce. Insecurity caused by insurgency and the security measures of the government and military further compound the issue (H., personal communication, 11 October 2022). For insurgency to be brought under control, the localities in Borno must receive more support and cooperation from their communities.

In 2012, Boko Haram insurgents held control over vast areas in the north, south, Damboa, and, most notably, Borno State. During this time, the military conducted counterinsurgency campaigns as a significant aspect of its task force, in conjunction with the mobile police, other state security agencies, and local intelligence organisations (Bamidele, 2017). Due to the large size of Borno State, the military was unable to monitor the entire area adequately, resulting in a limitation of attention to bigger towns such as Maiduguri and the borders between Borno and Adamawa States (K., personal communication, 8 November 2022). This allowed Boko Haram to shift their focus to communities with fewer military personnel, where they could carry out their activities with less resistance. Boko Haram also established camps in vast savanna forests such as Sambisa (B., personal communication, 16 August 2022).

With an increased military presence in Borno, the military used roadblocks and patrol operationteams to drive out the insurgents from portions of these communities (S., personal communication, 8 July 2022). This approach proved successful in ousting the insurgents from some areas and limiting their movements in others. According to a senior military officer interviewee:

> *The military operation in Borno is ongoing. However albeit some information on the circumstance in Borno is filtering out despite everything, we do not have a nitty gritty general picture since the greater part of the cell phone systems have been turned off in the State under crisis. Information is mainly coming from squeeze reports in Maiduguri, the state capital; from individuals in regions bordering Cameroun who can cross the outskirt and make calls from that point; and from individuals leaving Borno State – including the individuals who are relocating to different parts of the nation* (B., personal communication, 8 September 2022).

It became evident that once the Boko Haram insurgents were expelled from the territories they controlled or where they camped, they tended to relocate to the outskirts of Borno and neighbouring communities along the border. The Gwoza Hills, which is an extension of the Mandara Mountains that straddle Borno State, were severely affected by this, including the Sambisa Forest Reserve and the surrounding communities. Christians and non-Christians alike in a few communities within the Gwoza Hills and Gwoza community were assaulted, and both prominent and nonprominent locals were assassinated by presumed Boko Haram insurgents who had relocated to the mountains, forests, and undergrowth in the region. As a result, the vast majority of inhabitants left the Gwoza community and relocated to the northern part of Adamawa, with some even moving further into Yobe State (F., personal communication, 8 July 2022). The military was deployed in the Gwoza Hills to search for guerrilla Boko Haram insurgents in the caves, while the northern and local territories of Borno, where people had been displaced, also witnessed military counterinsurgency operations.

The Boko Haram jihadists were pushed to the fringes, specifically into the Lake Chad region and border areas of the state (A., personal communication, 21 November 2022). Another notable development is that most of the young community groups in Maiduguri, such as the CJTF, identified, arrested, and handed over suspected Boko Haram members to the military. However, over time, the military lost much of the local support owing to its obtuse strategies, which further strengthened the reason for the emergence of the CJTF (B., personal communication, 13 October 2022). A local community member from Borno State testified to this effect:

> *CJTF constitute youths of Maiduguri who came together owing to what is happening because the army and others do not know who they are*

*fighting, and they cannot differentiate who is Boko Haram and who is not a member of Boko Haram among them. By so doing, after we saw how the activities of Boko Haram got worse, we now resolve to pick our sticks and knives going after the people we knew they are members of Boko Haram, we will now catch them and handover them to soldiers. Inspired by what we are doing, the youth in Borno State all came out together to join forces with the army to go after Boko Haram. And as such, there is no hiding place for them as far as they are within the town* (F., personal communication, 26 September 2022).

Another interviewee from the Askira community stated the following:

*They have seen the pertinence of this community security option to the heap of security challenges assailing states and communities in Borno State, because success has been recorded thus far as people can go about doing their business without fear while the CJTF remains alert monitoring the movement of visitors coming into town so as to hinder the insurgents from having field day in Maiduguri. Because if the soldiers are left alone to combat Boko Haram, the insurgents cannot be defeated, due to their inability to differentiate between the lawful abiding citizen and the insurgents* (M., personal communication, 29 August 2022).

In the Shani Uba community, a CJTF respondent disclosed: "*CJTF constitute informants who volunteer to provide security for their community, following incessant Boko Haram attacks*" (A., personal communication, 11 November 2022). In addition, the interviewee mentioned that the Yan Banga (hunters), some of whom had been displaced from their homes by the insurgents, were working with the CJTF and the military, returning to their communities and capturing the insurgents (H., personal communication, 28 November 2022). The respondent said, "*What makes the group a fundamental component in winning the war is the fact that they live among them, and soldiers do not know as such. CJTF resolves to fish them out and hand them over to the military*" (Y., personal communication, 18 June 2022). In addition, there have been reported instances of community resistance against Boko Haram in Damboa and along the borders between communities in Borno State. The Yan Banga and CJTF groups have been actively resisting the insurgents since 2009, armed with bows, arrows, sticks, and machetes. Furthermore, in 2009, the vigilante men in Damboa handed over a key supporter of the Borno State Religious Affairs Commissioner, Alhaji Buji Foi, to the military due to their strong disdain for Boko Haram. Foi was subsequently executed extrajudicially in Maiduguri by the military (G., personal communication, 24 October 2022). Figures 6.5 and 6.6 below show the locations and numbers of Boko Haram conflict incidents and fatalities between 2009 and 2021.

**Figure 6.7**: Locations of Boko Haram-related conflict in Borno, 2009–2021.

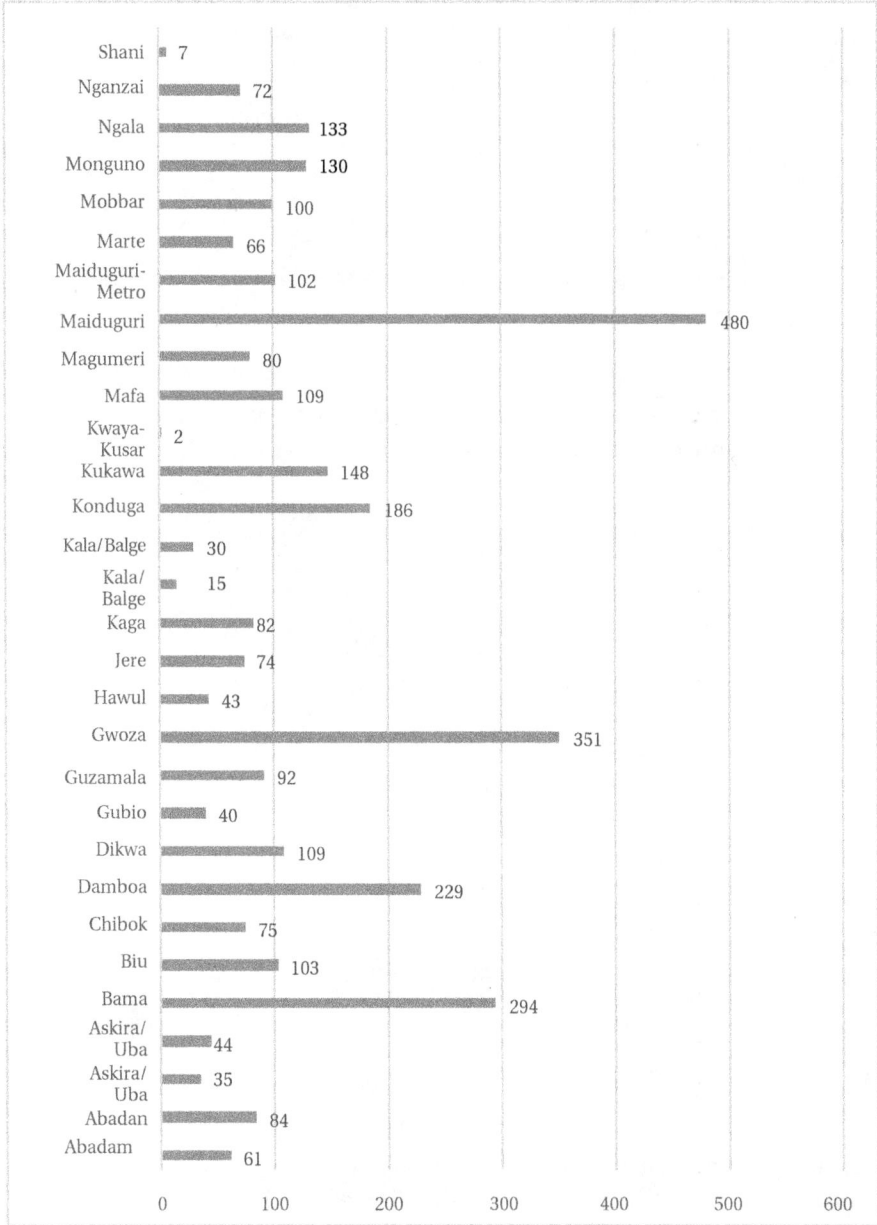

| Location | Value |
|---|---|
| Shani | 7 |
| Nganzai | 72 |
| Ngala | 133 |
| Monguno | 130 |
| Mobbar | 100 |
| Marte | 66 |
| Maiduguri-Metro | 102 |
| Maiduguri | 480 |
| Magumeri | 80 |
| Mafa | 109 |
| Kwaya-Kusar | 2 |
| Kukawa | 148 |
| Konduga | 186 |
| Kala/Balge | 30 |
| Kala/Balge | 15 |
| Kaga | 82 |
| Jere | 74 |
| Hawul | 43 |
| Gwoza | 351 |
| Guzamala | 92 |
| Gubio | 40 |
| Dikwa | 109 |
| Damboa | 229 |
| Chibok | 75 |
| Biu | 103 |
| Bama | 294 |
| Askira/Uba | 44 |
| Askira/Uba | 35 |
| Abadan | 84 |
| Abadam | 61 |

*Source*: Author

**Figure 6.8**: Location of fatalities due to Boko Haram conflict in Borno, 2009–2021.

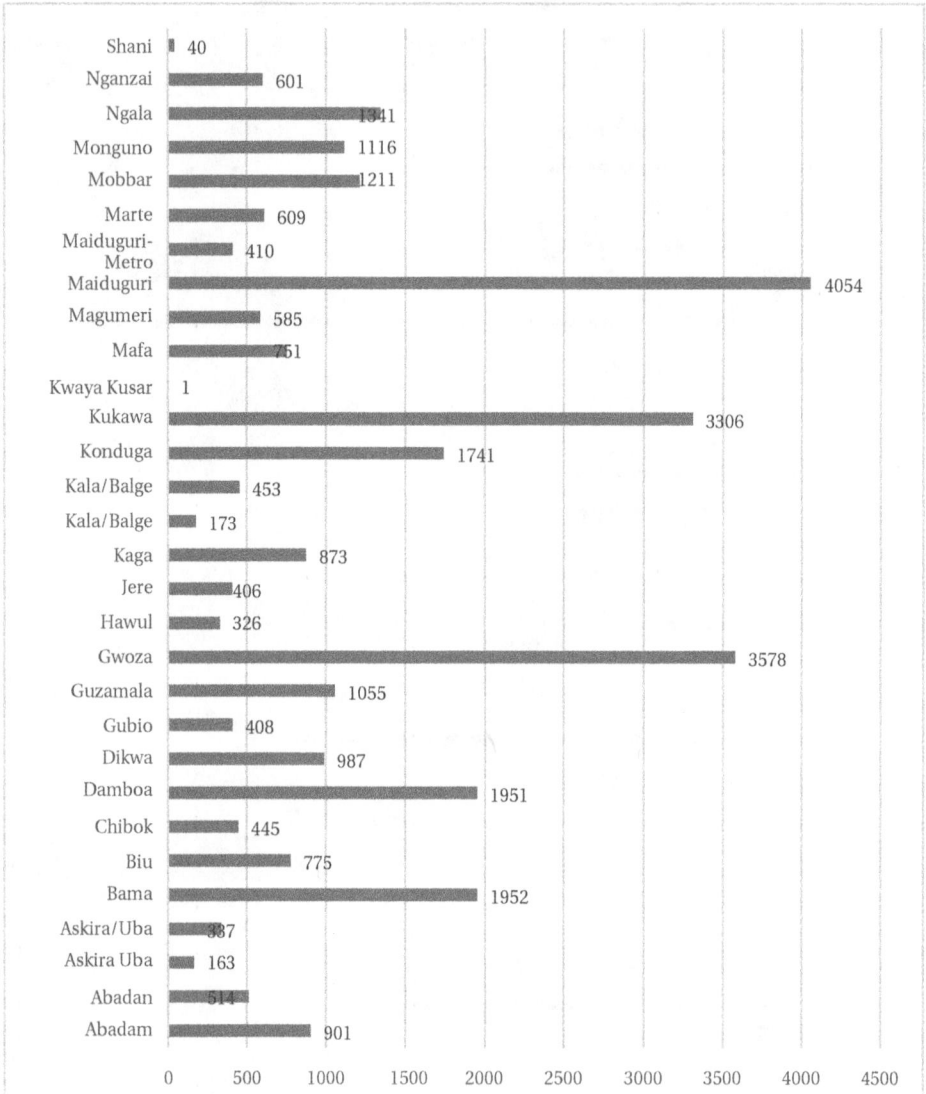

*Source*: Author

In the fight against the insurgency in Nigeria, one significant challenge was the difficulty in determining the size of the local forces fighting against the insurgents. This made it challenging to plan and execute effective military operations. In response to this challenge, the formalisation of the CJTF into a formal structure determined the force size and provided a framework for organising and coordinating the activities of local security groups. Before the formalisation, localsecurity forces were a loose association of volunteers who provided information to the military on an ad hoc basis. The lack of a formal structure made it challenging to determine the number of volunteers available and their capabilities (M., personal communication, 11 October 2022).

The formalisation of the CJTF took place in 2013. Before 2013, the CJTF was an informal association of local volunteers who provided support to the Nigerian military in their fight against Boko Haram. However, in response to the increasing threat of Boko Haram, the Nigerian government and military recognised the need to formalise and integrate the CJTF into their counterinsurgency efforts. The formalisation process involved the registration of group members, training, and the establishment of a clear chain of command.

With the formalisation of the CJTF, the Nigerian military was able to work closely with the group's leadership to develop a more structured approach to insurgent peace. This allowed for the registration of group members, which made it easier to determine the number of volunteers available and their capabilities. The formalisation also helped to provide training for CJTF members to improve their effectiveness and ensure that they adhered to human rights standards. Furthermore, the formalisation of the CJTF helped to establish a clear chain of command, which improved coordination and communication between the group and the military.

As a result, the military was better able to integrate the CJTF into its operations and leverage its local knowledge and support in the fight against Boko Haram (G., personal communication, 3 November 2022). Before the formalisation of the CJTF, the military relied on local community members for information, especially in areas outside Maiduguri in Borno State (M., personal communication, 7 November 2022). However, most of the information received about extensive attacks, particularly in remote areas, was often incorrect, unsubstantiated, or one-sided (A., personal communication, 19 October 2022).

Before the formalisation of the CJTF in 2013, Boko Haram-controlled areas often resulted in the destruction of all state-owned facilities, including office buildings and schools, which were termed "makarantun boko" by the insurgents. This was a term used to describe state-owned facilities that were destroyed by Boko Haram in areas under their control. It is a Hausa phrase whereby the word "makaranta" means school, and "boko" is a reference to Western education, which Boko Haram opposes. Therefore, the phrase "makarantun boko" could be translated as "Western education schools", and the destruction of such facilities was an attempt by Boko Haram to eliminate Western education in the areas under their control. However, the insurgents' control of various areas and the destruction of state facilities were counteracted by the CJTF's formalised intervention from 2013 onwards (S., personal communication, 9 November 2022).

As previously noted, relying solely on military intervention, regardless of the strategy adopted, was not sufficient to defeat the Boko Haram insurgency. In addition, the military's continued reliance on the CJTF's insurgent peace operations has made counterinsurgency operations intricately interdependent in many communities in the affected states (A., personal communication, 11 July 2022). Therefore, a comprehensive approach involving the military and communities was essential to address the insurgency effectively.

### Formative process of the Civilian Joint Task Force

Various indigenous grassroots security groups in Borno State share similar characteristics with the CJTF. While some of these groups may be referred to as "community informants" in certain areas, this term is not commonly used to describe these groups across the state. Nevertheless, the CJTF and these groups follow a similar formative process that involves the mobilisation and organisation of local volunteers to support the Nigerian military in its fight against Boko Haram by providing local intelligence, conducting patrols, and securing communities against insurgent attacks. A member of a CJTF group in Benisheik asserted the following:

> *Here in Gwoza, we do not have CJTF like that of Maiduguri. On the contrary, we have vigilantes and hunters who have been operating in the town for quite a long time. The rise of Boko Haram and its activities created the need for us to play our part in securing our communities* (I., personal communication, 21 July 2022).

An affirmation of local security initiatives highlights the shared goal of combatting the insurgency threatening communal existence. This underscores the importance of grassroots efforts in complementing existing military strategies, as the limitations in the latter have necessitated a collaborative approach. As a result, the CJTF emerged as a key player in counterinsurgency efforts, working closely with other grassroots security initiatives to provide vital intelligence, conduct patrols, and secure communities against Boko Haram attacks. When asked about the primary military strategy behind involving the CJTF, the following insight was provided:

> *We are not involved in operation alongside the military, but we help in complementing their efforts by alerting them on any possible attack and we are stationed at various schools, markets and any social gathering to provide security* (I., personal communication, 22 July 2022).

The need for a community alert system capable of detecting possible attacks at close range was one of the driving factors behind the local option for combatting the Boko Haram insurgency in Borno State. In addition, the constant presence of military personnel in crowded areas, such as schools and markets, was deemed necessary to enhance security. Thus, the CJTF plays a critical role by collaborating with the military to provide security in affected communities. However, it was noted that, in areas where the CJTF is absent, local hunters often assume similar responsibilities (H., personal communication, 24 October 2022). They take the place of the CJTF to contribute to the furtherance of military efforts and avoid any gap which the enemies can exploit. According to a female CJTF, the rationale behind the formation of the hunter groups is the need for effective insurgency-related peace strategies, owing to incessant Boko Haram attacks (H., personal communication, 26 June 2022).

The military also engages the locals in other ways, such as through the provision of knowledge-based information about the inhabitants of the local community, which helps with intelligence gathering. The significance of this strategy cannot be overstated, as it forms a critical part of the locals' security scheme. As the natives know their communities better than anyone else, their involvement in intelligence gathering has proven highly effective in determining the cause and uniformity of operations and plans of the insurgents. The military's knowledge of the locale has led to the belief that local involvement or engagement is the most effective security strategy for community defence (D., personal communication, 24 August 2022).

This view is supported by the findings of several studies, including a study by Bamidele (2017, 2018, 2024), which found that locals can provide valuable intelligence about the activities of insurgents in affected communities. Another study by Bamidele (2018) also noted the importance of involving locals in intelligence gathering, as they possess knowledge of the terrain and community that is critical to successful military operations against insurgents.

Interviews with the CJTF revealed that the councils of the Damboa, Dimka, and Biu emirates (administrative subdivisions of Borno State headed by traditional rulers known as emirs, who serve as custodians of the state's cultural heritage and play important roles in the governance and development of their respective emirates). The councils had raised various issues regarding the emergence of the CJTF as a local insurgent peace group. These issues include the growing frustration and desperation among the affected locals, the military's need for additional manpower to address its lack of knowledge about Boko Haram's hideouts, and the necessity to secure recovered or recaptured towns and villages through extensive 24-hour checks. According to one account:

*CJTF is just a group of civilians who took their sticks according to native language Kanuri (gora) in which they use in fighting the Boko Haram. Thus, what compel them to kick against the activities of Boko Haram activities is frustration, due to the frequent attacks on people... Inspired by the zeal of CJTF, government now recognize their efforts and gave them support* (A., personal communication, 9 August 2022).

Another respondent, a CJTF leader of Command Sector 3, also affirmed, "CJTF is completely voluntary, even as they insisted on assisting the military, in spite of some ethno- religious-based refusal. Another key factor that sustained this voluntary native participation is the Borno State government's acknowledgement as well as financial and material aid" (S., personal communication, 9 August 2022). According to one source (personal communication, 7 August 2022), a CJTF member in Command Sector 8 stated, "CJTF constitutes youths volunteered to provide local security for their community, following incessant Boko Haram attacks".

The young and energetic members of the local community provided selfless support, as security needs persisted despite the military's presence. The respondents cited in the previous paragraph repeatedly emphasised the voluntary nature of the local population's involvement in insurgency-related peace efforts and noted that it was a local initiative driven by the urgent need for the survival of the community. In essence, the local option was a last resort in the counterstrategies and responses to the Boko Haram insurgency. In addition, as the respondent emphasised, only the local security group could provide accurate information to the military and thus strengthen efforts to protect communities against the insurgents' ethnoreligious cleansing ambitions, which were a source of desperation for many. By working together, the community was able to resist these destructive forces and preserve their way of life.

According to another member of the CJTF from Borno State, the local option emerged as a result of the local population's frustration with the military's persistent failures. The group was formed to engage in guerrilla warfare against the sworn killers to protect their community from further harm (Y., personal communication, 27 September 2022). They committed that "if they perish, they perish" (Y., personal communication, 30 November 2022). When inquired about the inspiration behind the inception of the CJTF, the source explained:

*What inspired the youths in my community to join CJTF is nothing rather than the Boko Haram insurgency that have been tormenting the people of the state. And when the youths are fed up with the killings on daily basis, they now mobilize themselves to go after the members of the Boko*

*Haram since they live among them* (Y., personal communication, 10 November 2022).

The above information suggests that the CJTF was formed in response to the local population's frustration and desperation in the face of ongoing tragedy. Rather than giving up, the young locals decided to take action and fight back against Boko Haram. Another member of the CJTF from Borno State described it as a fight against the extremist group. He went on to explain that when the young locals became fed up with the activities of the insurgents, they made a resolution to track them down, flush them out, and turn them over to the military for justice (M., personal communication, 10 November 2022). This echoes other statements made by the CJTF indicating that the group was formed in response to the challenges posed by Boko Haram's activities. Ignoring the threat would have resulted in significant setbacks for their communities. The concept of insurgent peace, introduced by David Galula in 1964, supports this action by emphasising the need to entrust urgent and vital but local tasks to the locals, rather than relying solely on the military. In other words, soldiers should be confined to purely military tasks, while other tasks are performed by the locals.

The most critical factor sustaining this approach has been the Borno State government's support for the local fighters. This confirms the argument that it is the responsibility of the state to secure its citizens from harm and welcome their support in overcoming insurgency, thereby preventing collateral damage and shielding locals from harm in a broader sense. A CJTF member in Jere added:

> *Within the context of Maiduguri, the government and the community stakeholders are the initiators. Why? Because when the government saw how the whole thing began, the government now recognized their efforts by regarding them as part of the ongoing operation* (S., personal communication, 18 November 2022).

According to the above respondent's testimony, the key parties involved in the emergence of the CJTF in Borno State, referred to as the "initiators", are the locals and the state government. Local security is an efficient way of utilising the resources of the state's security institutions, and locals can adequately aid the military in preventing all forms of insurgency arising from the local population. Thus, the role played by the state government in encouraging local efforts has led to the more organised and effective CJTF of today. Without proper funding and support from the state and community leaders, the radical native setup could have remained an amateur effort. The Borno State government's involvement in the scheme includes providing monthly salaries, training, vehicles, uniforms, and even cars in recent times.

Before government support, however, the CJTF was an unprofessional endeavour and a grassroots undertaking. A CJTF member at its state headquarters affirmed the original spontaneity in the group's establishment as a counterreaction to the prevailing insecurity in the local space, despite the presence of the military:

*CJTFs starts from nowhere, and as a matter of fact, it is just a group of civilians who took their sticks, according to native language Hausa, gora which they used in fighting the Boko Haram. Thus, what compelled them to kick against the activities of Boko Haram is frustration, due to the frequent attacks on people* (A., personal communication, 10 June 2022).

A source continued:

*As a matter of fact, owing to the insurgency bedeviling Borno State, when the situations worsened and the citizens were frustrated, they then resolved to fight back those that caused the mayhem in the state, which are the Boko Haram terrorists* (A., personal communication, 5 June 2022).

From the above, it is evident that there was no official government delegation or legal enforcement to establish the CJTF. As the members of the CJTF have emphasised, the locals' frustrations, desperation, and fear of total annihilation were the primary drivers behind the voluntary, local security initiative in the affected communities. The communities took it upon themselves to ensure their safety and that of their children. The respondent (B., personal communication, 10 June 2022) stated that the communities demanded to be part of the military operations despite initial resistance based on the traditional security system, as they were desperate for their survival. He pointed out the weaknesses in the military's operations, which became more apparent with every unsuccessful insurgency-related peace attempt. Moreover, he affirmed that the military's confusion about the actual perpetrators and the need for more personnel led to the creation of CJTF. Another member of the CJTF also stressed the voluntary nature of the local security group:

*It all started as a volunteer work in which the youth in the town were fed up, because as of then, there was a state of emergency and the treatment the military was giving to the citizens in Maiduguri metropolis was that kind of brutal treatment and the masses now said they were tired and since they actually knew those people who were doing this things, so they came up grouped themselves and were later accepted by the military's to be part of the operation. So that's how its initiation came about* (G., personal communication, 21 June 2022).

A markedly distinct account of the factors that catalysed the formation of the local security group was provided, linking them to a specific victim of the insurgents. This victim had tragically lost their entire family at the hands of the attackers:

> *What inspired CJTF to begin its operation is quite a long story but let me just make it brief. What actually happened was there was a guy who was threatened by the Boko Haram group, that they would kill him. Then, they went further and wiped out his family. His father was killed, his mother has killed as well as his siblings. After the incidence, the guy now opened up to police and army by informing them. He now came up and volunteered that he knew them and that he was willing to expose them, that some of them were his friends around, and that's how he started exposing them and they were all arrested and inspired by his courage and zeal other young people in the town who are fed up with Boko Haram activities followed suit. And that's how the whole thing begun* (I., personal communication, 25 June 2022).

The statement confirms that rising frustration and desperation among locals were crucial in the formation of the CJTF. It cites a tragic incident, where an entire family was killed by insurgents, as a key motivator for seeking revenge and collaborating with the military to track down the perpetrators. The grief and tragedy experienced by many locals due to the Boko Haram insurgency quickly became known within the communities, fuelling a passion to curb the violence. This collective sense of determination and bravery was evident across all emirate councils and played a crucial role in bolstering the strength of the CJTF.

A member of the CJTF shared his observations during a tour of Askira Uba, describing the group as a collection of energetic young people who voluntarily undertook the task of tracking down insurgents and supporting the military in their operations (Y., personal communication, 26 June 2022). The name "CJTF" reflects this mission of pursuing and confronting the enemy, he explained. In the Kanuri langue, the term "*durza*" means a "brave man" while the "*ka*" means "a big stick". Hence, the phrase "a brave man with a big stick" was appropriate at the beginning of the fight, as the group members were using only sticks to fight Boko Haram. It was added that the primary strategy in the group's operations involves close collaboration with the military to safeguard communities from attacks. Emphasis was placed on the fact that the CJTF's effectiveness depends significantly on cooperation with various stakeholders.

A member of the CJTF in Maiduguri, Command Sector 10, noted that the emergence of the local security group was partly due to the need to differentiate between Boko Haram insurgents and innocent community members. He further explained that collaboration with the military was essential because the insurgents' skill in camouflage and deception undermined the military's efforts, highlighting the need for local input. In addition, he emphasised the importance of intelligence, which was lacking at the time.

Within the context of the Boko Haram insurgency, intelligence refers to the information that could be gathered about the insurgent group, including their members, locations, plans, and tactics (A., personal communication, 25 August 2022). Intelligence is critical in any counterinsurgency operation, because it enables the security forces to anticipate and prevent attacks, track down and apprehend or eliminate insurgent members, and disrupt the group's ability to operate. In the case of the CJTF, the military was struggling to gather reliable intelligence about Boko Haram due to a lack of trust and cooperation from the local communities, who saw the military as an external force and often feared retaliation from the insurgents (A., personal communication, 25 June 2022). The locals, however, had a better understanding of the terrain, culture, and social dynamics of their communities, which allowed them to gather more accurate intelligence about Boko Haram and its activities. By collaborating with the military, the CJTF was able to provide valuable intelligence that significantly enhanced the effectiveness of military operations against Boko Haram. The early, challenging days of Command Sector 7 were marked by profound sadness:

> *CJTF constitutes of young people of Maiduguri who came together owing to what is happening because the police and military do not know who they are fighting, and they cannot differentiate who is Boko Haram and who is not a member of Boko Haram amongthem. By so doing, after we saw how the activities of Boko Haram got worse, we now resolved to pick our sticks and knives to go after the people we knew were members of Boko Haram, we would then catch them and hand them over to the soldiers. Inspired by what we are doing, the youth in Borno State all came out together to join forces with the Army to go after Boko Haram. And as such, there is no hiding place for them as far as they are within the town* (L., personal communication, 25 September 2022).

The testimony highlights that the military's intervention in combatting the insurgency before the formation of the CJTF led to the arrest of innocent local members and the tragic loss of some of their relatives. This indicates that, rather than ending the catastrophic events and ensuring security, the military's actions inadvertently caused additional suffering for the locals. This was due to a lack of trust and cooperation between the military and the local communities as well as the military's limited understanding of the local terrain and social dynamics.

As explained by another CJTF member, local involvement in the fight against insurgency was crucial, because locals had a better understanding of the terrain and culture, which allowed them to provide valuable intelligence to the military. The team used their knowledge of the local terrain to guide the military to Boko Haram's hideouts. The aim of gathering intelligence was to prevent surprise attacks and enhance the military's operational effectiveness. This collaboration between the military and the CJTF significantly contributed to restoring peace and security in the affected communities. Another CJTF member noted that the communities plagued by insurgency were mired in tragedy and confusion until the local youths stepped forward to join the struggle for peace:

> *How it all started was when Boko Haram will come and kill people's brothers and parents, and soldiers will come and kill any person they found within the area Boko Haram attacked, not minding whether one is innocent or not. This is what led us to start exposing Boko Haram because we knew them, and they were living among us. So we now gave soldiers our support in the ongoing operation to the extent that Boko Haram left the metropolis and went to the bush. The fact that they ran to the bush did not let us to relent in the fight because we go after them. As a result of this, they now resorted to the use of bomb. And with the help of God, they do not succeed at times* (H., personal communication, 29 September 2022).

The testimony highlights that the military's difficulty in distinguishing between Boko Haram insurgents and local inhabitants was largely due to a lack of information-sharing and trust with the affected communities. Coupled with delayed responses to attacks, this situation indicated a limited understanding of the local environment, resulting in the mistaken identification of nearly everyone in the area as a potential suspect. Therefore, the involvement of willing natives in the CJTF, who provided crucial intelligence and a sense of direction to the military, highlighted the significance of enlisting locals in the fight against Boko Haram's insurgent acts. The natives' intelligence efforts also resulted in a significant change in the insurgent peace battle. As a result, Boko Haram insurgents resorted to the use of explosives to prevent being wiped out, as indicated by the respondent.

In addition to intelligence gathering, another critical factor that led to the emergence of the local security group was the need for routine and standby security checks for the maintenance of recovered towns and communities and overall insurgent peace operations. A CJTF member stated that the locals were actively involved in day-to-day security operations, going from house to house and area to area, chasing away insurgents and arresting those who were not fortunate enough to escape, promptly handing them over to the military. This level of collaboration between the military and the locals led to a more effective security system.

Given the vast area affected by Boko Haram attacks, it would have been challenging for the military to search thoroughly, considering their numbers. Thus, the need arose for close-range security checks, which were buttressed by the critical role the CJTF played in their collaborativesecurity operations:

> *Their role in the state now constitute staying alert to checkmate the activities of the dreaded Islamic sect Boko Haram by manning the checkpoints, they are also stationed at IDPs camps, and at out-skirts of the town together with the military to monitor movement of people coming in and going out of the town* (B., personal communication, 29 August 2022).

To enhance the security network and ensure tighter surveillance, the military increased the number of roadblocks and checkpoints, which required a larger workforce than they could provide alone. This demand was met by the local youths who joined the CJTF. A female member of the CJTF stated that the group recognised that its members needed to play the role of criminal investigators and assume the responsibility of monitoring the movement of locals, particularly in the markets, after a previous suicide bombing incident. In other words, it was evident from the casualty statistics that the military's operational strategies alone had too many loopholes, which the CJTF needed to address.

The military's continuous presence at centres of daily interaction, such as markets, gave the locals a sense of peace and security. However, some military officers considered this belittling, which highlighted the need for the CJTF to assume the role of security watch in the market squares. This point was raised by a CJTF member in Command Sector 2, Maiduguri, who highlighted the need to institute the local security team. To describe why the group is a crucial element in winning the war against Boko Haram, a source emphasised the urgent need for support the military in their anti-insurgency efforts:

> *The predominant police and army strategy on the involvement of CJTFs in the operation involves using them as fighting force alongside the police and army. I myself was one of the CJTF that went after Boko Haram at Sambisa forest, where I spent one month and a week going from one village to another in pursuit of Boko Haram* (K., personal communication, 20 August 2022).

One notable example of successful collaboration between the CJTF youth volunteers and the military in the fight against Boko Haram is detailed in a testimony describing a month-long battle in the Sambisa Forest, a known stronghold of the insurgents. This joint effort was highly effective in achieving the shared objective of enhancing security in the region:

> *What makes the group a fundamental component in the battle against Boko Haram insurgency is its support given to the police and army, more also with the support of God who saw us through when we were chasing them out from Maiduguri down to the bush and killing them. Moreover, the full support we gave to the police and army also plays a vital role, because as it stands today, whenever the soldiers ask us to go to bush alongside them, we agree* (B., personal communication, 21 November 2022).

The successful involvement of CJTF members in supporting the military's insurgency-related peace operations has highlighted the effectiveness of grassroots participation in decision-making and battle initiatives. It is now evident that the collective efforts of local volunteers can significantly contribute to the success of security operations, alongside the military's efforts.

### Conclusion

This chapter examines the factors contributing to the emergence of the CJTF and its role in addressing the Boko Haram insurgency through insurgency-related peace operations. It is argued that the CJTF has potential beyond Borno State and that understanding its role requires a contextual rather than generalised approach. The significance of state-society relations in the effectiveness of local initiatives is emphasised, with the lack of trust in the military's capacity to address Boko Haram insurgents leading to the establishment of the CJTF as a local security force in Borno State.

The structure of the CJTF is reviewed, highlighting the necessity of enhanced scrutiny, complementarity, collaboration, and effective service integration between local insurgent peace strategies and military operations. The security of local populations is a critical component of the CJTF's peace efforts, which have contributed to countering Boko Haram insurgents in affected communities. The origins and ideology of the CJTF are linked to the military's heavy-handed approach in the fight against Boko Haram. The chapter underscores the importance of balancing top-down and bottom-up approaches in counterinsurgency efforts, advocating for closer collaboration between the military and community-based initiatives. Additionally, it addresses the need to critically evaluate and deconstruct negative narratives associated with certain CJTF elements.

The success of some CJTF members in information sharing and auxiliary combat roles has fostered a greater need for local collaboration. Consequently, the fight against Boko Haram has seen significant progress due to the CJTF's active engagements and collaboration with the military. The limited military intervention reflects the locals' increasing proficiency in managing insurgency issues. Overall, the CJTF is presented as having considerable potential to serve as an effective tool in combatting insurgencies extending beyond Borno State.

# CHAPTER SEVEN
# ORGANISATIONAL STRUCTURE AND OPERATIONAL STRATEGIES OF THE CIVILIAN JOINT TASK FORCE

## Introduction

In this chapter, the focus is on two main themes: the CJTF's organisational structure and its operational strategies. At the operational level, the mode of operation, intelligence gathering, and information management are investigated. In addition, the structure of the organisation and the distribution of tasks and responsibilities among members are explained.

The chapter specifically explores the inclusive, committal system that characterises the CJTF's approach to dealing with insurgents at the operational level. This collaborative approach involves either referring or transferring suspects to state security agencies (military) for further questioning, investigation, and prosecution. The system is characterised by a commitment to working with government security agencies, contributing to the recognition and legitimacy of the CJTF as an insurgency-related peace force.

Fieldwork observations reveal that the CJTF's willingness to cooperate with military forces and submit Boko Haram insurgents to them seems to contradict the group's original formation as a revenge mission against the insurgents who killed the leader's father. The group's initial enthusiasm to apprehend Boko Haram members increased drastically after the death of the leader's mother, who had previously dissuaded the group from seeking revenge. This enthusiasm led to the Borno State government's invitation for the CJTF to cooperate with the military in fighting the insurgents. Although revenge may have influenced the group's formation, it was not the primary motivation later when collaborating with insurgency-related peace operations in the state, leading to the confiscation of ammunition and the killing of many Boko Haram insurgents. The joint operations of the CJTF and the state's apparatuses have significantly hampered Boko Haram's actions in Borno State. The military has affirmed the successful intervention of the CJTF in insurgency-related peace operations, recognising them as a group well-suited for such efforts and thus contributing to their legitimacy as an insurgency-related peace force.

In this chapter, the review focuses on the CJTF's operational strategies for promoting insurgent peace, such as monitoring IDPs, relocating communities under siege or at risk of Boko Haram attacks, and manning posts or stations in most towns in collaboration with the military. CJTF members are present in many areas, covertly reshaping and revitalising the military's previously stagnant system. They act as community watchers due to their familiarity with rural villages. Initially, there was contention due to a conflict of interest between the CJTF and the military, leading to the military's reluctance to approve or accept the CJTF. The group's oath of allegiance and commitment also caused disarray, maltreatment, and disagreements among various security apparatuses. However, acceptance grew as the CJTF began operations with the military, being recognised as a pro-government force tasked with working closely with the military to gather intelligence and perform auxiliary roles.

The evaluation covers how the CJTF has performed in its alliance with the military, which remains divided on the legitimacy of the CJTF's operations. Some lower-ranking military personnel strongly believe that the CJTF's activities are effective in addressing Boko Haram's insurgency, while higher-ranking officers hold differing opinions.

## Organisational structure of the CJTF

In the local government areas of Borno State, the CJTF has established 10 command sectors, each headed by a commander appointed as the overall leader. Every command sector has a subchairman and 10 wards with a chairman as well as an average of 25 persons working in each ward, comprising approximately 250 to 300 people attached to a command sector. The state has 27 local government areas, which are administratively and religiously controlled by eight emirate councils (Borno, Damboa, Dikwa, Biu, Askira, Gwoza, Shani, and Uba). After completing the paramilitary training organised by the military, members of the CJTF group are deployed in the local government areas (see Figure 7.1 below).

**Figure 7.1**: Paramilitary training of CJTF members.

*Source*: Author

**Figure 7.2**: Paramilitary training of CJTF members.

*Source*: Author

**Figure 7.3**: CJTF members in a joint operation with the military.

*Source:* Author.

**Figure 7.4**: CJTF members in a joint operation with the military.

*Source:* Author

The institutional structure of the CJTF includes the president, a general as chairman, an operational commander/head of intelligence, and an operational commander/head of operation. In addition, 231 women are recorded as staff in the operational department, intelligence guarding unit, rehabilitation training centre, and welfare department of the CJTF. Some are deployed to various local government areas across the state. Each command sector or unit has a leader who is linked to the overall headquarters at the Post Office in the former NITEL Building, Maiduguri.

The unit responsible for maintaining discipline and providing rapid response in cases of Boko Haram insurgency and civil wrongs in Borno State and neighbouring communities receives reports of such incidents. To fulfil its duties and responsibilities, the unit has discretionary and assimilating privileges. CJTF members often accompany local security operatives and the military during counterinsurgency operations in the state. In these cases, the chairman leads the preparation for a counterattack. If Boko Haram insurgent incidents are reported, the unit refers them to Battalion (Army) 251, 195, or 7 Division Military Intelligence Department for further action.

A designated office handles the pursuit of the struggle and cases of civil wrongs. Community and religious leaders are involved in the panel of judges who interrogate suspects and refer the cases to state security agencies for further investigation. These agencies include the Nigerian Police Force, Nigerian Army, Nigerian Navy, Department of State Security, Nigerian Civil Defense Services, Nigerian Customs Services, and Nigerian Immigration Service.

According to historical accounts, Jafar Lawan's father was reportedly killed by Boko Haram members, which may have motivated him to seek revenge against the group (B.A., personal communication, 21 July 2022). His mother reportedly prevented him from taking action, but after her death, he began identifying Boko Haram members in the locality. He gained support from local members and was eventually invited by the Borno State government to collaborate with the military in combatting Boko Haram. This led to the formation of the CJTF insurgent peace group, with Jafar Lawan as its initiator and base in Hausari (B.A., personal communication, 15 July 2022). His role as the initiator made him the first leader to chair the CJTF. During an interview with a CJTF member about interventions and command in the Damboa Emirate Council area, the following statement was made:

> With regard to policy making, due to the fact that those CJTF members are civilians and illiterates, they are not really involved in it, because like I said you need a lot of technicality to deal with these civilians as a result of their different ideas and views. So the reason why the CJTF members record a lot of success in the counterinsurgency operation was that they are always in line with the instructions from the government security officers because a lot of them are illiterate and

had never been to such a war before, they have never been into any security issue before, by so doing, they are lacking in terms of policy formulation. And the policy making here is highly centralized and it is the government security officers that actually bring out the policy supported by their headquarters (A., personal communication, 26 July 2022).

As highlighted in previous sections, the success of the military's operations in Borno State is closely linked to the interventionist role played by CJTF members. A particularly noteworthy example of their effectiveness is demonstrated by their actions in the communities of Bnisheik, Damboa, Bama, Gambororu Ngala, and Monguro, where CJTF members have successfully recovered large caches of ammunition (see Figure 7.2 below) and eliminated a significant number of Boko Haram insurgents in collaborative insurgency-related peace operations (S., personal communication, 24 July 2022).

**Figure 7.5**: Recovering Boko Haram caches of ammunition.

*Source:* Author

Evidence shows that the CJTF's interventions in insurgency-related peace operations with the military have significantly impeded the activities of Boko Haram insurgents in all local government areas of Borno State. A military operative interviewed in the Shani Emirate Council area attested the following:

*With regard to the ways CJTF members are involved in the counterinsurgency operation with the military, I will like to affirm that yes they are often involved in the ongoing operation, like I have said earlier, if not for the effort of CJTF members, the Boko Haraminsurgency would have been futile, their coming has brought tremendous achievements in the counter insurgence, like the major way they got involved as I said earlier they were able to fish out individually those who were involved in those acts and as well using diabolically means as constituting fighting force. In short, then, it was CJTF members that were doing the spy work, the soldiers were relaxed. Another way they are involved has to do with manning checkpoints to ensure that laws are not violated* (Y., personal communication, 17 June 2022).

Findings show that joint operations between the CJTF and the military in the state have significantly impacted the actions of Boko Haram insurgents. The CJTF's successful interventions in military insurgency-related peace operations demonstrate that the group is a valuable asset in preplanned and strategically structured counterinsurgency efforts. Respondents noted that the integration of the CJTF and the military has limited Boko Haram's activities, forcing them to primarily select soft targets through suicide bombings in various locations in Borno State. The CJTF's intelligence gathering and local initiatives have proven effective against Boko Haram's attacks on local government areas in the state. One community member shared this view in an interview:

*Regarding interventionist roles of CJTF members method of counterinsurgency with those of the police officers, I would like to acknowledge the fact that the CJTF members have tried a lot because they are not trained personnel, likewise the military who are trained for such operation, and are well equipped with weapons knowing the tactics of how to go about the operation while possessing the skills. But in the case of CJTF members, they are just common civilians who do not have the knowledge of how to go about tackling security issues, but their local initiatives are well fit into the operation. But they remain part of the operation* (M., personal communication, 10 October 2022).

The intervention of the CJTF in the military's insurgency-related peace operations is widely recognised and appreciated by the local communities that are under attack by Boko Haram insurgents. This positive reaction from the locals is a significant development and has greatly assisted insurgency-related peace operations in Borno State. With the assistance of the CJTF insurgent peace group, the military is making a significant impact and is expected to continue doing well. Galula's (1964) insurgent peace theory argues that no state can effectively combat insurgency or eliminate the threat posed by insurgents without the support of the local population. Therefore, based on the feedback from the respondents, the military must continue working collaboratively with the locals to ensure the complete eradication of insurgency in Borno State.

## Insurgency peace and CJTF's operational strategies

In this section, the roles of the CJTF in counterinsurgency operations alongside the military are explained. According to a CJTF member, the group's roles include participating in battlefield operations armed with locally made guns taken from Boko Haram members killed in combat. Another CJTF member (see Figure 7.3 below) notes that each CJTF command sector is regulated by guard commanders who oversee no fewer than 50 members. The guard commanders are responsible for providing instructions and directives on conducting insurgency-related peace operations. Other key roles include the secretary and public relations officers.

**Figure 7.6**: Author (left) with Research Assistant, late Abubakar Musa (right).

*Source*: Author.

During the interviews, the operations commander and head of operations expressed a strong belief that the Borno State government did not prioritise the overall improvement and security of the CJTF as a whole. It was noted that the government's focus was primarily on the security and development of the CJTF members registered under BOYES, who received essential resources such as uniforms, weapons, and vehicles. As a result, the CJTF has developed its own resources and strategies to enhance its effectiveness against the Boko Haram insurgency. One such strategy is "Operation Deep Punch", which involves actively pursuing and engaging insurgents in their bush hideouts. By relying on its own resources, the CJTF aims to effectively combat the insurgency and contribute to restoring peace and security in Borno State.

A female group member stated that the CJTF not only participates in counterinsurgency operations but also provides humanitarian assistance, including monitoring and relocating IDPs. She highlighted the CJTF's role in relocating communities under siege or at risk of Boko Haram attacks and recounted instances where timely interventions prevented tragedies in IDP camps in Damboa, Bama, and Monguno. She also described an incident in Gamboru Ngala where a CJTF member sacrificed his life to stop a suicide bomber, ensuring the safety of local residents. In addition, she noted that CJTF efforts have helped keep markets in major communities across Borno State operational.

Based on the analysis, it is clear that both the CJTF and military view the current counterinsurgency strategies as promising for both social and political advancement. Fieldwork revealed that military leaders and commanders in Maiduguri have supported the CJTF by addressing their needs. CJTF commanders are influential figures in Maiduguri and have been instrumental when required. Interviews indicated a strong unity between the CJTF and the military in addressing the Boko Haram crisis. Despite the absence of military posts or stations in many towns, CJTF groups are widespread, providing support in villages and towns and contributing to maintaining peace. In addition, intermediaries are crucial in supporting the military, as confirmed by a member who stated:

> *For instance, if someone has vital information to give about Boko Haram, they prefer approaching us with it before we can notify the security agencies and we also serve as Criminal Investigation Department in the community* (B.A., personal communication, 17 October 2022).

The involvement of the CJTF in peace operations in Borno State is straightforward due to the group's well-defined roles and responsibilities. The CJTF is structured to function as a community-based security force against Boko Haram insurgents, working in a humanitarian capacity. The Borno State government has permitted the group's participation in these operations, provided that all members are officially registered and recognised by the military in the areas where they operate.

An interview with a CJTF member from Command Sector 8 revealed that the group's structure includes the chairman as the highest-ranking member, followed by the deputy chairman and other ranks (H., personal communication, 10

October 2022). These officers coordinate CJTF activities, alert the military as per instructions, and ensure that the group's operations align with its mandate.

However, there has been conflict between the CJTF and the military, partly due to some military personnel's reluctance to pursue insurgents (H., personal communication, 9 September 2022). This reluctance may stem from being overwhelmed by the insurgency's challenging conditions and risks, differences in strategies or tactics between the military and CJTF, or personal or political motivations such as fear of retaliation or sympathy for the insurgents. These issues have led to communication and trust breakdowns between the military and CJTF, underscoring the need for clear coordination and understanding between different security forces during joint operations.

Disorganisation, mistreatment, and disagreements among various security forces have beenreported during their operations against insurgency in Borno State, Nigeria. The inclusion of the CJTF has also led to some grievances. Despite these challenges, CJTF members remain committed, having taken an oath of allegiance and commitment. They have chosen not to publicly express their grievances and to continue following military orders. As noted, "*the military know that we are not happy about the tactics used by them, but they let us understand that military works on command*" (T., personal communication, 23 June 2022).

The traditional approach to combatting Boko Haram involves offensive attacks and pursuing insurgents in the bush, typically carried out collaboratively by various security forces. However, at the CJTF headquarters, it was evident that the group also participates in street patrols with the military and monitors their immediate and neighbouring communities. In addition, the CJTF, with its local knowledge of the terrain, culture, and people, provides the military with strategic and tactical intelligence on insurgent activities in rural communities. This local insight aids in launching successful operations.

The CJTF's involvement in insurgency-related peace operations has enhanced trust between the military and local communities. CJTF members are seen as part of the communities they serve, leading to a sense of shared responsibility for security and fostering collaboration between the military and local residents. This cooperation has contributed to successful insurgency-related peace operations. Figure 7.4 below shows a group of CJTF members before embarking on an operation.

**Figure 7.7**: CJTF members.

*Source:* Author

The CJTF's ability to carry out insurgency-related peace operations that the military may not be able to perform, along with their local knowledge and understanding of the communities they serve, make them an invaluable partner in the fight against the Boko Haram insurgency. In essence, the involvement of the CJTF has expanded the scope of insurgency-related peace operations in Borno State, as it complements the military's efforts and provides valuable intelligence and security to the local communities. This was confirmed by a unit leader in CJTF Command Sector 7, who said, "*Military know what we do, and they need us; they need our local technical intelligence*" (Y., personal communication, 22 November 2022). He also stated that the methods and systems utilised in combatting Boko Haram include the military and CJTF patrols as well as manhunts in pursuit of Boko Haram insurgents in the bush.

## The nature and implications of collaboration

The CJTF and the military in Borno State have developed a close relationship. However, the dominant military presence in the region has meant that CJTF activities have received relatively little attention in insurgency-related peace operations, particularly in Borno State. Despite this, the CJTF has played a crucial role in reshaping the approach to addressing the Boko Haram insurgency in the three states where it operates. As noted by a CJTF member, "*Since we have been in support of security officers in all the villages and local areas, the officers have been receiving some success, and through the collaboration, many weapons have been recovered from Boko Haram members"* (S., personal communication, 11 June 2022).

Focus group discussions revealed that strict rules govern the conduct of CJTF members during interventions. They are prohibited from taking the law into their own hands and must report any known Boko Haram insurgents to the military. According to a member, if a CJTF member captures a Boko Haram insurgent, the rule is to hand the insurgent over to the military (D., personal communication, 3 August 2022). This indicates that the CJTF primarily operates as a pro-government force, working closely with the military to gather intelligence and perform auxiliary military tasks against Boko Haram.

In discussions with Maiduguri residents, it emerged that the military frequently relies on CJTF members for insurgency-related peace operations, particularly in challenging terrains and rural communities with which they are less familiar. The military heavily depends on the CJTF in its operations in Borno State. Despite being unarmed, CJTF members have been at the forefront of the fight against Boko Haram and have paid a heavy price, with hundreds killed since 2013. During a visit to the CJTF headquarters, it was observed that, despite challenges and losses, the group remains committed to local security, with the military continuing to lead the insurgency- related peace operations.

Despite its supportive role, the CJTF has significantly influenced and revitalised the military's insurgency-related peace strategy, transforming it into an effective framework for combatting Boko Haram's insurgency. This influence has led to notable successes in combat and demonstrates the group's unwavering commitment to eradicating local insurgency. As a result, the CJTF is recognised as a cohesive and widespread local security force with considerable impact on local security and the future stability of rural communities affected by the Boko Haram crisis in Borno State. Interviews revealed that both the federal and Borno State governments support the CJTF's role in peace operations, providing necessary financial and material aid. Key informant interviews at the Borno State border described the CJTF's intervention role as follows:

> *In my own village state, CJTF do not have much power to intervene because of the limited activities of the Boko Haram insurgency group in the state and majorities of the atrocities committed by the group is limited to the borders between the state of Borno and Adamawa and rural communities, and in most cases, they are in unanimity with the security officers, but only two-third of them adhere to the law and the guideline of the military counterinsurgency operations* (B., personal communication, 27 July 2022).

Nevertheless, on the subject of intervention, another respondent said the following:

> *You know community members' inhabitants are meant to enjoy support and protection from both of us and so all the community stakeholders partake and add to the importance and values of the security and according to our working plan, both of us (i.e., CJTF members and security officers) need "safety" also and community have been given some safety rights, those rights are what CJTF, and security agents is giving them. Military officers are the ones who are outsiders to the communities and the main target of the Boko Haram insurgents in the location since the community locations are so vast and cannot be effectively policed and captured by the security officers, CJTF will just be in one part of the location doing what can also protect their people. And you know, "whoever knows the intrigues of the road path within the Boko Haram insurgency location is the person that enters it". CJTF assist the security officers to settle and strategize in the different locations because they are familiar with every nook and cranny of the communities. Although the military officers always claim to be working for us, but we are also protecting them through our little operation and cooperation* (M., personal communication, 11 September 2022).

Referring to the strategies of CJTF members in Borno State that resulted in controlling the Boko Haram menace, another interviewee made the following comment:

> *We have advised the security officers to find ways to incorporate all the members of CJTF so that we can easily locate the hideouts of Boko Haram insurgents and all the hideouts in different locations of the communities. But there are cultural restraints as CJTF are under some restrictions, in whom the territorial control of those security officers are vested. This is because they believe that it is conflicting with the standard security officers' counterinsurgency operations, and as such can be negating to the general objective of the security officers in the locations* (L., personal communication, 11 November 2022).

During an interview in Biu, a participant highlighted the essential role of the CJTF in countering Boko Haram activities, stating that the "*CJTF's responsibility is to support the military and maintain peace in the community*" (U., personal communication, 28 August 2022). This perspective supports the argument made by many scholars that local security forces, such as the CJTF, who have deep knowledge of rural areas and terrain, are crucial in addressing the security issues in Borno State, particularly in these regions.

The effectiveness of using local security forces to address the various security threats in Borno State has been proven, with significant progress made in counterinsurgency operations. This progress has allowed locals to go about their daily lives with greater safety. CJTF members remain vigilant, monitoring the movement of outsiders and visitors in cities, towns, and rural areas to prevent insurgents from gaining control. The cooperation between the military and CJTF has been vital for the success of these counterinsurgency efforts. As noted in a focus group discussion, if the military were to combat Boko Haram alone, it would face difficulties distinguishing between law-abiding residents and insurgents. Despite any reservations the military may have about the CJTF's presence in the urban and rural areas of Borno State, it often relies on the group's information, guidance, and intelligence, as reflected in the following comment:

> *The role of CJTF includes fighting Boko Haram, exposing them and monitoring of people's movement, because virtually all of the areas in the urban and rural that have CJTF and as such they know who a stranger is, once he/she comes into their area and many insurgents members have been arrested through this means and a good number of weapons has been recovered from them* (S., personal communication, 28 June 2022).

CJTF members receive official support from the military in their operations. One member explained that the primary strategy of involving the CJTF in insurgency-related peace operations is to utilise the group both as informants and as a combat force. In addition, the CJTF manages many of the auxiliary peace operations. It remains unclear whether the support from CJTF members is voluntary or driven by fear or pressure from the military. Nonetheless, their assistance has been crucial for the success of insurgency-related peace efforts against Boko Haram in Borno State. A study conducted in Biu indicates that the military views the CJTF as a crucial yet ordinary component in the state's peace efforts, regularly incorporating the group into assessments of the insurgency situation.

### Emerging polemics on the CJTF's identity in the military structure

At the CJTF headquarters in the Post Office area of Maiduguri, Borno State, it was discovered that the group plays a significant role in peace operations against insurgents, including participating in combat alongside the military. The military consistently praises joint operations with the CJTF, noting that their involvement boosts confidence and shows strong community support for the fight against Boko Haram. Therefore, any claims that the CJTF is unfit for these operations do not reflect the actual situation.

Interviews conducted in Dikwa and the Biu Emirate Council revealed that the CJTF is often perceived merely as a group of hunters. According to a CJTF member and hunter in the Biu Emirate area, the group's strategy for regaining control involved leading military troops to reclaimed communities, particularly in rural areas (S., personal communication, 8 June 2022). This approach proved effective in instilling fear in Boko Haram fighters, who were aware that some CJTF members employed charms (magical powers).

The primary reason for involving locals in the fight against Boko Haram is their ability to act as informants due to their deep knowledge of the insurgents. However, there is ongoing debate about the best way to utilise the CJTF in insurgency-related peace operations in Borno State. An elderly community member noted that CJTF members are organised into command sectors within the metropolis, and each local government area has its own CJTF units operating under strict military instructions (Z., personal communication, 28 September 2022).

An interview with a CJTF member in Dikwa highlighted that the group's success can be attributed to its large numbers, which resulted from the Borno State government's decision to train and integrate them into the fight against Boko Haram. This government decision significantly increased the number of CJTF members involved in insurgency-related peace operations, contributing to the group's success in combatting Boko Haram. The interviewee also noted that this decision influenced the group's perception of their role in the conflict, as the training provided helped them understand their involvement as a means of protecting their communities from insurgency.

By empowering the CJTF to actively counter the insurgency, the Borno State government not only enhanced the group's capabilities but also instilled a sense of ownership over community security. This empowerment fostered a level of determination and commitment among CJTF members that may not have been achieved if they had been mere recipients of government support. The interview revealed that the Borno State government's strategy of training and involving local security groups played a crucial role in countering the Boko Haram insurgency, building resilience, and encouraging a collective responsibility for security within the communities.

Moreover, the CJTF members have demonstrated a level of determination and commitment that would likely not have been achieved if they were merely passive recipients of government support. The CJTF group is a crucial element in the fight against insurgents because they offer a practical perspective that helps the military develop effective strategies to address the insurgents' dominance in the state. Being closely integrated with the local communities, CJTF members can differentiate between guilty individuals and innocent locals, a task that military officials might struggle with on their own.

Both the Borno State government and lower-cadre military officials have recognised the CJTF group as an essential guide for the military during counterinsurgency operations.

Regardless of facing indiscriminate attacks and losses, the CJTF remains vital in achieving the objective of countering the insurgency and securing a victory over the state's enemies. The effectiveness and conventional role of the CJTF in insurgency-related peace operations are evident from the progress made in restoring normalcy despite numerous Boko Haram assaults. Therefore, the intervention of the CJTF in these operations is justified and necessary for the state's security efforts.

## Conclusion

This chapter has thoroughly examined the organisation and strategies of the CJTF, highlighting its effectiveness in the fight against insurgency. It underscores the importance of locally based insurgent peace groups in insurgency-related peace operations and the necessity for federal government involvement in these efforts. The study has focused on the CJTF's role in intelligence gathering, information management, and its integration into the military's operational structure for countering insurgency in Nigeria. While locally based insurgent peace groups such as the CJTF offer a promising model for countering the Boko Haram insurgency in Borno State and potentially beyond, it is essential to recognise and account for contextual differences to avoid overgeneralisation.

Locally based insurgent peace operations have complemented state-centric military responses by playing a crucial interventionist role. The fieldwork has established that CJTF operates under military supervision, maintaining a cooperative relationship across Borno State's local government areas. The trust between the military, CJTF, and local communities has fostered confidence in the fight against insurgency.

The examination of the CJTF's organisation and strategies has shown the group's effectiveness in insurgency-related peace. Beyond engaging in punitive actions against insurgents, the CJTF has demonstrated competence in routine joint patrols and roadblocks. Earlier chapters provided a comprehensive understanding of the CJTF's role in local security within the Nigerian context.

A key finding from this investigation is how the CJTF's operations have evolved through partnerships and coordination. The group's success is attributed to its synergy with the military and local communities, creating a mutually reinforcing effect in combatting insurgency.

Studying the CJTF's operations solely within a military framework may overlook an important aspect of insurgency-related peace – empowering local communities to address the root causes of insurgency. Engaging local communities in identifying and resolving underlying issues such as economic marginalisation, social inequality, and political disenfranchisement is crucial for long- term peace. Decentralising insurgency-related peace efforts in Borno State could enhance the effectiveness of local security campaigns and contribute to lasting peace.

Local involvement in insurgency-related peace is vital for empowering communities to address insurgency issues and prevent future conflicts. This approach also helps build trust between the government and local communities, which is essential for sustainable peace. Therefore, while military operations provide necessary security, they should be complemented by broader strategies that involve local communities in addressing the underlying causes of insurgency. This comprehensive approach is crucial for achieving enduring peace and addressing the complex issues contributing to the ongoing conflict in Borno State and beyond.

# CHAPTER EIGHT
# CIVILIAN JOINT TASK FORCE'S INTERVENTIONISM AND INSURGENT PEACE IN BORNO STATE

## Introduction

The evaluation of interventionist approaches to insurgency peace in the northeast has been a central topic in discussions about insurgency-related peace, yet a detailed analysis of the CJTF's role remains underexplored. This chapter addresses this gap by examining interventionism through various frameworks, arguing that the CJTF effectively fills a critical gap left by the military. Previous chapters have reinforced this argument, showing that the military's operational strategies alone were insufficient to overcome the insurgent threat due to the porous nature of the local community and complex local security dynamics.

The term "porousness" describes how a community's boundaries permit external influences – both positive and negative – to penetrate due to factors such as weak social cohesion, a lack of shared values, and significant diversity that hampers the establishment of common ground. Within the context of local security, the porousness of a community can affect its ability to safeguard itself from external threats and maintain internal stability and safety.

The concept of epistemic security and its influence on local communities is also crucial. Epistemic security involves protecting knowledge, information, and communication systems from external threats such as hacking or misinformation. Conversely, transversal local security pertains to the physical safety and well-being of individuals within a community, considering social, cultural, and economic factors that influence security concerns. While epistemic security focuses on safeguarding information and knowledge, transversal security prioritises the tangible safety and stability of people, taking into account their sociocultural and economic contexts.

The establishment of the CJTF group was deemed crucial, given the need to engage with the local community to ensure their safety. The group works closely with residents to identify and address security concerns, foster trust, and establish effective communication channels. This engagement justified the creation of the CJTF, especially in areas lacking military intervention or where state forces struggled to maintain peace. The CJTF proved effective in these regions due to its deep local knowledge and its ability to provide intelligence where the military's presence was weak.

Throughout this book, it has been established that the CJTF's interventionist role involved collaborating with the military, albeit with limited responsibility for local security from Boko Haram insurgents. The CJTF significantly contributed by gathering crucial intelligence, which complemented the military's counterinsurgency efforts. Initially, the federal and state military setups did not fully recognise the CJTF's role until the group began actively screening, gathering information about Boko Haram and guiding military forces to insurgent hideouts. The CJTF's linguistic profiling and identification skills became invaluable, addressing challenges such as language barriers that previously hindered military operations (K., personal communication, 14 July 2022).

Analysis reveals that the CJTF's approach to maintaining local security was both practical and functional making it highly effective and preferred among the local community. By filling the security gap left by state forces, the CJTF offered a proactive solution to security concerns. Its close community ties and rapid response capabilities rendered it a highly effective and symbolic local security approach. The group's success in restoring peace and security has made it a beacon of hope and resilience for the region.

Discussions held at the CJTF headquarters revealed that the group addressed the gaps left by the military, despite initial doubts about its suitability for a collaborative interventionist role. The CJTF demonstrated its capacity to handle security challenges and insurgency effectively at both urban and rural levels. For instance, the group operated covertly, using disguises to infiltrate Boko Haram insurgents' hideouts. By acting as undercover agents, CJTF members gathered intelligence and disrupted insurgents' activities, which they then shared with security forces, contributing significantly to regional peace and security. This clandestine approach was crucial in preempting insurgent attacks and minimising risks to community operations. The CJTF's ability to blend in with insurgents and gather strategic intelligence has been crucial in identifying insurgent plans and targets, contributing to successful counterinsurgency efforts. While questions regarding the CJTF's effectiveness alongside the military persist, the military generally supports the group's role in enhancing security. For instance, the CJTF's efforts in retaking territories captured by Boko Haram, despite lacking advanced weapons or military support, have improved local security and increased community confidence.

This study supports the views of other researchers (Galula, 1964; Omeni, 2017; Gawthorpe, 2017), affirming that achieving peace would be challenging without the CJTF's intervention, especially in collaboration with the military. During fieldwork, the CJTF, working with the military, recovered 70 motorcycles loaded with explosives, 430 rifles, and 870 pistols from Boko Haram insurgents. The group also played a vital role in neutralising Boko Haram's stronghold in the Sambisa Forest, highlighting the importance of interventionism and the CJTF's effectiveness in restoring peace in Borno State, northeast Nigeria.

## CJTF's intervention in military operations

The military continues to support the CJTF's interventionist role in countering Boko Haram in Borno State. This ongoing collaboration underscores the combined effort of the military and local communities, a synergy highlighted by interviews with emirate councils and supported by scholarly works, including those by Galula (1964) and Gawthorpe (2017). The CJTF has proven effective in mitigating the impact of the insurgents, making it essential for the military to prioritise this partnership.

Galula's (1964) theoretical framework emphasises the need for local involvement in insurgency-related peace operations, asserting that a purely military approach is insufficient in a community characterised by "porousness". The CJTF's interaction with local populations, including those with ties to Boko Haram, is vital for effective counterinsurgency. This perspective is corroborated by scholars such as Hassan (2015) and Bamidele (2024).

CJTF members excel in areas where the military lacks local knowledge and intelligence. Their role in counterinsurgency operations has been pivotal, especially in villages where the military's information-gathering capabilities fall short. Bamidele (2018, 2022) supports the bottom-up approach, which fills the gaps left by the military's deficiencies in information collection. Despite some CJTF members feeling undervalued by federal and state authorities, security officers interviewed acknowledged the group's significant contributions. CJTF members are instrumental in gathering intelligence, screening for information about Boko Haram operations, and guiding military efforts to insurgent hideouts. Their role remains crucial in the local counterinsurgency strategy, a fact consistently supported by the aforementioned scholars.

The CJTF has been acknowledged as a vital player in maintaining peace and security in Borno State, although its role does not encompass all military counterinsurgency operations. During an interview with a CJTF member, it was revealed that the group employs a distinctive method of linguistic identification (M., personal communication, 23 July 2022). CJTF members use coded language to differentiate between outsiders and Boko Haram insurgents, a technique that is unique to them and serves as a strategic asset.

The use of coded language enables CJTF members to communicate securely, preventing eavesdropping or understanding by outsiders or potential infiltrators.

This identification method is crucial for the group's effectiveness in safeguarding their communities and disrupting Boko Haram's activities. It fosters a strong sense of unity and cultural preservation within the CJTF while enhancing its operational security.

As noted by various sources, CJTF members are tasked with questioning suspicious individuals in their communities to verify their intentions (personal communication, 25 August 2022). If individuals provide satisfactory responses, they are allowed to continue with their activities. However, if someone is suspected of being an intruder or sleeper spy and fails to provide acceptable answers, CJTF members are responsible for handing them over to the military. A sleeper spy is defined as a deep-cover agent who remains inactive for extended periods to gather intelligence and conduct covert operations without detection. These spies can be activated at any time for missions such as sabotage or espionage, making the CJTF's role in identifying and managing such threats crucial.

The intervention of the CJTF in Borno State has proven particularly effective in regions where the military's competence and intelligence are limited. The military is advised to prioritise its partnership with CJTF members when addressing the Boko Haram insurgency. However, the CJTF's intervention should not be seen as a replacement for military operations but rather as a complementary bottom-up approach involving local populations.

The CJTF's involvement in counterinsurgency operations has been commendable. When the group expressed its interest in combatting Boko Haram, it formed a dedicated interventionist force. With support from security officers, CJTF members engaged in intense operations, searching for insurgents street by street. Their motivation stemmed from personal knowledge of those responsible for violence in Maiduguri. Key roles of the CJTF included identifying and exposing Boko Haram members, manning checkpoints, and monitoring the movement of individuals.

The roles of CJTF members and the military, though aligned in the common goal of countering Boko Haram, differ significantly. CJTF members operate based on instructions from their command sectors and local authorities, while the military follows directives from various headquarters. In joint operations, CJTF members adhere to military commands while maintaining their own command structure. Interviews with locals in Mafa, near Maiduguri, reveal that CJTF members received approval from local authorities for their operations and had established command sectors in areas severely affected by Boko Haram, such as Konduga, Mafa, and Bama (S., personal communication, 13 July 2022). This organisational structure ensures effective coordination and collaboration between the CJTF and the military in their combined efforts against the insurgency.

The complexity of the CJTF's interventionist roles compared to those of the military arises from the difference in their backgrounds and training. CJTF members, being ordinary civilians, initially lacked formal military training, whereas security officers were trained professionals withextensive experience. Despite this disparity, the CJTF's involvement in counterinsurgency operations has been crucial.

The success of the military's insurgency-related peace efforts in Borno State is significantly attributed to the effective collaboration with CJTF members. This partnership has been effective in both rural and urban areas. For instance, when Boko Haram insurgents attacked Biu town, the prompt action of CJTF members stationed there successfully thwarted the attack and prevented the insurgents from infiltrating the town. Such examples highlight the effective synergy between the military and CJTF in achieving their common goal of combatting the insurgency in Borno State.

### Debating the CJTF's interventionist role

The CJTF has been widely discussed in scholarly literature (Bamidele, 2017a&b, 2018, 2020, 2023; Idris et al., 2014; Olonisakin, 2016; Ibrahim & Bala, 2018). While some scholars view the group as a crucial local insurgent peace force addressing the military's shortcomings, others question its effectiveness in insurgent peace operations in Borno State (Onapajo & Ozden, 2020; Onuoha et al., 2020). Despite these debates, analysis from various perspectives, including the advantages and disadvantages of bottom-up versus top-down approaches, confirms that the CJTF's presence in the state is justified due to its effective security maintenance in both urban and rural areas.

One notable strength of the CJTF group is its ability to infiltrate Boko Haram insurgents' hideouts, gather intelligence, and blend into their territories. This capability allows the CJTF to provide critical information to the military, aiding in the planning and execution of successful counterattacks against the insurgents. The group's effectiveness as informants and undercover agents underscores its significant role in supporting the military's efforts to establish peace operations in Borno State.

The military's challenges in engaging effectively with local communities limit its intelligence-gathering capabilities against Boko Haram. The CJTF's close interaction with locals provides a deeper understanding of insurgent operations, which is crucial for successful insurgency-related peace efforts. Consequently, the partnership between the CJTF and the military is essential for achieving effective insurgent peace operations in Borno State.

The CJTF's capacity to fight alongside the military during counterattacks has been a topic ofdebate. However, an interview with a CJTF member in Borno

State revealed that the military's strategy involves actively engaging the CJTF group during counterattacks to support efforts towards achieving insurgent peace. The member recounted spending over a month in Sambisa Forest, moving from village to village in pursuit of Boko Haram insurgents. He explained that the CJTF operates in well-organised battalions, each responsible for specific geographic areas, with members highly trained and dedicated to maintaining local peace and security (U., personal communication, 29 August 2022).

Although previously assigned to different command sectors, the member is currently working with Army Battalion 251, 195, or the Division Military Intelligence Department. This battalion structure allows the CJTF to cover larger areas and respond promptly to security threats, enhancing its role in counterinsurgency operations alongside the military.

Interviews with CJTF members revealed that the Borno State government had initiated a training programme for them, highlighting their recognised role as interventionists in the military's insurgency peace plan (B., personal communication, 11 September 2022). This training has strengthened the CJTF's effectiveness in collaboration with the military, contributing to a more peaceful environment in Maiduguri. It was noted that there had been no conflicts between the CJTF and the military since their collaboration began. The CJTF's primary role in Maiduguri has been to secure the area against Boko Haram encroachment, and they remain committed to supporting the military's efforts against the insurgents.

## CJTF's productive insurgent peace interventions

Insights underscore the CJTF's crucial role in facilitating the return of locals to their farms and businesses in areas previously under Boko Haram control. Despite their effectiveness, there is a strong emphasis on the need for continued government support, including funding, equipment, and training, to sustain and enhance their operations. In addition, it is important for the government to ensure the welfare of CJTF members by providing basic necessities and support for their families in case of injury or death.

The CJTF's success in collaborating with the military, even without advanced weaponry, reflects their commitment and understanding of local dynamics. Their ability to adhere to military guidelines and operate independently when necessary further demonstrates their vital role in maintaining peace and security in Borno State. The ongoing training and support for CJTF members are crucial for sustaining their effectiveness in insurgency-related peace efforts.

Comments highlight the CJTF's crucial role in ensuring local security, particularly in areas where the military's presence was lacking. This observation reinforces the importance of collaboration between the CJTF, the military, and local communities in countering Boko Haram. The partnership has proven effective in reducing insurgent attacks and maintaining peace in Borno State (A., personal communication, 17 September 2022. Bamidele (2017a&b, 2018, 2020) emphasises that achieving insurgent peace necessitates the involvement of locals, as their knowledge of local geography and dynamics is invaluable:

> *Indeed, there are many things that make our group (CJTF) a fundamental component in the intervention in this Boko Haram crisis, because you see these Boko Haram people the military do not know them, and we the people of Borno community knew them, and they live among us. At first you dare not point them because if you dare, they will kill you. As their activities got worst and the locals are now pushed to the wall, that is how we came in supporting the weak areas of the military in various areas, though Hausari area is the main root of where it began, so I can say the intervention came lately from the locals, that is Lawan Jafar the overall Chairman of Borno State, he was the pioneer of how CJTF came to be, and he went further to notify other areas to follow same suit to the extent all locals in various areas to come out for the operation which we tag "operation flush Boko Haram"* (I., personal communication, 16 July 2022).

The interviews suggest that the CJTF is seen by locals as a complement rather than a competitor to the military's efforts. The effective collaboration between the CJTF and the military has led to a notable reduction in insurgency activities in Borno State. This collaboration highlights the value of integrating local initiatives with formal military operations in insurgency-related peace efforts. Bamidele (2020) and other scholars point out that local initiatives such as the CJTF play a crucial role in insurgent peace processes, often providing insights and support that complement traditional military approaches. The collective engagement of CJTF members has proven effective, reinforcing the idea that local involvement is essential for achieving and sustaining peace and security in conflict zones.

## Collective insurgent peace achievements

To provide insight into the achievements of the military and the CJTF in promoting peace, a review of local security records at the CJTF headquarters on Post Office Road in Maiduguri was conducted. These records revealed that the CJTF's interventionist role had been notably effective, especially considering the military's initial struggle to address the Boko Haram crisis in Borno State. The records supported the findings from interviews, highlighting that the partnership with the CJTF, which employed operational tactics such as a semi-auxiliary fighting force, intelligence gathering, and the identification of Boko Haram members, was crucial to the success of military peace operations against insurgents.

Focus group discussions with local residents and interviews with CJTF members and military commanders conducted in August 2022 further underscored the CJTF's critical role in the conflict. The CJTF was instrumental in apprehending Boko Haram insurgents, rescuing women and children, and recovering ammunition and grenades from various localities and border areas. The collaboration between the CJTF and the military significantly disrupted Boko Haram's activities in the state, leading to the reclamation of numerous rural communities from insurgent control. Despite ongoing attacks on vulnerable targets through hit-and-run strikes and suicide bombings, the CJTF's strategic interventions effectively countered these threats.

The CJTF's efforts in combatting Boko Haram insurgents have resulted in several notable achievements. One significant success was the retrieval and recapturing of weapons and other items from insurgents between 2013 and 2022. For example, in Gamboru Village, Borno State, the CJTF, in coordination with the military, successfully recovered 70 motorcycles laden with explosives, small arms and light weapons, 430 rifles, and 870 pistols from Boko Haram insurgents. Another notable operation, as detailed in a report from the CJTF headquarters, occurred in the Zabarmari ward, where a collaborative effort led to the recovery of 300 AK-47 rifles and numerous locally made Dane guns from Boko Haram insurgents (CJTF Unpublished Report, 2021).

In addition, the CJTF achieved notable success in apprehending numerous Boko Haram insurgents without military assistance. For instance, the group captured over 20 insurgents disguised as local residents in the Biu Emirate Council near the border and seized 245 AK-47 rifles from them (CJTF Unpublished Report, 2021).

The CJTF's achievements in combatting Boko Haram have been substantial. In Bundun Village, a joint effort with the military led to the discovery of a significant cache of Boko Haram ammunition and grenades, resulting in the recovery of 650 AK-47 rifles and 80 additional rifles. In the Maiduguri metropolis, a collaborative operation with the military resulted in the deaths of over eight Boko Haram insurgents, who were armed with locally made Dane guns, and the successful rescue of numerous hostages, including men, women, and children.

In the Biu Emirate Council area, the CJTF independently captured over 20 insurgents disguised as locals and recovered 245 AK-47 rifles. Another combined operation in Borno State resulted in the confiscation of 500 AK-47 rifles with loaded magazines and 230 locally made Dane guns from insurgents. In addition, in Durubajuwe, Wala, and Rugga Fulani, another joint operation led to the confiscation of 690 Dane guns and 56 AK-49 rifles (CJTF Unpublished Report, 2021).

In a significant insurgent attack, the military killed 34 Boko Haram insurgents, freed over 400 hostages, and seized 767 AK-47 rifles and over 50 motorcycles (CJTF Unpublished Report, 2021). In communities such as Jeje, Diba, and Huyum, the CJTF, working with the military, displaced Boko Haram members from their hiding spots, leading to the abandonment of over 23 hostages and several ammunition caches, which were subsequently retrieved. Notably, during the military's Operation Lafia Dole (Peace by Force) in Borno, CJTF members played a crucial role in recovering large amounts of ammunition hidden underground in communities such as Brogozo-Alagardo.

The interventionist role of the CJTF has markedly advanced peacekeeping efforts against Boko Haram insurgents in Borno State and its surrounding areas, including the former stronghold of Sambisa Forest. In Alagarno Forest, the CJTF seized substantial caches of ammunition capable of arming an entire military battalion. The recovered items included a 5x20 Lyra beefcake mixture of 7.62mm (NATO) ammunition, 36 boxes of .51mm calibre ammunition, a considerable amount of 7.62mm (special) ammunition, and one 81mm mortar tube. In addition, significant quantities of ammunition were discovered hidden in insurgent camps in Abu Fatima, Gursum, and Kadiri (CJTF Unpublished Report, 2021).

Another notable operation in Alagarno Forest led to the seizure of 12 vehicles, nine AK-47 rifles, 27 motorcycles, sniper rifles, three Fabrique Nationale rifles, a fabricated rocket bomb, solar panels, and five locally made Dane guns. Furthermore, approximately 20 locals held captive by Boko Haram insurgents were rescued (CJTF Unpublished Report, 2021). With CJTF support, the army's 112th Battalion also confiscated weapons, medical supplies, fuel tanks, water pumps, generators, 340 AK-49s, and various explosive mechanisms. In total, over 56 Boko Haram insurgents were arrested during military and CJTF operations in Borno State.

The joint operations in Dikwa showcased another level of CJTF intervention. Key items seized included lorries carrying vital health supplies, explosive devices, generators, fuel pumps, and mechanical workshop machines. The 192nd Battalion of the army, collaborating with CJTF members, successfully neutralised over 10 Boko Haram insurgents and discovered a belt containing 42 rounds of 7.62mm (NATO) ammunition and two multipurpose machine guns (CJTF Unpublished Report, 2021). These operations underscore the significant impact of CJTF efforts in the ongoing fight against terrorism and reflect the community's resolute commitment to ensuring regional safety.

## Conclusion

This chapter examined the interventionist role of the CJTF in promoting peace and its collaboration with the military in counter-Boko Haram operations in Borno State. The CJTF functions as an auxiliary fighting force, focusing on information gathering and sharing, local problem-solving, and other supportive activities. The findings from the fieldwork demonstrated that the success of the CJTF's intervention has fostered a strong trust relationship with the military. This trust has led to the CJTF's frequent involvement in peace operations, including arrests, raids, and even illegal renditions – defined as the forcible abduction or transfer of individuals between countries without legal process or judicial oversight.

The CJTF's role has enhanced its relationship with the military, positioning Borno State as a crucial player in the fight against Boko Haram. Effective insurgency-related peace requires a balance between top-down (direct) and bottom-up (indirect) approaches. Thus, it is essential for the military to combine direct force with collaboration with local communities to address the root causes of insurgency. Employing both approaches will help address the Boko Haram insurgency more effectively and contribute to lasting peace in the region.

# CHAPTER NINE
# ASSESSMENT OF CIVILIAN JOINT TASK FORCE'S EFFECTIVENESS

## Introduction

This chapter assesses the effectiveness of the CJTF in its insurgent peace interventions in Borno, focusing on the factors contributing to the initiative's success and strategies for managing the Boko Haram crisis. The analysis reveals that the factors driving the CJTF's success align closely with those found in military-led peace operations. A key element of the CJTF's effectiveness is the collaboration between the military and local communities, a factor often underappreciated by governments until security issues become severe and persistent. The effectiveness of the CJTF justifies its recognition and accolades as a notable local peace initiative, setting a precedent for addressing insecurity and banditry through local solutions.

Galula's (1964) framework provides a basis for evaluating the CJTF's insurgent peace efforts through five key attributes:

1.  Initiation of Local Security: This involves the motivation of CJTF members to establish and maintain security and order within their communities.

2.  Integration for Enhanced Response: This refers to the incorporation of CJTF members into the broader state security framework, facilitating a coordinated response to the insurgency.

3.  Responsiveness: This encompasses the state's readiness and ability to address the needs and concerns of CJTF members.

4.  Capability to Execute Peace Tasks: This involves the CJTF's ability to effectively carry out tasks related to peace and stability.

5.  Quality of Provisions: This refers to the standard of weapons, equipment, and resources provided to the CJTF by the state.

Galula (1964) suggests that the effectiveness of the CJTF's interventions can be measured by how well these attributes are implemented. These attributes are integral to the CJTF's operations and closely related to the hearts-and-minds strategy employed by the group.

This study addresses several concerns surrounding the operations of the CJTF, including allegations that their activities have endangered local lives, involved human rights abuses and looting, and caused tensions with the

military. These issues underscore the complex nature of the CJTF's role in
the conflict against Boko Haram and the potential negative impacts on local
communities. Such concerns necessitate a thorough examination of the
challenges that might arise following the cessation of insurgent peace
operations.

A significant issue is the potential difficulties the CJTF may face upon the
end of their combat role. Proposed solutions to address these challenges
include reintegration into civilian life, comprehensive disarmament to
prevent remobilisation, and the training and incorporation of members into
formal security forces such as the military or police. In addition, empowering
CJTF members with job skills and providing compensation for their lost roles
as combatants are recommended to facilitate their transition to civilian life.
These measures aim to mitigate the risks associated with disbanding the CJTF
and help integrate them productively into society.

Despite the CJTF's contribution to combatting Boko Haram, uncertainties
remain regarding its long-term future. Addressing underlying social issues
such as illiteracy, unemployment, and poverty is crucial, as these factors
could significantly impact CJTF members once the conflict ends. Failure to
address these issues may exacerbate the challenges faced by former CJTF
members and hinder their reintegration into society.

There are also concerns about the potential misuse of power by CJTF
members if left unregulated. Without proper oversight, some members might
use their acquired power to intimidate personal adversaries rather than
focusing on insurgency-related peace efforts. This risk highlights the necessity
for strict regulations and monitoring to prevent the emergence of new threats
similar to the Boko Haram insurgents. While the CJTF has played a crucial
role in the fight against Boko Haram, careful consideration and planning are
required to address the social and security challenges that may arise once
their combat role concludes. Implementing the proposed solutions and
addressing broader socioeconomic issues will be essential in ensuring a stable
transition for CJTF members and preventing potential future threats.

## CJTF's effectiveness in insurgent peace

To effectively evaluate the CJTF group's insurgent peace initiative, several
critical questions must be addressed. First, what specific factors have
contributed to the success of the CJTF's efforts? Understanding these factors
can provide insights into the elements that make the initiative effective.
Second, are there adequate measures in place in Borno State to manage the
ongoing Boko Haram insurgency crisis? Assessing the current strategies and

their efficacy will help determine if additional actions are needed to support the CJTF's objectives.

The factors determining the success of insurgent peace initiatives largely overlap with those essential for effective military insurgency-related peace operations. Both approaches require a deep understanding of the local context, strategic planning, and coordinated efforts to address the insurgent threat. However, in an insurgent peace initiative, the primary distinction is that the local communities directly affected by the insurgency take a leading role in their own protection.

While other external support may be available, it is the host communities that bear the primary responsibility for their own security. This local ownership is critical for the success of the initiative, as those directly facing the threat are often best positioned to implement effective defensive strategies and countermeasures.

Evaluating the effectiveness of the CJTF's initiative involves examining how well these locally led efforts are integrated with broader security measures and the support provided by external actors. Identifying successful strategies and areas needing improvement can guide future initiatives and ensure a more robust response to the insurgency. Understanding the factors behind the success of the CJTF initiative and assessing the effectiveness of current measures in Borno State is essential for evaluating the initiative's overall impact. The local leadership in insurgent peace initiatives is crucial, and their role in self-protection, supported by external measures, determines the overall success of the initiative.

### Frameworks for assessment

To ensure the effectiveness of an insurgent peace intervention, the attributes identified by Galula (1964) are essential, and the CJTF appears to embody these in its local security initiative. Initially, during the early stages of the Boko Haram insurgency, the Borno State government and Nigerian military did not recognise the need for local intervention. This oversight highlighted the potential benefits of a collaborative approach from the beginning, suggesting that the CJTF's model aligns well with successful local insurgent peace initiatives by allowing local solutions to address local problems.

Galula's (1964) framework is particularly notable among various approaches to local security measures in counterinsurgency warfare. It emphasises the importance of leveraging local resources and power to enhance the effectiveness of counterinsurgency operations. According to Galula, five criteria are crucial, though any one of these attributes alone can significantly impact the effectiveness of local security groups. This framework articulates how local empowerment can be a key factor in successful insurgent peace initiatives.

In comparison, Kilcullen (2005) offers a framework that includes not only the plan of action but also the strategic, operational, and political outcomes of insurgent peace interventions. This approach underscores the necessity of a well-defined plan that aligns operational implementation with the political objectives of the government. Evaluating the CJTF using Kilcullen's framework would involve assessing how effectively their strategies achieve the intended political goals of insurgent peace.

Kiras (2010) explores various strategies to maximise the effectiveness of local forces, such as those within the CJTF, during different levels of insurgency. The "hearts-and-minds" strategy, endorsed by scholars such as Kilcullen (2005) and Galula (1964), focuses on legal and ethical compliance to enhance local effectiveness. In contrast, the "draining-the-sea" approach, which relies on brutality and noncompliance with laws, is less favoured due to its adverse impact on local support and effectiveness. Firsthand interviews with military and CJTF members reveal that the latter approach undermines local cooperation and effectiveness.

By applying Galula's (1964) framework and incorporating insights from Kilcullen (2005) and Kiras (2010), this analysis investigates the impact of CJTF members on the overall effectiveness of military operations in insurgent peace efforts. The evidence suggests that the CJTF's adherence to the "hearts-and-minds" strategy contributes positively to its effectiveness, aligning with Galula's emphasis on local engagement and empowerment in counterinsurgency operations.

## Balancing effectiveness with accountability

An interview with the military at a checkpoint in Borno State highlighted several concerns about CJTF members, including perceived issues with discipline, human rights abuses, and personal vendettas. Despite these issues, the CJTF's contributions to improving security in an area previously plagued by daily violence cannot be overlooked (senior military officer, personal communication, 10 July 2022). Their effectiveness in supporting military operations against insurgents is evident. However, the potential for lawlessness and misuse of their resources poses significant risks once their role in the operations concludes.

The CJTF's access to valuable local information and weaponry raises concerns about the potential misuse of these assets for personal gain or furthering their interests if not properly managed. The absence of strict accountability and oversight could exacerbate these risks, leading to noncompliance with established rules and regulations governing security forces. If the CJTFis not disbanded in an organised manner, there is a possibility that they could continue operating as vigilante groups or even become a threat to the military or government.

To address these issues, a comprehensive plan is needed for the termination of the CJTF's involvement in military operations. This plan should include strategies for disarmament, demobilisation, and reintegration to ensure a smooth transition and prevent the CJTF from posing future security threats. Accountability measures must be in place to address any unlawful actions committed by CJTF members during their tenure, thus safeguarding the integrity of the operations and mitigating potential long-term security challenges.

The military and government must establish clear guidelines and regulations for the CJTF's continued involvement, specifying their roles, responsibilities, and rules of engagement. Effective oversight and accountability mechanisms are crucial to ensure that CJTF members adhere to legal and ethical standards. Proper training and equipping of CJTF members are essential to ensure that they can perform their roles effectively and within the boundaries of the law. In addition, a clear timeline for the CJTF's involvement must be established, with a controlled disbandment process once their role is no longer deemed necessary. This includes strategies for the safe disposal of weapons and ammunition and ensuring a smooth reintegration of members into civilian life. By addressing these aspects, the military and government can enhance the benefits of the CJTF's involvement while mitigating risks and ensuring long-term stability.

### Future of the CJTF after insurgent peace operations

During an interview conducted at the CJTF headquarters in Borno State, members revealed that the state government had promised their incorporation into the military following the end of the Boko Haram crisis. Additionally, the federal government pledged to recruit active CJTF members with potential into the military and police force. Given that many CJTF members possess high academic qualifications, including university degrees, there is significant potential for their formal recruitment into the military, which would allow them to continue contributing to regional peacebuilding efforts.

Such a recruitment strategy offers a constructive path for individuals who might otherwise be vulnerable to involvement in violent conflict. Even with higher academic qualifications, CJTF members are not immune to the socioeconomic challenges that might push them towards extremist groups. Factors such as limited job opportunities, widespread poverty, and societal discrimination can exacerbate feelings of frustration and marginalisation. By offering viable alternatives such as employment and social inclusion, the government can help steer these individuals away from extremist ideologies towards peaceful and productive roles.

The promise made by the government appears to be materialising, as CJTF members have begun integrating into the military. Reports indicate that 850 CJTF members have been incorporated into various military ranks, from lance corporal to cadet, based on their qualifications (CJTF Unpublish Report, 2021). This integration underscores the potential for CJTF members to transition effectively into formal security roles. Focus group discussions, including military personnel, have highlighted the CJTF's significant contribution to military operations through local intelligence and community trust.

The local nature of CJTF members, being residents of the communities they serve, adds another dimension to their role. Their integration into the military upon the completion of the peace operations seems likely, but the timing for disbanding the CJTF remains uncertain and dependent on the ongoing success of the peace efforts. Despite their critical role, there have been reports from locals indicating that some CJTF operations have involved violence, with some individuals narrowly escaping death. This suggests a complex and potentially troubling aspect of their involvement, even as they aim to contribute to peace. While the CJTF's integration into the military and their role in local security efforts highlight significant opportunities for peacebuilding, it is essential to address the reported incidents of violence and ensure a well-managed transition process. Clear plans for disarmament, demobilisation, and reintegration, alongside continued oversight and accountability, are crucial to harnessing the CJTF's positive impact while mitigating potential risks associated with their involvement. Therefore, it should be closely monitored to address further violence or danger due to members' actions. In an interview, a community member said the following:

> There was a claim laid by one Hajiya Yagana Muazu, a former Commissioner in Borno State who alleged that 2 of her security personnel got dead within the hands of the CJTF members with local guns as she and her kids ran for their lives. She pleads with the President Buhari administration to control the insurgent peace operations of CJTF (U., personal communication, 26 July 2022).

In an interview, it was stated that the individuals responsible for killing Hajiya Yagana Muazu's military personnel were thugs, not CJTF members. Additionally, in another interview, the chief security officer and special adviser on security matters to the Borno State government provided the following clarification:

> Although CJTF members have their shortcomings but the present administration in Borno State is also aware of their contributions in

*combating the Boko Haram insurgents. In 2013 through the Governor Kassim Shettima and the administration in partnership with military mobilized and trained over 26,000 personnel under the pay-roll of Borno State Government from the Ministry of Youth Empowerment Scheme* (A., personal communication, 18 June 2022).

Kashim Shettima, a former governor of Borno State, demonstrated support for the CJTF by providing over 20 vehicles to aid their peace efforts in the region (B.A., personal communication, 9 July 2022). This support was aimed at boosting the morale and operational capacity of CJTF members in their fight against the insurgency. However, while this assistance has likely improved the CJTF's effectiveness, it is crucial that their activities remain coordinated with broader insurgent peace efforts both now and in the future. Effective coordination ensures that CJTF actions support, rather than undermine, the overall peace process.

To maintain alignment with peace efforts, ongoing monitoring and dialogue with CJTF members are essential. This will help prevent any potential issues, such as violent actions that could harm locals or exacerbate regional conflicts. CJTF members must adhere to established protocols and guidelines set forth by government authorities, military leadership, and other stakeholders involved in the peacebuilding process. By following these protocols, CJTF members can significantly contribute to sustainable peace both during and after insurgent operations.

Regardless of the CJTF's notable success in countering Boko Haram, the group's long-term prospects remain uncertain. Interviewees have raised concerns about allegations of human rights abuses and tensions with the military, prompting policymakers to consider the implications of CJTF activities for postinsurgency reconstruction and development. There are also fears that, if not properly regulated, the CJTF might misuse its power for personal vendettas rather than continuing its role in counterinsurgency, potentially becoming a threat similar to Boko Haram.

Addressing these concerns requires addressing broader socioeconomic issues in Borno State, such as unemployment, hunger, and financial instability, which affect CJTF members. The federal government's establishment of the Northeast Development Commission (NEDC) aims to facilitate community reconstruction and member rehabilitation. As the national coordinator for humanitarian and transformative efforts in northeastern Nigeria, the NEDC plays a critical role in integrating CJTF members into the broader peacebuilding and rehabilitation framework.

Despite these efforts, challenges remain due to a lack of effective linkages, coordination, and monitoring of insurgent peace activities, particularly among local security members. Addressing these challenges is vital for ensuring that CJTF contributions to peacebuilding are sustained and that their transition into postconflict roles is managed effectively.

The postinsurgent peace initiative, unfortunately, fell short in addressing the reintegration needs of CJTF members, limiting the overall effectiveness of the policy. Interviews with CJTF members in Borno State reveal concerns about their future once the insurgency ends. Currently, some members are employed full-time and receive monthly payments from the Borno State government, though these payments are inconsistent and limited to those with official identity cards and affiliation with the Borno State Youth Association for Peace and Justice (BYAPJ). Those excluded from this support are increasingly questioning what the federal government plans to do for them postconflict, given the ongoing BOYES programme in the state.

A leader in Borno State emphasised that CJTF members, who have played a crucial role in safeguarding the state's integrity during the Boko Haram insurgency, should not be abandoned by the government. He argued that the Borno State government should facilitate their transition to postinsurgency roles, reflecting the sentiment of many who believe they deserve continued support due to their significant contributions (Z., personal communication, 16 October 2022).

Interviews conducted at the CJTF headquarters revealed varied expectations among members regarding their postconflict roles. Some members are eager to secure state employment after their security duties, while others prefer to be deployed elsewhere. There is a common hope that their service against Boko Haram will secure them employment or recognition in the postconflict period. Many CJTF members anticipate rewards from the state government, such as employment opportunities, scholarships, or cash payments upon demobilisation. They feel they have earned these rewards through their commitment to the fight against Boko Haram. Some members even draw comparisons to the amnesty programme in the Niger Delta region, where locals who supported the military were recruited into the Nigerian Navy and Air Force, provided educational opportunities, and placed on government payrolls. This comparison underscores their belief that they should receive similar recognition and support for their service.

The observed expectation among CJTF members for postconflict rewards highlights a need for a comprehensive reintegration strategy. Addressing these expectations through targeted employment opportunities, educational programmes, and other forms of support can ensure a smoother transition for CJTF members and leverage their experience in contributing to lasting peace in the region.

During interviews, several CJTF members reported severe casualties in their fight against Boko Haram, including over 1,007 deaths, 233 hospitalisations, and 311 injuries (B.A., personal communication, 13 June 2022). In addition, their families became targets for Boko Haram insurgents, who spied on them and threatened attacks due to the CJTF's effectiveness in the conflict. These experiences have led many CJTF members to seek compensation from the state government. While the Borno State government has provided some relief to widows and families of fallen CJTF members through humanitarian agencies, the issue of postconflict rewards remains contentious.

The disarmament of CJTF members is a priority for both the federal and Borno State governments, as highlighted in interviews with military officials. However, any disarmament strategy needs to be implemented promptly to avoid future risks. CJTF members must be prevented from misusing their power, as well as the small arms and light weapons they acquired from Boko Haram. There is concern that some members may refuse to surrender recovered arms and monies, as reported by a CJTF member at a checkpoint near Gwazo Road.

Fragmentation within the CJTF ranks has become a significant issue, particularly in Borno State. Focus group discussions revealed that some members feel marginalised by senior officials, leading to reorganisation efforts that created new positions, such as Borno State coordinators. Despite these efforts, factionalism persists within the group. Disputes over state government resources and the sharing of spoils from operations, such as proceeds from cattle sales and seized cash, have contributed to this division and highlighted elements of criminality.

According to Sec. 14(2)(b) of the Nigerian Constitution (Federal Republic of Nigeria, 1999), the federal government's priority is the security and welfare of its citizens. State security agencies are responsible for crime detection, offender apprehension, law and order preservation, and the protection of lives and property. In addition, Sec. 217(2)(c) tasks the military with suppressing insurgencies and supporting civil authorities, including the police and judiciary, to restore order. These constitutional provisions ensure that the federal government and its agencies, including the military, address social problems such as local insurgency while promoting the security and welfare of citizens.

The CJTF's role, supported by the state, was crucial in areas where the military struggled to suppress Boko Haram. This official backing granted the CJTF legal authority to provide security, aligning with Nigeria's democratic principles. However, ensuring that CJTF members are appropriately integrated and managed postconflict remains essential to maintain peace and stability in the region. In an interview, the leader of the CJTF in Ubi town emphasised the need for constitutional backing for any action related to security, stating, "*Any kind of action, whetheror not within the interest of security, should have constitutional backing, and any aberration fromthis could be thought of as a criminal offence against the state*" (B., personal communication, 15 August 2022). He further referenced Sec. 12 of the General Public Order Act, Cap. 382, Laws of the Federation 1990, which stipulates that "no association ought to organise or train or equip persons for the aim of sanctioning any such person to be used in usurping the functions of the national security of the Federation". This underscores that, while locals are responsible for reporting crimes and aiding security agencies, they do not have the authority to enforce laws independently.

Even with the CJTF's significant contributions alongside military efforts in countering Boko Haram since 2013, there have been instances where CJTF members acted independently. They have conducted attacks, rescued hostages, and reclaimed lost territories on their own, leading to improved safety in some areas. However, it is important to recognise that the insurgent peace operations in Nigeria have also been associated with human rights violations, dislocation, and exploitation of locals by both the military and CJTF. This dual impact has compounded the suffering of those already affected by Boko Haram's actions.

Although the CJTF's local insurgent peace initiative has been crucial in combatting Boko Haram, it presents potential issues for the future. The initiative, while not entirely impulsive or unjust, may lead to challenges if not managed properly. The lack of clear constitutional and legal frameworks for local security actions could result in future complications, including potential misuse of power by CJTF members. To address these concerns, it is essential to establish clear guidelines and legal frameworks for the CJTF's actions. This would ensure that their operations are conducted within the bounds of the law and prevent potential abuses. In addition, integrating CJTF members into formal security structures with proper oversight could mitigate risks associated with their future involvement in peacekeeping efforts.

The CJTF has played a vital role in the fight against Boko Haram; careful consideration and planning are needed to ensure that their contributions do not lead to further issues. This includes addressing potential human rights violations and ensuring that their actions align with established legal and constitutional standards.

### Treatment of Boko Haram detainees

CJTF imprisonment centres hold Boko Haram insurgents who have killed or violated locals. During focus group discussions in Borno State, community members expressed concerns about these detention facilities, noting issues such as overcrowding and inadequate resources. Some facilities are reportedly used to repress and oppress suspected locals who may not be involved with Boko Haram, causing additional suffering for innocent individuals already traumatised by the conflict. Prolonged detention of some suspects, including those wrongly accused, raises further concerns about potential human rights abuses within these facilities.

The CJTF is also recruiting former low-risk Boko Haram members through Operation Safe Corridor, a clemency programme aimed at reintegrating individuals who have renounced violence. This programme is currently the only amnesty offered to Boko Haram defectors after detention and plays a key role in reducing insurgency and fostering reconciliation.

However, the programme conflicts with the existing legal framework, which criminalises any affiliation with Boko Haram without exceptions. This framework does not account for individuals who may have been coerced into cooperation with Boko Haram under threat of execution. As a result, the CJTF's approach, which involves engaging with former Boko Haram members, breaches this law.

Strict enforcement of the current laws without flexibility can undermine military efforts to combat Boko Haram. Individuals might be reluctant to cooperate or come forward due to fear of punishment, which hampers intelligence gathering and counterinsurgency efforts. A more nuanced legal framework is needed to address these challenges, allowing for exceptions where individuals have been forced to cooperate or seek to defect.

Another issue with the Operation Safe Corridor programme is its restrictive eligibility criteria, which limit acceptance to low-risk defectors who have repented. Low-risk defectors are those who have abandoned their allegiance to a militant group such as Boko Haram and are considered to have had a lower level of involvement in the group's violent activities. These individuals may include women and children who were forcibly recruited or abducted, as well as men who were coerced into joining or supporting the group under duress. In contrast, high-risk defectors, who have played more active roles or held leadership positions, may face legal consequences for theiractions.

The programme's criteria also overlook locals who were unwillingly subjected to insurgent rule and were victims of circumstances. These locals were initially used by Boko Haram as informants, suppliers, and fighters, and later by the Nigerian state for similar purposes. The CJTF often distrusts and rejects these individuals, viewing them as opportunists who may not be loyal. As a result, they are excluded from the clemency programme.

The CJTF's screening process lacks clarity, especially in defining what constitutes a low-risk individual. This uncertainty makes it difficult for potential defectors to understand their status and the risks involved in surrendering. Some individuals identified as low-risk have been rearrested and reclassified as high-risk, leading to further concerns about the programme's consistency and effectiveness.

Participants in the amnesty programme often face extended waiting periods with no clear timeline for release. They might also face violent retaliation from Boko Haram and even from CJTF members or locals upon release. Amnesty International has raised concerns about the ostracism faced by defectors, even those with limited involvement.

To address these issues, the government should provide comprehensive support to those who complete the amnesty programme. This support could include job training and skills acquisition to improve employment prospects, financial aid or loans to help start businesses, and counselling or mental health support to address trauma. Such measures would help reintegrate individuals more effectively and address the broader challenges they face.

### Distrust of the CJTF

Observations at checkpoints and borders reveal that people are often harassed, extorted, and forced to pay fees for passage, leading to distrust and tension between locals and CJTF members. In addition, many of the arms and ammunition seized from Boko Haram insurgents are circulating among CJTF members, which could increase distrust for several reasons. There may be suspicions that CJTF members are either colluding with Boko Haram or supporting their activities. Concerns may also arise about the CJTF's ability to control and manage weapons, potentially using them for extortion or violence against locals. There might also be fears that the CJTF is becoming increasingly militarised, posing a threat to local safety and security. These factors can contribute to a breakdown of trust between the CJTF and locals, impacting the effectiveness of local security initiatives against Boko Haram.

The local community closely scrutinises the actions and motivations of the CJTF. Any perceived deviation from their primary responsibility of community protection may lead to increased mistrust and tension. Locals might question whether the CJTF is more focused on its own interests rather than fulfilling its duty to protect the community in collaboration with the Nigerian military.

A conflict of interest between the CJTF and Boko Haram can further contribute to local distrust. If the CJTF is perceived as being too aligned with the military or government, they may be viewed as an extension of the state's security apparatus, causing distrust among those suspicious of the government's intentions. Conversely, if the CJTF is seen as compromising or collaborating with Boko Haram, some locals may consider them to be traitors, leading to doubts about their loyalty and commitment to community security. This can create divisions within the community and hinder efforts to build trust and cooperation.

If the CJTF is viewed as ineffective in countering Boko Haram or protecting the community, locals may lose faith in their ability to provide adequate security and turn to other groups or individuals for protection. This can further erode trust in the CJTF, complicating efforts to build effective local security and counter violent extremism.

The locals may view the government's focus on insurgent peace operations as neglecting crucial issues such as hunger, poverty, illiteracy, and environmental concerns. This perception could lead to distrust of the CJTF, as the group is involved in these operations and may seem to prioritise them over local needs. It is recommended that the government address both insurgent peace and governance issues equally to meet the needs and concerns of Borno State residents through military and CJTF interventions.

The military and CJTF could work together to address basic needs by implementing programmes that address hunger; provide food, water, shelter, and healthcare; and also conduct insurgent peace operations. They could deploy personnel to collaborate with local communities on providing amenities and engage in community development, such as building schools and offering educational resources to combat illiteracy. In addition, they could implement environmental conservation programmes and promote sustainable agricultural practices to address environmental concerns and stimulate economic development. Engaging actively with local communities and addressing their basic needs can help the military and CJTF build trust and credibility, leading to a more effective approach to insurgency and peace operations in Borno State.

The trend among CJTF members to grant amnesty and rehabilitation to Boko Haram insurgents is concerning and contributes to local distrust. This policy may seem to prioritise the interests of former terrorists over the safety of the local population, causing grievances and a sense of abandonment. There is also fear that these former terrorists might still hold radical beliefs and pose a risk of reengaging in violent activities. In addition, locals may feel their opinions are disregarded in the decision-making process regarding amnesty and rehabilitation. To address this, the CJTF should involve the local population in consultations, improving the quality of the rehabilitation process and ensuring that the safety and security of the locals remain a top priority.

### CJTF reintegration and disarmament

The reintegration and disarmament of inactive CJTF members once the Boko Haram insurgency ends are critical for maintaining peace and preventing the potential remobilisation of the group as local insurgents. Neglecting these actions could lead to distrust among locals of the group and the government. CJTF members, due to their involvement in political power and interactions with Boko Haram insurgents, possess unique knowledge and experience that could be misused. For example, they might exploit their connections with former insurgents for personal gain or manipulate the situation to increase funding or support by exaggerating threats or falsely reporting incidents.

If CJTF members are not properly disarmed and reintegrated into society when the insurgency is over, there is a risk that they could form a local insurgency group themselves, using their skills and experience to launch attacks or gain power. Therefore, the government must closely monitor and regulate the involvement of CJTF members in political and security operations to prevent potential abuse of their knowledge. Failure to address this issue could lead to further distrust and security threats, undermining the progress made towards peace.

The government must prioritise the reintegration and disarmament of CJTF members who have become inactive after the insurgency ends. This should be a key component of postinsurgency efforts to ensure that these members do not become remobilised as local insurgents. Proper reintegration and disarmament will also prevent their use by other violent groups due to their valuable knowledge and experience. Ignoring the status and knowledge of CJTF members could result in increased distrust among the local population and pose threats to the peace achieved.

### Conclusion

When assessing the effectiveness of CJTF's insurgent peace interventions, one key question is the value of financial support. Discussions with respondents in all locations reveal concerns about whether the resources provided to the group are being used for their intended purposes. Analysis of the data gathered from these discussions shows that locals tend to gather resources, including funding, and direct them towards supporting insurgent peace initiatives. This demonstrates a willingness on the part of locals to actively participate in peacebuilding efforts. The resources are used to support the initiatives of the CJTF insurgency group and other locally based efforts aimed at preventing attacks by Boko Haram insurgents.

Questions arise regarding whether the resources are being used for their intended purposes and whether there is adequate transparency and accountability in their use by the CJTF, who are expected to promote peace and stability in the region. However, the success of these operations is hindered by some members who seem more interested in benefitting themselves rather than supporting the overall goal of the peace operations. This lack of cooperation leads to initiatives being implemented that do not work well. Not all insurgent peace initiatives are effective, but they are still implemented as part of the larger peacebuilding process. The peace operations team considers it important to make some progress towards their goals, even if it is not as effective as hoped.

During fieldwork, it was discovered that providing CJTF members with only a short military training course on identifying Boko Haram insurgents, without engaging them in insurgent peace training, is ineffective. Feedback from respondents highlights the limitations of military training in addressing the challenges of insurgency in the region. There is a need for more practical and long-term insurgent peace interventions between the military and the CJTF insurgency group.

The implication is that military training alone is insufficient to address the complex and multifaceted issues of insurgency in the region. Military training may help identify and counter violent activities but may not address the underlying causes of insurgency or promote sustainablepeace and stability in the long run. Therefore, respondents suggest that more practical and long-term interventions aimed at promoting peace and stability should be considered. This may involve engaging with the CJTF group in peace initiatives that address the root causes of insurgency, such as poverty, unemployment, and lack of access to education and healthcare. Such interventions may also involve providing economic opportunities and social services to communities affected by insurgency, which may reduce their susceptibility to extremist ideologies and activities.

Feedback from respondents highlights the need for a more comprehensive and holistic approach to addressing the challenges of insurgency in the region, which should go beyond military training and focus on addressing the root causes of the problem with practical and long-term interventions aimed at promoting peace and stability.

Respondents suggest that relying solely on continuous local security measures, such as maintaining a military or police presence in high-risk areas, is insufficient to address the challenges of insurgency in the region. Instead, a more comprehensive approach is proposed, including local empowerment through military and CJTF training coupled with financial support to address the underlying root causes of the conflict and build long-term stability.

An additional challenge to the effectiveness of insurgent peace operations is the porousness of the initiatives across the state. Multiple locally based initiatives are already underway and, in some instances, would benefit from merging. However, if the initiatives are poles apart, the result would be a myriad of insurgent peace interventions lacking synergy and collaboration, thereby jeopardising their effectiveness.

# CHAPTER TEN
# CHALLENGES TO THE CIVILIAN JOINT TASK FORCE'S IMPLEMENTATION OF NIGERIA'S LOCAL SECURITY POLICY

## Introduction

In this study, the challenges faced by the CJTF in implementing the state's policy on local security are examined. These challenges include legal issues, inadequate training, ill-equipped fighters, a lack of combat capability, and nonadherence to the rules of engagement. Legal challenges are explored within the context of the Nigerian legal framework, specifically Sec. 14(2)(b) of the 1999 Constitution (as amended), which states that all security operations should be solely within the purview of the Nigerian military. This implies that the CJTF's operations were illegal. However, despite this, the group eventually gained governmental support, affecting military operations and the human rights of citizens.

The study reveals that the CJTF's insufficient information and nonadherence to the rules of engagement led to violations of international humanitarian law and unauthorised, indiscriminate attacks on suspected Boko Haram members in the Baga area of Borno State as well as assaults on communities suspected of supporting the insurgents. In 2013 and 2014, the group was also under investigation for the unlawful execution of suspects in their custody.

The joint peace operations of the CJTF and the military in Borno State faced several challenges, including difficulty in deciding on appropriate strategies, unclear reasons for locals' greater receptivity to the CJTF compared to the military, and debates between the two groups. Selection and training processes, a lack of accountability, and minimal involvement of women in peace initiatives were problematic. Poor funding and a lack of incentives were major challenges, with members using their own resources, spending extensive time in meetings, and still needing to care for their families. Locals' distrust of the CJTF was significant, with accusations of arson, murder, looting, and rape. The military's conduct was also undermined by the CJTF's deficient information sharing. Despite these issues, the group contributed to improved security in the state, though the CJTF's involvement in insurgent peace arrangements remained subject to criticism.

## Challenges of narratives and counternarratives

The Boko Haram insurgency in Nigeria has been characterised by a complex interplay of narratives and counternarratives. Narratives provide specific interpretations of events, while counternarratives challenge these interpretations and present alternative views. Within the context of the insurgency, these narratives and counternarratives have significantly influenced public opinion, mobilised support, and impacted policy decisions. This study addresses the challenges of navigating these narratives and counternarratives, particularly in efforts to combat the insurgency.

Evidence revealed that the CJTF had the potential to contribute to the fight against Boko Haram in Borno State but faced challenges in collaborating with the military for peace. Difficulties included selecting the best strategy and addressing why the CJTF was preferred over the military, despite both groups working towards peace. The narratives surrounding the peace process often highlighted the CJTF's efforts without acknowledging the contributions of local people. In addition, debates arose about whether locals or the government should lead the peace process, creating divisions and feelings of exclusion among those who felt marginalised. The discussions frequently centred on local versus government power dynamics and overlooked other influential factors. To address these issues and achieve peace, a comprehensive and inclusive approach involving all perspectives and stakeholders was necessary.

Another challenge facing the CJTF's implementation of the state's insurgent peace policy was the disagreement between local groups, such as the CJTF, and the government (represented by the military). The local group often believed that aggressive action was necessary to combat Boko Haram, while the government focused on gaining local support and accurately understanding the local context to build trust and cooperation between the military and the locals. In Borno State, certain leaders criticised the ongoing debates between the two groups for hindering the achievement of peace. The disagreement between the locals (represented by the CJTF) and the state (represented by the military) was primarily due to operational differences –essentially about the best approach to and execution of the peace operation – rather than a conflict of fundamentally irreconcilable views.

This chapter on Borno State also highlighted that the CJTF's credibility was a significant challenge to achieving insurgent peace. The group's credibility was crucial to the peace efforts, but their contributions were often viewed as unreliable by both the military and locals. This led to negative perceptions, with some referring to them as sell-outs when they collaborated with the military. Such derogatory terms undermined the group's legitimacy. Locals were expected to handle the peace operation independently, and collaboration with the military was considered unconventional and inconsistent. This lack of alignment with the group's original values adversely affected peace operations, with collaboration perceived negatively by locals and contributing to the challenges in achieving peace.

## Challenges of incorporating the CJTF into military operations

In this section, the issue of incorporating the CJTF into the military insurgent peace operation is addressed. The aim was to enhance the group's credibility, but this incorporation has remained problematic despite the federal and state government's announcement of a recruitment programme for CJTF members into the regular military in 2018 (U., personal communication, 8 August, 2022). An interview highlighted that the recruitment programme lacked effective insurgent peace strategies and postinsurgent strategies for reintegrating CJTF members into society after their involvement in the insurgency.

The programme was poorly planned, leading to various challenges during insurgent peace operations. The respondent noted that the programme failed to address the root causes of the insurgency and engage effectively with the local community. In addition, the recruitment and posting of CJTF members were poorly managed, and there was inadequate training in insurgent peace strategies.

Since 2016, a total of 250 CJTF members have been enlisted in the state's security forces, including the Nigerian Army, State Security Services, and Nigeria Police Force (B.A., personal communication, 10 July 2022). However, concerns have been raised that CJTF members fear dismissal or relocation after the Boko Haram insurgency ends, as they worry that the federal and state governments might view them as a nuisance, a perception they faced before their military involvement.

The enlistment process involves an oath that binds CJTF members to their assignments, requiring them to fulfil their roles and responsibilities without deviation. This secrecy reinforces their reluctance to reveal their identities or engage in activities that could jeopardise national security. This adds a layer of difficulty in engaging with the local population or gathering crucial intelligence while also challenging the military's ability to monitor their activities and ensure that they fulfil their roles.

Focus group discussions and individual interviews revealed that the group posed challenges to insurgent peace operations. One issue was the nondisclosure of vital information by some members, which could have preempted Boko Haram attacks on locals. Some members, who had previously been part of Boko Haram and subsequently repented, were unable to report information to the military due to fear of repercussions from Boko Haram. This history of involvement with Boko Haram, along with potential remaining connections or sympathies, posed a security risk.

Despite local scepticism about the collaboration between the military and the CJTF, one respondent argued that the partnership was justified as it did not hinder insurgent peace but rather ensured local security:

> *The local knows the already die-hard locals, but they shy away from disclosing to the military for fear of being killed or punished. If CJTF members were to discover that one has reported to the military, then one will be killed. This fear is impacting on information flow necessary for fighting Boko Haram insurgency on the part of CJTF members* (M., personal communication, 23 September 2022).

Respondents expressed concerns regarding the trustworthiness of certain members of the CJTF's local security structure in maintaining peace and security in the region. This scepticism stemmed from the fact that some CJTF members had children who were involved in the Boko Haram insurgency. It was believed that these individuals might withhold critical information from both their CJTF colleagues and the military, thus impeding the group's effectiveness in upholding peace and security. As one respondent from Borno State noted:

> *The locals are aware of who poses a threat to their peace and security. The challenge with local security initiatives is that some CJTF members, including leaders, have sonsor daughters involved with Boko Haram. A parent or guardian would likely refrain from disclosing sensitive information that could negatively impact their children, leading to a reluctance to share crucial information with the military* (A., personal communication, 16 September 2022).

Further concerns were raised about the character of certain CJTF members, particularly those with criminal records. Given the severity of the insurgency, there were apprehensions about the reliability of these individuals in contributing to peace efforts. Consequently, respondents advocated for the implementation of security vetting measures for local volunteers engaged in insurgent peace or local security roles. Such measures were anticipated to ensure that only individuals deemed trustworthy and reliable would be assigned critical responsibilities. One respondent remarked:

> *It is troubling to find convicted criminals among local security members, supported by their communities. The question arises as to how such individuals can be trusted to share information and participate effectively in peace efforts. If convicted criminals are involved, there is a risk of*

*inadequate or misleading information. Therefore, vetting local insurgent peace or security members (CJTF) is essential to ensure that only reputable individuals are involved* (D., personal communication, 4 July 2022).

Interviews and focus group discussions also revealed issues related to a lack of accountability within the CJTF's implementation of Nigeria's local security policy. Some respondents indicated that local volunteers were performing roles beyond their qualifications, such as those typically associated with police officers. This overreach alienated the communities they were meant to serve, indicating a failure in accountability. For instance, if volunteers were tasked with basic security and reporting suspicious activity, their assumption of additional roles – such as making arrests or using excessive force – was problematic. In addition, there were instances of coercive behaviour, including pressuring locals to pay bribes under threat of police fines. Such conduct not only violated legal standards but also eroded the trust and confidence of the community in the local security or insurgent peace structures.

This behaviour could have led to distrust and alienation from the very communities the volunteers were meant to protect and serve, potentially undermining the overall objectives of the peacebuilding efforts. The negative impact on the relationship between volunteers and the communities further compromised the peacebuilding process. Clearly defining the roles of local volunteers and ensuring accountability for their actions were essential to rebuilding community trust and achieving effective peacebuilding outcomes.

One military officer highlighted these issues:

*Local security has not been very effective in this area. Volunteer members have been abusing their roles, and some CJTF members have acted as spies for Boko Haram and as spoilers of insurgent peace efforts. We believe that offenders are in various locations, not in military custody. CJTF members are supposed to make weekly reports to the military. There was a particular incident where two CJTF members fought over control of a location in Borno and began extorting protection money. Such experiences undermine the effectiveness of local security* (M., personal communication, 21 June 2022).

A local leader in Borno also noted the problem of accountability:

*Some members of local security (CJTF members) have been taking bribes and behaving as though they were part of the Nigeria Police Force. This behavior has diminished their credibility. In some areas, insurgent peace efforts have functioned like vigilantes* (U., personal communication, 10 July 2022).

Another significant challenge identified in Borno State was the minimal involvement of women in peace initiatives. Discussions with women revealed that their exclusion from peace operations was perceived as a violation of their rights. Women argued that their inclusion could have increased the acceptability of peace strategies. However, social norms and perceptions that women were unsuitable for such roles, as well as concerns from CJTF members about potential risks, contributed to their exclusion.

Interviews with women also disclosed that they faced harassment from CJTF members, which eroded their trust in the group and impeded their willingness to engage in military collaborations and local security efforts. Trust is a critical component in effective CJTF relations, and its absence hindered the realisation of insurgent peace.

The involvement of women in insurgent peace initiatives must be prioritised, and a safe space should be created to facilitate their collaboration with the military and local security groups. In addition, individuals who engage in harassment or other inappropriate behaviour towards women must be held accountable in order to foster trust and enhance collaboration between genders in peace efforts.

It is evident that the CJTF has neither fully recognised nor valued the diverse and significant  roles that women play in society. For a comprehensive and enduring insurgent peace in Borno State, the contributions of women must be acknowledged. Viewing women's roles solely through their traditional functions as wives and mothers is inadequate. Women hold significant positions globally, including in Nigeria, and possess insightful and progressive perspectives. These qualities enable them to identify signs of insurgent activity and influence counteractions, especially within their families; excluding women from peace operations risks undermining lasting peace, which requires the full participation of both men and women. In Borno State, women should be actively involved in decision-making and various aspects of the fight against Boko Haram. Their participation can also challenge gender inequality and the concentration of power in men's hands.

Evidence suggests that women could be valuable contributors to insurgent peace operations. Although some women might choose to remain silent rather than act counterproductively, their involvement is crucial. A woman from the CJTF group in Borno State expressed  this perspective:

> *Women can sometimes be interventionists. Within a community, women might be aware of Boko Haram members but may choose to remain silent about it. Their silence can be attributed to their nature and social norms in Borno State* (A., personal communication, 10 November 2022).

## Challenges of poor funding and incentives

Insufficient funding and inadequate incentives pose significant challenges to the sustainability of the insurgent peace initiatives led by the CJTF group. The group primarily depends on financial support from the Borno State government, which complicates efforts to maintain and advance local security initiatives. A prominent leader within the CJTF recently noted the organisation's heavy reliance on state government funding to sustain its operations (U., personal communication, 25 August 2022). Other participants corroborated this view, highlighting that the CJTF's sustainability is precarious due to its dependence on the state government's funding, which is subject to shifts in governmental priorities.

Despite some respondents downplaying the impact of funding issues, it is clear that a continuous and reliable source of funding is crucial for the group's ongoing operations. Without adequate financial support, the realisation of insurgent peace efforts is at risk. A female resident of Gwazo, Borno State, illustrated this challenge by recounting how a valuable insurgent peace programme, which aired on a popular local Hausa radio station, was discontinued due to a lack of funds, as the state government did not support the CJTF group financially. She recalled:

> *I remember an insurgent peace intervention on a local Hausa radio station that was quite effective. The host featured mentors who addressed various social issues, including the Boko Haram insurgency crisis. It was a very useful intervention that resonated with the challenges our community faced. However, when state government funding stopped, we were left without support* (A., personal communication, 16 August 2022).

This statement underscores the critical role of funding in sustaining the CJTF's insurgent peace initiatives, as confirmed by respondents at the group's headquarters in Borno State. Local initiatives focused on insurgent peace are often reliant on periodic funding from the state government. To maintain their operations, one leader had to continuously seek alternative funding sources. Aligning their efforts with the state's shifting priorities and interests posed an additional challenge, potentially undermining the sustainability of the peace initiatives. While local initiatives such as the CJTF are crucial for achieving peace, their dependence on government funding can negatively impact their effectiveness. The group often operated on a voluntary basis due to insufficient budgetary support from the state government, relying only on occasional donor funding to cover expenses such as transportation and meals for meetings.

The lack of funding represents a major challenge to the sustainability of the CJTF group's insurgent peace initiatives. Consequently, members must often rely on their personal resources and commitment to participate in various activities. Evidence from Borno State reveals that local-level initiators within the CJTF lack motivating incentives, leading many participants to view their involvement as unpaid labour. This lack of motivation is exacerbated by additional expenses such as transportation, meals, and communication costs with the military. Respondents emphasised the need for state government support to provide incentives that would sustain the commitment of local security volunteers.

Given the evolving nature of the Boko Haram insurgency in Borno State, which is influenced by factors such as Islamisation, religious intolerance, and severe poverty, insurgent peace initiatives must be sustained over the long term. The lack of consistent funding and motivating incentives impedes the CJTF group's ability to achieve lasting impact and sustain progress. Therefore, it is crucial for the state government and other stakeholders to prioritise funding and provide appropriate incentives to support local-level initiatives aimed at achieving peace.

A member of the CJTF group in Borno State highlighted these issues:

> One of the concerns we have as members of the CJTF group, including those who previously served in local security as night watchmen (now renamed vigilante group), is the lack of facilitation. There is no transportation or even a bottle of water provided when we come for meetings. Our participation in local security can only be termed volunteerism. Imagine spending the entire day in a meeting while still having to support a family (B., personal communication, 12 September 2022).

This statement underscores the significant sacrifices made by local volunteers and the challenges associated with their unpaid involvement. Members of the CJTF balance attending meetings and local events with fulfilling family obligations. The absence of external support or compensation creates obstacles that could hinder the establishment of insurgent peace. Since the CJTF group's commitment is voluntary and uncompensated, the potential for demotivation is high. Providing appropriate compensation could significantly boost morale and dedication. While the CJTF does not seek monthly salaries, reasonable compensation would help sustain their efforts towards achieving peace.

### Locals' distrust of CJTF

The locals in Borno State are facing what they believe is collective punishment as a result of the activities of both the military and CJTF members. There is an uneasy relationship between the locals, the military, and CJTF. However, it is important to note that the genesis of the CJTF group in Borno in 2013 can be directly traced to the locals' attempts to inhibit the devastating activities of the Boko Haram insurgency. They realised that they could not rely solely on the military to provide the necessary security.

The locals' lack of trust in the military stems from incidents of harassment of innocent locals, who are occasionally mistaken for Boko Haram insurgents. This lack of trust also extends to CJTF members whom they believe are members of the military or Boko Haram spies. The situation is further complicated by the fact that some members of the CJTF are former Boko Haram members who have surrendered and are now working with the group to establish peace.

The strained relationship between the locals, military, and CJTF underscores the significant challenges in achieving insurgent peace in Borno State. This situation highlights the urgent need for trust-building measures to foster cooperation among the various stakeholders involved in the quest for lasting peace in the region. According to a respondent from the University of Maiduguri:

> *The establishment of the CJTF group has led to debates that are turning communities against each other, particularly in Borno State, and causing friction between the military and the CJTF group. This discord arises from the actions of CJTF members concerning Boko Haram insurgency activities. As a result, both the military and the locals have become more insular, reducing their levels of cooperation with the CJTF, and consequently fostering mistrust* (W., personal communication, 14 July 2022).

This statement highlights the detrimental effects of mistrust between the military, CJTF, and local communities, which negatively impacts insurgent peace efforts. The growing mistrust has created a divide between the military and CJTF, complicating efforts to develop unified strategies against the Boko Haram insurgency. The lack of confidence-building measures has intensified feelings of victimisation, discrimination, and alienation among the local population. Actions taken by the CJTF, intended to preemptively address insurgency, have further diminished trust and led to the derogatory language being used against them. A respondent commented on this issue:

> *CJTF members in parts of Borno State are referred to derogatorily as 'Rapers.' Whenever CJTF members are seen, they are called 'Rapers the killers.' There is even a song that has been produced focusing on the atrocities, primarily linked to CJTF members' harassment in Borno State* (I., personal communication, 17 October 2022).

This statement underscores the negative perceptions some locals hold towards the CJTF, contributing to a hostile environment where the group is seen as a threat rather than a protector. The situation is exacerbated by incidents of harassment and rape, which undermine the group's effectiveness and hinder peace efforts. The relationship between the CJTF, military, and local communities has become increasingly strained, impeding progress towards insurgent peace.

The negative actions of the CJTF, including criminal behaviour while they are supposed to be establishing peace, have severely limited the cooperation necessary for insurgency peace and local security. Reports of discrimination against CJTF members, particularly following grenade attacks in 2015, have further strained relations. A respondent recounted an incident where her involvement with the local security group led to passengers avoiding her on public transport due to unfounded fears (H., personal communication, 13 June 2022). This negative perception has exacerbated the distance between locals and the CJTF, leading to friction with the military and undermining efforts towards peace.

To build peace within the context of insurgency, it is essential to establish trust and cooperation among all stakeholders. Community dialogues, targeted training programmes, and initiatives to bridge gaps between the military, CJTF, and local populations are crucial. These measures will help rebuild trust, mitigate accusations, and foster a collaborative approach to insurgency peace, thereby creating a stable environment conducive to achieving lasting peace.

## Challenge of inadequate strategic communication

Timely and accurate information sharing, coupled with strong coordination with the military, are critical strategies for effectively countering and undermining the Boko Haram insurgency. For example, the military can play a preventive role by alerting the CJTF to the potential repercussions of actions such as aligning with Boko Haram or mimicking their behaviours. This could help deter such actions and, if necessary, facilitate preemptive arrests based on credible intelligence suggesting that a CJTF member may defect to Boko Haram. Ensuring that all relevant information is communicated to the military is crucial for establishing peace and minimising loss of life.

However, ensuring the timely and accurate relaying of information poses significant challenges. It necessitates effective communication and a high level of trust between the  military and the CJTF. Despite this, some CJTF members, particularly leaders, have earned credibility, making their information valuable. Yet, problems have arisen from the military's occasional authoritarian responses, which can alienate the local population. Accounts from Borno State during early 2013 reveal how insurgent peace efforts have occasionally led to alienation due to practices such as arbitrary arrests and military raids that disproportionately affected innocent civilians. The perception that information from the CJTF led to repressive military actions has been compounded by operations such as Operation Lafia Dole, which targeted innocent locals following the Chibok schoolgirls' kidnapping. Such actions have resulted in human rights violations and wrongful detentions, undermining the effectiveness of the CJTF's efforts over time.

Another significant challenge is the CJTF's capacity to address operational issues effectively. If the CJTF fails to understand and address the dynamics of Boko Haram's threats, including their methods and rationale, it will struggle to provide actionable intelligence to the military. This inefficiency hampers the development of effective counterinsurgency strategies.

Moreover, the CJTF's implementation of the state's insurgent peace policy has been hindered by an inadequate understanding of justice. Justice, within this context, involves fair and equitable treatment for all parties involved in the conflict, including victims, perpetrators, and affected communities. It requires recognising and safeguarding the rights of all stakeholders and establishing mechanisms to hold individuals and groups accountable for any rights violations. Without a robust understanding and application of justice, the CJTF's peace initiatives are likely to fall short in addressing the broader needs of the conflict-affected region. Within the context of the CJTF's implementation of the state's insurgent peace policy, justice is a vitalelement for achieving sustainable peace in the conflict zone. Without a robust commitment to justice, the CJTF's efforts may be perceived as biased, unfair, and lacking in legitimacy. This perception could arise if the CJTF appears to favour particular religious, ethnic, or political groups, lacks transparency, fails to engage adequately with stakeholders, or administers unjust treatment during its operations.

Ensuring justice in the peace process entails addressing the root causes of conflict, promoting reconciliation and healing, and establishing effective mechanisms for accountability and redress. It also involves including all stakeholders in the peace process and considering their perspectives and concerns. As highlighted by a respondent:

> *In these spaces, we want each of the military to identify what they want to change or address with respect to the fight against Boko Haram insurgency crisis. We want them then to prioritize both short-term and long-term insurgent peace operational goals and then collaborate towards that insurgent peace goal* (Y., personal communication, 10 July 2022).

This statement underscores the CJTF's desire for the military to clearly define and prioritise its objectives in combatting the Boko Haram insurgency, and to work collaboratively towards achieving these goals. Such an approach fosters justice by ensuring that all stakeholders have a voice in the peace process and that decisions are made inclusively and participatorily.

## Effect of CJTF on insurgent peace

The CJTF's operations and their impact on insurgents have been extensively studied (Bamidele, 2018, 2020, 2023). The disarmament, reintegration, and rehabilitation of the CJTF are critical for the success of any future amnesty deal with Boko Haram and the broader insurgent peace efforts. The CJTF is integral to the effectiveness of the ongoing Boko Haram defectors' programme, Operation Safe Corridor, as they are positioned to facilitate the reintegration and rehabilitation of defectors and locals previously under insurgent control. Their relationships with the community are essential for creating an environment conducive to defectors' reintegration as well as for fostering trust and security within the communities.

Despite some locals viewing CJTF members as protectors from the insurgency, the group has also become a source of insecurity and various threats. A growing sense of neglect from the Borno State government has led some CJTF members to engage in criminal activities, including extortion, theft, cattle rustling, robbery, and drug peddling. The military's supervision of the CJTF is limited and hampered by weak leadership in the command sectors of Borno State.

While the CJTF's involvement in insurgent peace initiatives in Borno State has been subject to criticism, it has also contributed to improved security, with areas previously plagued by violence now experiencing relative peace. The effectiveness of any future amnesty deal with Boko Haram and its factions will depend significantly on the successful disarmament, reintegration, and rehabilitation of the CJTF group.

## Addressing the CJTF's operational challenges

As the Boko Haram insurgency crisis nears its resolution, the CJTF group continues to grapple with significant operational challenges in its efforts to achieve lasting peace. Addressing these challenges is crucial for a successful transition to the postconflict period and for preventing future issues. Despite these difficulties, the CJTF has made notable contributions, including reducing the frequency of attacks by Boko Haram insurgents and overcoming them in Borno State.

One major challenge involves criticism from elite elder statesmen in Borno, organised under the umbrella of BELT. Between 2011 and 2022, BELT accused the military of heavy-handed tactics and of inciting the CJTF to act against local interests. These accusations fostered perceptions of bias and illegitimacy surrounding the CJTF, undermining their peacebuilding efforts and leading to calls for their withdrawal from the state. To address this challenge, the CJTF must confront these accusations directly and work towards establishing transparent and impartial operations.

In addition, BELT accused both the military and the CJTF of indiscriminate violence, including arson, murder, looting, and the rape of young women, attributing these actions to inadequate information from the CJTF that failed to distinguish Boko Haram insurgents from civilians. Despite these allegations, the CJTF has occasionally succeeded in aiding identification efforts, in line with its intended purpose. However, there are concerns that the group has mirrored Boko Haram's violent actions, as highlighted by a CJTF leader (see Chapter 7).

Another operational challenge is the frequent targeting of CJTF-active areas by Boko Haram, likely intended to deter the group from collaborating with the military. A focus group discussion revealed a statement from Boko Haram insurgents:

> *We have established that the locals in Borno State are currently against our cause. They have allied with security operatives and are actively supporting the government in its war against us. We intend to declare complete war on you as a result of your alliance with the military and police to fight our brethren* (A., personal communication, 3 August 2022).

In response to these threats, Boko Haram insurgents killed approximately 22 locals, including students and fishermen, demonstrating the seriousness of their threats. The escalation of violence can be attributed to a lack of cooperation and trust between the CJTF and the military. A military officer emphasised the need for cooperation between the military and local communities, stating:

> *Boko Haram insurgency is a social phenomenon; before you grow and become an insurgent, the local community and the state have responsibilities to fulfill. There is a need for cooperation between the military and locals. If the locals are capacitated, supportive, and trust the military, they can share information with the CJTF group* (M., personal communication, 13 November 2022).

According to the military officer, deficiencies in teamwork and information sharing have compromised the effectiveness of the CJTF and military collaboration. The officer highlighted that corruption within the military has contributed to weakened trust and potential information leaks:

> *CJTF group has a weak link with the military. It is caused by corruption linked to the military. CJTF members are people like us; they want money, and they can leak information to the Boko Haram insurgents. They can pass the shared information to the Boko Haram insurgents. Therein lies the danger of cooperation* (A., personal communication, 14 July 2022).

CJTF members themselves have acknowledged that their involvement in corrupt practices, such as accepting bribes, has contributed to the erosion of trust between the CJTF and the military. One CJTF member noted:

> *The assessment and view of the military is largely negative about our members. There is a view already out there that CJTF group is corrupt... it is out there but there are also real scenarios where CJTF members are participating in bribe taking. The military would lose trust with CJTF group and therefore hamper information sharing* (M., personal communication, 19 November 2022).

To address these operational challenges, it is crucial for the CJTF to focus on rebuilding trust with the military. Timely and effective information sharing can play a key role in disrupting Boko Haram's plans and preventing further violence. By overcoming these issues and fostering a more transparent and cooperative relationship, the CJTF can contribute significantly to the successful establishment of peace in the postconflict period and mitigate future problems.

## Conclusion

The challenges facing the CJTF in implementing Nigeria's local security policy in the fight against the Boko Haram insurgency have been examined. Despite collaboration between the CJTF and the military, several significant obstacles persist, including a lack of trust between these groups, negative perceptions of the CJTF's activities within the community, and deficiencies in effective information sharing. In addition, the broader community often struggles with mistrust of both the CJTF and the military, further complicating the security dynamics.

Addressing these issues necessitates a strategic shift towards more noncoercive, locally focused approaches. Emphasising transparency, accountability, and community engagement is essential for fostering stronger relationships and rebuilding trust among all stakeholders. It is crucial for the CJTF and military to adopt practices that are not only legally compliant but also sensitive to the needs and perceptions of the local populace. Future studies should investigate how collective problem-solving and cooperative strategies can be adapted to different settings, particularly comparing urban and rural contexts.

Generally, overcoming these challenges and establishing trust between local security groups and the military is vital for effective collaboration and the successful establishment of long-term peace. By focusing on inclusive and transparent practices, the CJTF and its partners can enhance their effectiveness and contribute significantly to achieving sustainable peace in the region.

# CHAPTER ELEVEN
# CONCLUSION AND RECAPTURING

## Introduction

After its formation, the CJTF was co-opted by the military to gather intelligence and collaborate with local communities during the Boko Haram insurgency. Both the federal and state governments recognise the group's value and provide members with organisational support, including training and arms. The militarisation of the CJTF involves giving it access to sophisticated weapons, upgrading traditional weapons such as bows, arrows, spears, and local guns. As an auxiliary force with close ties to the military and locals, the CJTF not only provides intelligence due to its knowledge of local communities, including their language and culture, but also participates in long-range patrols and offensive operations. The CJTF remains an asset in the fight against Boko Haram due to its collaboration with the military and insight into the insurgency.

This chapter summarises the concerns raised in previous chapters about the CJTF's misconduct, including human rights violations, violent acts, extortion, threats, and erroneous profiling of innocent locals. These issues have become regular problems associated with the group, potentially resulting from its collaboration with the military, given similar accusations against the military forces. Despite these reports of misconduct, the CJTF's interventions in insurgent peace have been beneficial to the state. Although the group has admitted to instances of torture, extortion, and sexual violence committed by members, these do not invalidate its contribution to the struggle against Boko Haram.

Previous chapters also mention that dealing with the CJTF after insurgent peace is established requires careful consideration and planning. The government and military need to develop strategies that address the group's disarmament and integration into the state's security apparatus, ensuring that the process does not trigger violence or create new security threats. Close coordination and communication with the group's leaders and members are necessary to build trust and facilitate a smooth transition. Addressing issues faced by disbanded members, such as poverty, unemployment, and marginalisation, is essential to prevent the emergence of a new armed group.

While the CJTF has made significant contributions to the fight against insurgency in Borno State, challenges remain, such as the lack of a robust training programme, navigating areas where Boko Haram hides, poor funding, and inadequate support from federal and state governments. Therefore, this chapter recommends solutions, such as legalising and institutionalising the CJTF to ensure holistic local security.

## Summary of findings

### Initiation of the CJTF

The chapter revealed that Borno State has a long history of local participation in countering insurgency threats, including religious and ethnic insurgencies. As such, it is not surprising that the CJTF group plays a significant role in the ongoing fight against Boko Haram insurgents in Borno State. However, while the locals work with the CJTF group, there is mistrust on both sides, which means that trust and cooperation need to be developed to combat the insurgency effectively.

The CJTF started with about 500 members in 2013 when it was formally launched in Yerwa-Maiduguri. It has since grown to become a force to reckon with, with an estimated 26,000 members. The military recognised the potential benefits of working with the locals, particularly in the area of intelligence gathering and therefore offered support to organise, train, equip, and operationalise the CJTF. As such, the group has become an auxiliary force recognised throughout the state with robust ties to the military and locals. Moreover, over time, the group has matured and become increasingly complex with its stratified structures.

### CJTF's activities

The CJTF performs diverse tasks, including maintaining checkpoints, gathering intelligence, patrolling, initiating arrests of suspected Boko Haram insurgents, and defending recently liberated communities from being retaken by the insurgents. The military often integrates CJTF members on long-range patrols or offensive operations to make effective use of their knowledge of communities, language, and culture. However, while the CJTF has been instrumental in pushing back the Boko Haram insurgency, its growth in numbers and capability comes with some risks due to its increased access to sophisticated weapons through its collaboration with the military.

While the group's members previously had access to bows, spears, and locally made guns, they now have access to automatic rifles, and there have been reports of some members privately acquiring firearms or making rifles for themselves. This has raised concerns about the implications of the existence of the CJTF, with some observers perceiving the group as a potential national security risk. While the CJTF group's contribution to the fight against the Boko Haram insurgency cannot be overemphasised, it is essential to manage their growth and access to weapons to prevent any negative outcomes. In addition, when the conflict has ended, the government and military need to develop strategies to integrate the group into the state's security apparatus, disarm them effectively, and address any potential conflicts that may arise during the process.

The CJTF group has been reported to violate human rights, including extortion, threats, and perpetration of violent acts against suspected insurgents. Although the group has admitted to these violations, it has also been claimed that they are less likely to abuse locals due to their local community ties. Moreover, the military contributes to reducing the frequency of abuse. However, opinions differ on whether the CJTF has played out its role or is still required for future operations. Disassembling the group currently would not be a simple task due to retributive attacks by Boko Haram and the group's reluctance to comply with disarmament. In addition, the group may be politicised, endangering insurgent peace in the state. The CJTF could resort to predation as a survival strategy if state support wanes. Despite these challenges, many members of the group have already been recruited into the military, which could contribute to continued assistance in checking insurrectional activities in Borno State.

CJTF has played an important role in preventing Boko Haram insurgents from disseminating information to locals. In addition, the group's interventions have helped to improve relations between the military and locals and increased the flow of information reaching the military. Due to their active involvement in local communities, CJTF members are familiar with the daily routines of locals. As a result, they can identify individuals who are absent without explanation or whose movements are suspicious. This makes it more difficult for Boko Haram to conduct underground, covert, or clandestine activities, such as planning and carrying out attacks, planting bombs, and recruiting new members, because the CJTF can alert the military to any potential threats. Furthermore, the group's strong networking in every corner of the state has weakened the insurgents' strength and hindered their territorial ambitions. Overall, the CJTF has been a vital resource in breaking down the resilience of the insurgents.

## Challenges to the CJTF's interventions

The CJTF's interventionist role is not without challenges and shortcomings. These challenges are mainly operational, technical, and institutional. Operational challenges include a lack of robust training in insurgent peace, which could help CJTF members understand the complex nature of the conflict and how to engage with the community. Without proper training, CJTF members may not have the necessary skills and knowledge to carry out their duties.

In the case of the CJTF, an insufficient number of members is also a significant operational challenge, as it can limit the group's ability to carry out its mandate. With fewer members available to carry out operations, the CJTF may struggle to cover all areas and respond to potential threats promptly. This can hinder the group's ability to protect the locals, reduce deaths, and prevent the recurrence of Boko Haram insurgency activities in the region.

Technical challenges relate to the tools, equipment, and technology required to effectively carry out the CJTF's operations. For example, technical challenges such as a lack of access to reliable communication equipment, inadequate surveillance technology to monitor Boko Haram activities, and insufficient resources to conduct proper intelligence gathering would affect the success of the CJTF's interventions. A lack of specialised skills among CJTF members, such as bomb disposal, cybersecurity, or other technical expertise, could be critical in countering Boko Haram's tactics and might impact the CJTF's ability to carry out its mandate of protecting the locals and reducing deaths.

Technical challenges also arise due to the specific terrain and environment in which CJTF operates. Borno State, where the group operates, has a difficult terrain with vast stretches of desert and rugged terrain, which makes it challenging for both the military and CJTF to navigate and conduct their operations effectively. This terrain also provides cover for Boko Haram insurgents to launch their attacks and hide from the authorities. With rugged terrain and limited infrastructure, CJTF members may struggle to access certain areas and respond to potential threats on time. This can hinder their ability to protect the locals, reduce deaths, and prevent the recurrence of Boko Haram insurgency activities in the region.

Institutional challenges include poor funding and inadequate support from the federal and state governments, as well as the locals, which hinder the group's ability to carry out their duties effectively. Without adequate funding and support, the CJTF may struggle to access the resources and expertise needed to carry out its mandate effectively. This can hinder their ability to protect the locals, reduce deaths, and prevent the recurrence of Boko Haram insurgency activities in the region.

The above challenges have made it impossible for the CJTF's insurgent peace operation to accomplish some of its main goals in tandem with the military. While insurgent peace has prevailed in Borno State and prevented the establishment of a caliphate by the insurgents, the CJTF's core mandate of protecting the locals, reducing deaths, and ensuring the nonrecurrence of Boko Haram insurgency activities has been grossly underachieved.

## Militarisation of the CJTF

Although it became militarised and equipped with army resources to work with the military, the CJTF group was initially established to assist locals in identifying and apprehending Boko Haram insurgents due to growing insecurity in Borno State. At first, the group was not equipped with sophisticated weapons and, for example, relied on sticks and machetes. However, over time, members accumulated homemade Dane guns to help man checkpoints. Thus, the group can be seen as a distinct category of locally based insurgent peace initiatives, emerging from local populations frustrated with the military's inability to address security challenges in their communities.

As the CJTF evolved from a locally based insurgent peace initiative into a full insurgent peace operation and began to work alongside the military, they were provided with sophisticated weaponry. This new level of power and weaponry could have the potential to be misused and could pose a threat to the stability of the country, especially if the group were to use its weapons against the state or other groups. This would be a possibility, because CJTF members may not be as well trained or disciplined as the military, and their actions could cause further unrest and destabilisation in the state. Therefore, to address this, many CJTF members were recruited into the military for post-Boko Haram insurgency operations. However, the management of the CJTF group in the postinsurgent peace context will require careful consideration from both federal and state governments.

Overall, the militarisation of the CJTF group and its implications for peace and security in BornoState need to be carefully considered. The group has the potential to assist in maintaining peace and security in the region, but its management and effectiveness require attention to ensure that they do not become a threat to the stability of Borno State and the country as a whole.

Investigations into allegations of unlawful killings and human rights violations by members of the CJTF have forced them to adopt military tactics in their security control and intelligence-gathering activities. This has caused the group to operate on the fringes of the Nigerian state, blurring the lines between the state and locals in their insurgent peace operations. This study also found that the CJTF has a propensity for violence, which highlights the need for the federal and state governments to consider the strategic reintegration of members into their communities.

Various options for this reintegration have been explored in Borno State, and the state needs to ensure that the CJTF's transition back into its communities is successful and does not lead to further violence or instability.

## Recommendations

I make the following recommendations based on the study findings summarised above.

### Legalisation and institutionalisation of the CJTF

It is recommended that the CJTF be legalised and institutionalised as a complementary force to the military to strengthen the overall insurgent peace operations in Borno State. To institutionalise something means to establish it as a formal, organised, and accepted part of a system or organisation. This means establishing the CJTF group as a recognised and formal entity within the military or government structure in Borno State.

To legalise something means to make it legal or permissible under the law. This means that legalising the CJTF would mean recognising its existence and operations under the law and granting it legal status and protection. This would give the group a level of legitimacy and make it accountable to the law, thereby making it easier for it to collaborate with the military and government in Borno State. Thus, locally established insurgent peace apparatuses should be established for each location, as part of a broader strategy. The synergy between the CJTF group and the military would be systematised to make their joint operations more effective, with a well-grounded insurgent peace mechanism emerging from this collaboration. However, the military should adopt a technique to demilitarise members of the CJTF who cannot be absorbed into mainstream military formations, while simultaneously instilling respect for the rule of law and human rights in these members.

### Continued localisation of the CJTF

In addition to its role as a military organisation, the CJTF should have a locally based security focus, rather than being fixated solely on military insurgent peace operations. The group should be reengineered and professionalised in its dealings with the locals, particularly within the post-Boko Haram insurgency context. Furthermore, a disarmament, demobilisation, and reintegration framework should be established for CJTF members in Borno State, with a focus on their economic reintegration through incentives for small-scale and medium-sized enterprises. The Borno State government should provide organisational, institutional, and technical backing for this.

The state government should also consolidate the CJTF group by including them in a formal local security framework that focuses on reducing latent crimes resulting from the Boko Haram insurgency, such as arms proliferation and human trafficking. Coaching establishments for the group should be improved, well funded, and properly equipped, providing capacity building, training, compensation, and the acquisition of necessary instruments for the proper management of disorders resulting from insurgency activities. The CJTF code of conduct should also be reviewed to enhance standards, ethics, and compliance with human rights and humanitarian laws.

To improve the CJTF relationships with locals, regular interactive forums should be held to provide avenues for the discussion of key issues and the building of confidence. In addition, finally, to balance bottom-up and top-down insurgent peace responses to the Boko Haram insurgency and prevent the continuous mobilisation of youths from localities already plagued by violence and displacement, local capacity should be incrementally strengthened through stronger involvement of the state government and other relevant agencies to reconstruct the CJTF group and ensure its local relevance. In addition, the locals in the state should regard the CJTF aslegitimate members of the state. Therefore, alleged abuses by the CJTF should be dealt with publicly and immediately. For the group to be relevant, they must enjoy the confidence and trust of the locals.

## Numerical strength of the CJTF

The military requires many insurgent peace actors due to the large local population. This raises the question of the necessary numerical strength of the CJTF for effective insurgent peace interventions, as military personnel are not deployed in all the affected communities in Borno State. However, the continuous incorporation of CJTF members in the fight against Boko Haram requires flexibility and decentralised decision-making. What works in one area might not necessarily be effective in another.

The CJTF should be engaged solely in defensive roles during insurgent peace, focusing on protective defence, infrastructure security, and intelligence gathering. The group should not be used in offensive operations, except as guides in critical strongholds of Boko Haram. Additionally, the CJTF and other supportive locals should work together during insurgent peace. The CJTF was formed by locals in response to Boko Haram's brutal attacks; operations by locals, rather than indiscriminate military violence, have significantly contributed to the expulsion of Boko Haram insurgents from urban areas in Borno State. The CJTF and locals should  be regarded as protectors and defenders, not just as representatives conducting insurgent peace operations.

To gain a comprehensive understanding of insurgent peace operations, more qualitative and quantitative research on local security mechanisms in African countries and beyond is suggested. Countries such as Syria, Iraq, Afghanistan, Somalia, Yemen, Libya, Mali, the Philippines, Colombia, and India (especially Jammu and Kashmir and Northeast India) have recently experienced insurgency. Research could be conducted through several approaches:

Literature review: Conduct a comprehensive review of relevant literature, including academic publications, government reports, and media coverage, which were not covered in my research. This will lead to a broader understanding of the local security mechanisms and identify gaps in the existing knowledge.

Fieldwork: Conduct fieldwork in the area where the insurgent peace initiatives are taking place. This could involve interviews with key stakeholders, including local community members, government officials, military personnel, and insurgents themselves. This will provide firsthand insights into the peace initiatives and a more nuanced understanding of the local context.

Case studies: Select a few case studies of successful and unsuccessful insurgent peace initiatives and analyse them in-depth. This will identify common challenges and best practices that can be applied in other contexts.

Comparative analysis: Compare insurgent peace initiatives in various countries. This will identify factors that contribute either to success or failure and provide insights into the broader applicability of local peace mechanisms.

Participatory research: Engage with local communities and stakeholders to co-create knowledge about peace initiatives. This approach would emphasise the importance of local perspectives and knowledge and can build trust and legitimacy for the research.

## Contribution of the book

This book has provided insights into the relationship between the military and CJTF's unconventional approaches to insurgent peace. These insights should be useful to governments, especially state military, because the hybrid technique of fighting the insurgency I have explained could serve as a new and uniquely collaborative approach between locals and the military in insurgent peace. Moreover, my case study of locally led security mechanisms should be beneficial to international security and, in particular, to operatives in dire insurgency settings. Thus, I have provided insurgency and insurgent peace scholars with a unique template for understanding insurgency and insurgent peace operations. The outcome of my research should also prompt further studies on how to improve the strategies of operations to end insurgency expeditiously with minimal collateral damage and disruption of peace.

This study should inspire national, regional, and international authorities and other concerned stakeholders to review the insurgent peace initiatives I have described to embark on holistic local strategies to halt the human and material devastation already occasioned in several locales in Africa. Such local strategies emphasise local interests, knowledge, intelligence, and formalised, dedicated participation to maximise the benefits of synergy between locals and the military in insurgent peace situations.

This study offers important lessons on how insurgent peace in Borno State can be addressed effectively by leveraging the patriotic fervour of locals in the state. The lessons learnt from the management of the CJTF group in Borno State can be inculcated in other states where a similar local security group also operates. The other states in the northeastern region can even learn from the mistakes made by CJTF in Borno State once it is effectively managed or members are reintegrated into their different localities.

## Conclusion

The CJTF holds a crucial role in maintaining local security and combatting the Boko Haram insurgency in the region. However, without regular training and proper equipment, the CJTF may not be able to carry out its duties, which could result in increased casualties and a prolonged fight. However, it is not sufficient to rely solely on military approaches to address the issue. To achieve lasting peace and stability, local communities must be integrated into the efforts to defeat the insurgency, because they have a deep understanding of the social, economic, and political dynamics in their region and are best placed to identify the root causes of the insurgency and contribute to targeted solutions that address them. In addition, involving local communities in the peace process can build trust and promote reconciliation between different groups in the region, which will reduce the risk of future conflicts and promote lasting peace and stability.

The CJTF should also receive adequate support and resources from the government and international partners in the form of funding for operations and logistical support, such as the provision of transportation, communication equipment, and the delivery of supplies, including food, water, and medical equipment. In addition, the involvement of women in peace and security efforts should be prioritised, as they often bear the brunt of the conflict and can play a crucial role in promoting peace and reconciliation in the region. The international community should also play a supportive role in addressing the Boko Haram insurgency by providing humanitarian aid, technical assistance, and capacity building for the CJTF and other local security forces.

In any conflict, victims have suffered because of violence and instability. This is certainly true in the case of the Boko Haram insurgency, which has caused human suffering and displacement, with countless individuals and families affected by the conflict. Therefore, to promote lasting peace and stability in the region, it is crucial to ensure that justice is served for these victims. This means holding accountable those who have committed atrocities and human rights abuses, whether they are members of Boko Haram, security forces, or the CJTF who have acted unlawfully. By doing so, trust can be restored and reconciliation promoted in the region.

# BIBLIOGRAPHY

Abdullahi, A. (2015). Globalization, identity crisis and insurgency in Northern Nigeria: Trends, complexities and implications for security governance in Sahel, West Africa. *International Affairs and Global Strategy, 37*(1), 59–76.

Achumba, I. C., Ighomereho, O. S., & Akpor-Robaro, M. O. M. (2013). Security challenges in Nigeria and the implications for business activities and sustainable development. *Journal of Economics and Sustainable Development, 4*(2), 79–99. https://core.ac.uk/download/pdf/234645825.pdf

Ackah-Arthur, J. (2023). *The state, non-state actors, and populations: Security responses to insurgent attacks in Sub-Saharan Africa* [Doctoral thesis, London School of Economics and Political Science]. https://etheses.lse.ac.uk/4635/1/Ackah-Arthur_201812393.pdf

Adesoji, A. (2010). The Boko Haram uprising and Islamic revivalism in Nigeria. *African Spectrum, 45*(2), 95–108. https://doi.org/10.1177/000203971004500205

Adesoji, A. O. (2011). Between Maitatsine and Boko Haram: Islamic fundamentalism and the response of the Nigerian state. *Africa Australia, 579*(4), 99–119. https://doi.org/10.2979/africatoday.57.4.99

Adeyeye, P. (2020). Operation Safe Corridor and the misplaced investment on terrorism. *DataPhyt.* https://www.dataphyte.com/security/operation-safe-corridor-and-the- misplaced-investment-on-terrorism/ (Accessed 31 July 2020).

Agbiboa, D. E. (2018). Eyes on the street: Civilian Joint Task Force and the surveillance of Boko Haram in northeastern Nigeria. *Intelligence and National Security, 33*(7), 1022–1039. https://doi.org/10.1080/02684527.2018.1475892

Agbiboa, D. E. (2020). Vigilante youths and counterinsurgency in northeastern Nigeria: The Civilian Joint Task Force. *Oxford Development Studies, 48*(4), 360–372. https://doi.org/10.1080/13600818.2020.1837093

Agbiboa, D. E. (2021). The precariousness of protection: Civilian defense groups countering Boko Haram in northeastern Nigeria. *African Studies Review, 64*(1), 192–216. https://doi.org/10.1017/asr.2020.47

Agbiboa, D. E. (2021). The precariousness of protection: Civilian defense groups countering Boko Haram in northeastern Nigeria. *African Studies Review, 64*(1), 192–216. doi:10.1017/asr.2020.47

Akubo, A. A., & Okolo, B. I. (2019, December 5). Boko Haram insurgency in Nigeria: Implications for national security and restorative justice. *African Journal on Conflict Resolution.* https://www.accord.org.za/ajcr-issues/boko-haram-insurgency-in-nigeria/

Al-Hindawi, F. H., & Saffah, M. D. (2019). Literary pragmatics. *Arab World English Journal, 10*(2), 394–408. https://doi.org/10.24093/awej/vol10no2.30

Allen, N. D. F. (2023, August 9). African-led peace operations: A crucial tool for peace and security. *Africa Center for Strategic Studies.* https://africacenter.org/spotlight/african-led-peace-operations-a-crucial-tool-for-peace-and-security/

Anthony, B. (2024). The role of community engagement in urban innovation towards the co- creation of smart sustainable cities. *Journal of Knowledge Economy, 15,* 1592–1624. https://doi.org/10.1007/s13132-023-01176-1

Aydinli, E. (2018). *Violent non-state actors: From anarchists to jihadists* (1st ed.). Routledge. https://www.routledge.com/Violent-Non-State-Actors-From -Anarchists-to- Jihadists/Aydinli/p/book/9781138598409

Baldwin, D. A. (1997). The concept of security. *Review of International Studies, 23*(1), 5–26. https://doi.org/10.1017/S0260210597000053

Bamidele, O. (2016a). Combating terrorism: Socioeconomic issues, Boko Haram, and insecurity in the north-east region of Nigeria. *Military and Strategic Affairs, 8*(1), 109–131. Institute for National Security Studies, Tel Aviv University, Israel.

Bamidele, O. (2016b). Combating terrorism: Anti-terrorism law, Boko Haram, and insecurity in Nigeria. *African Journal of Democracy and Governance, 2*(3&4), 139–150. https://hdl.handle.net/10520/EJC186710

Bamidele, O. (2016c). Civilian Joint Task Force (CJTF) – A community security option: A comprehensive and proactive approach of reducing terrorism. *Journal of Deradicalisation, Summer 7,* 124–144. https://journals.sfu.ca/jd/index.php/jd/article/view/40

Bamidele, O. (2024b). On responsibility for the security of others: An ethnographic case study of Civilian Joint Task Force insurgent peace in Borno State, north-eastern region of Nigeria. In N. I. Erameh & V. Ojakorotu (Eds.), *Africa's engagement with the responsibility to protect in the 21st century* (pp. 93–111). Cham, Switzerland: Palgrave Macmillan. https://doi.org/10.1007/978-981-99-8163-2_6

Bamidele, S. (2017a). Creating the deserved protection: Reflections on Civilian Joint Task Force (CJTF) counter-insurgency operations in the north-eastern region of Nigeria. *Journal of Law, Society and Development, 4*(1), 1–22. https://doi.org/10.25159/2520-9515/1032

Bamidele, S. (2017b). The Civilian Joint Task Force and the struggle against insurgency in Borno State, Nigeria. *African Conflict and Peacebuilding Review, 7*(2), 85–98. https://doi.org/10.2979/africonfpeacrevi.7.2.04

Bamidele, S. (2018). Understanding insurgency in Nigeria: Interrogating religious categories of analysis. *Jadavpur Journal of International Relations, 22*(2), 189–207. https://doi.org/10.1177/0973598418783642

Bamidele, S. (2020a). "Sweat is invisible in the rain": Civilian Joint Task Force and counter-insurgency in Borno State, Nigeria. *Security and Defence Quarterly, 31*(4), 171–188. https://doi.org/10.35467/sdq/130867

Bamidele, S. (2020b). Islamic insurgency in Nigeria: Perceptions from religious ideologies. *International Journal on World Peace, 37*(2), 37–52. Paragon House Publishers.

Bamidele, S. (2021). Securing through the failure to secure? Civilian Joint Task Force and counter-insurgency operations in the north-eastern region of Nigeria. *Journal of African-Centered Solutions in Peace and Security, 4*(1), 104–122. Institute for Peace and Security Studies, Addis Ababa University, Ethiopia.

Bamidele, S. (2024a). The Boko Haram insurgency and Nigeria's long path towards peace and security: The Civilian Joint Task Force experience. In N.

I. Erameh & R. Agu (Eds.), *Nigeria's Republic at Sixty: Of dreams, travails and hopes.* Washington, DC: Academica Press.

Bellamy, A., & Williams, D. (2011). The new politics of protection? Côte d'Ivoire, Libya and the responsibility to protect. *International Affairs, 87*(4), 825–850. https://doi.org/10.1111/j.1468-2346.2011.01006.x

Bellamy, P. (2020). Threats to human security. In *Human security in world affairs: Problems and opportunities* (2nd ed.). https://opentextbc.ca/human security/chapter/threats-human-security/

Bello, M., & Oyedele, D. (2012). *Conflict, Nigeria, sustainable development, West Africa.* Leadership Newspapers.

Berard, P. (2018). *Managing revolution: Cold War counterinsurgency and liberal governance* [Electronic thesis or dissertation, Boston College]. http://hdl. handle.net/2345/bc- ir:108101

Bøås, M., & Dunn, K. C. (Eds.) (2017). *Africa's insurgents: Navigating an evolving landscape.* Lynne Rienner Publishers. https://www.rienner.com/uploads/ 58dbe48f5f497.pdf. https://doi.org/10.1515/9781626376526

Boege, V., Brown, A., Clements, K., & Nolan, A. (2008). On hybrid political orders and emerging states: State formation in the context of "fragility". In *Berghof Research Center for Constructive Conflict Management Handbook.* Berghof Foundation. http://www.berghof- foundation.org/fileadmin/redaktion/ Publications/Handbook/Articles/boege_etal_handboo k.pdf

Bot, D. E. (2023). Implementing a people-centred national security framework for Nigeria: The role of the Nigeria Police Force (NPF). *Journal of Human, Social & Political Science Research, 27*(6), 99–119. https://www.cambridge nigeriapub.com/wp-content/uploads/2023/04/SJHSPR_VOL27_NO6_MAR- 2023-8.pdf

Bramble, A., & Paffenholz, T. (2021). *Implementing peace agreements: From inclusive processes to inclusive outcomes?* Inclusive Peace & Transition Initiative, Graduate Institute of International and Development Studies, United Nations Development Programme Oslo Governance Centre. https://www.inclusive peace.org/wp-content/uploads/2021/05/report-inclusive-implementation- en.pdf

Bräuchler, B., & Naucke, P. (2024). Peacebuilding and conceptualisations of the local in social anthropology/anthropologie sociale. *Social Anthropology/ Anthropologie Sociale.* https://doi.org/10.1111/1469-8676.12454

Brechenmacher, S. (2019, May 3). Stabilizing northeast Nigeria after Boko Haram. *Carnegie Endowment for International Peace.* https://carnegieendowment. org/research/2019/05/stabilizing-northeast-nigeria-after-boko-haram?lang= en. https://doi.org/10.1515/sirius-2019-4007

Britannica, T. Editors of Encyclopaedia. (2023, November 27). Insurgency. *Encyclopedia Britannica.* https://www.britannica.com/topic/insurgency

Bromley, D. (1986). *The case-study method in psychology and related disciplines* (6th ed.). Wiley.

Brown, H. (1983). *Thinking about national security: Defense and foreign policy in a dangerous world.* As quoted in Watson, C. A. (2008). *U.S. national security: A reference handbook* (2nd revised ed., p. 281). ABC-CLIO.

Bryden, A., N'Diaye, B., & Olonisakin, F. (Eds.). (2008). *Challenges of security sector governance in West Africa.* Geneva Centre for the Democratic Control of Armed Forces (DCAF). https://www.dcaf.ch/sites/default/files/publications/documents/bm_WestAfrica_bryden_e n.pdf

Buchanan-Clarke, S., & Knoope, P. (2012). *The Boko Haram insurgency: From short term gains to long term solutions* (Occasional Paper 23). Institute for Justice and Reconciliation. https://www.ijr.org.za/home/wp-content/uploads/2012/07/Nigeria-Report-.pdf

Bundeswehr Center of Military History and Social Sciences. (2017). *Insurgency and counterinsurgency in modern war.* Nomos Verlagsgesellschaft.

Buzan, B. (1991). New patterns of global security in the twenty-first century. *International Affairs, 67*(3), 431–451. https://doi.org/10.2307/2621945

Buzan, B., & Wæver, O. (2003). *Regions and powers: The structure of international security.* Cambridge University Press. https://ir101.co.uk/wp-content/uploads/2018/11/Buzan-Waever-2003-Regions-and-Powers-The-Structure-of-International-Security.pdf. https://doi.org/10.1017/CBO9780511491252

Buzan, B., Wæver, O., & De Wilde, J. (1998). *Security: A new framework for analysis.* Lynne Rienner Publishers. https://doi.org/10.1515/9781685853808

Castells, M. (1997). *The power of identity* (Vol. 2). John Wiley & Sons.

Center for Preventive Action. (2024, February 14). Violent extremism in the Sahel. *Council on Foreign Relations.* https://www.cfr.org/global-conflict-tracker/conflict/violent- extremism-sahel

Chandler, D. (2018). Beyond neoliberalism: Resilience, the new art of governing complexity. *Resilience, 6*(1), 1–22.

Chen, H. (2018). *Local security governance in Chinese cities: Urban transformation and societal change.* Routledge.

Cilliers, J., & Solomon, H. (1997). Southern Africa and the quest for collective security. *Security Dialogue, 28*(2), 191–205. https://doi.org/10.1177/0967010697028002007

Community Policing Consortium. (1994). *Understanding community policing: A framework for action.* Bureau of Justice Assistance. https://www.ojp.gov/pdffiles/commp.pdf

Community Tool Box. (n.d.). Understanding and describing the community. In *Community assessment: Assessing community needs and resources* (Chapter 3, Section 2). https://ctb.ku.edu/en/table-of-contents/assessment/assessing-community-needs-and- resources/describe-the-community/main

Coquilhat, J. (2008, September). *Community policing: An international literature review.* Evaluation Team, Organisational Assurance, New Zealand Police. https://www.police.govt.nz/resources/2008/community-policing-lit-review/elements-of- com-policing.pdf

Corbin, J., & Strauss, A. (2008). *Basics of qualitative research: Techniques and procedures for developing grounded theory* (3rd ed.). Sage Publications. https://doi.org/10.4135/9781452230153

Crawford, A., & Hutchinson, S. (2016). Mapping the contours of again, fail better? War, the state, and the "everyday security": Time, space, and emotion. *British Journal of Criminology, 56*(6), 1184–1202. https://doi.org/10.1093/bjc/azv121

Creswell, J. W. (2007). *Qualitative inquiry and research design: Choosing among five approaches.* International Student Edition. Sage Publications.

Creswell, J. W. (2013). *Research design: Qualitative, quantitative, and mixed methods approaches* (4th ed.). Sage Publications.

Deci, E. L., & Ryan, R. M. (2000). The "what" and "why" of goal pursuits: Human needs and the self-determination of behavior. *Psychological Inquiry, 11*(4), 227–268. https://doi.org/10.1207/S15327965PLI1104_01

Dietrich, K. (2015). *When we can't see the enemy, civilians become the enemy: Living through Nigeria's six-year insurgency.* Center for Civilians in Conflict. https://civiliansinconflict.org/wp-content/uploads/2015/10/NigeriaReport_Web.pdf

Dixon, P. (2009). *Insurgent collective action and civil war in El Salvador.* Cambridge University Press.

Dreher, A., & Kreibaum, M. (2016). Weapons of choice: The effect of natural resources on terror and insurgencies. *Journal of Peace Research, 53*(4), 539–553. http://www.jstor.org/stable/43920608. https://doi.org/10.1177/0022343316634418

Esposito, J. L. (2011). Sharia and the state in the modern Muslim world. In R. Peters & A. O. Akyeampong (Eds.), *Modern Muslim societies* (pp. 221–235). Oxford University Press.

Evans, G., & Newnham, J. (1997). *The Penguin dictionary of international relations.* Penguin Books.

Faleg, G. (2012). Between knowledge and power: Epistemic communities and the emergence of security sector reform in the EU security architecture. *European Security, 21*(2), 161– 184. https://doi.org/10.1080/09662839.2012.665882

Federal Republic of Nigeria. (1986). *National Security Agencies Act 19 of 1986.* https://www.placng.org/lawsofnigeria/print.php?sn=336

Federal Republic of Nigeria. (1999). *The Constitution of the Federal Republic of Nigeria, 1999.* https://publicofficialsfinancialdisclosure.worldbank.org/sites/fdl/files/assets/law-library- files/Nigeria_Constitution_1999_en.pdf

Federal Republic of Nigeria. (2011). *The Terrorism (Prevention) Act, 2011.* https://www.unodc.org/res/cld/document/nga/terrorism-prevention-act-2011_html/Nigeria_Terrorism_Prevention_Act_2011.pdf

Federal Republic of Nigeria. (2013). *The Terrorism (Prevention) (Amendment) Act, 2013.* https://www.unodc.org/res/cld/document/nga/terrorism-prevention-amendment-act-2013_html/Nigeria_Terrorism_Prevention_Amendment_Act_2013.pdf

Federal Republic of Nigeria. (2019a). *National Security Strategy.* https://www.nsa.gov.ng/wp-content/uploads/2019/12/Nigeria-National-Security-Strategy-2019.pdf

Federal Republic of Nigeria. (2019b). *Nigeria Police Trust Fund Act, 2019.* https://nptf.gov.ng/nigeria-police-trust-fund-act-2019/

Feng, X. (2019). *Public security governance and community participation in China.* Springer.

Fitzsimmons, M. F. (2008). *Hard hearts and open minds? Governance, identity, and counterinsurgency strategy*. Institute for Defense Analyses. https://apps. dtic.mil/sti/pdfs/ADA491404.pdf. https://doi.org/10.1080/01402390802024692

Forde, S., Kappler, S., & Björkdahl, A. (2021). Peacebuilding, structural violence, and spatial reparations in post-colonial South Africa. *Journal of Intervention and Statebuilding, 15*(3), 327–346. https://doi.org/10.1080/17502977.2021. 1909297

Galula, D. (1964). *Counterinsurgency warfare: Theory and practice*. Library of Congress-in-Publication.

Gana, M. (2020). Strategy of Civilian Joint Task Force militia in combating Boko Haram in Northern Nigeria. *International Journal of Legal Studies (IJOLS), 7*(1), 345–360. https://doi.org/10.5604/01.3001.0014.3126

George, A., & Bennett, A. (2005). *Case studies and theory development in the social sciences*. MIT Press.

George, J., & Adelaja, A. (2022). Armed conflicts, forced displacement and food security in host communities. *World Development, 158,*105991. https:// doi.org/10.1016/j.worlddev.2022.105991

Giddens, A. (1990). *The consequences of modernity*. Stanford University Press.

Gillespie, S. (2017). *The psychological impact of terrorism: A guide to psychological first aid for disaster workers*. Routledge.

Global Partnership for the Prevention of Armed Conflict. (2019). *Handbook on human security: Module 5: Comparing approaches to security*. https://www. gppac.net/files/2019-02/Module%205.pdf

Gray, D. E. (2009). *Doing research in the real world* (2nd ed.). Sage Publications.

Grimmick, R. (2023, April 6). What is a security policy? Definition, elements, and examples. *Varonis*. https://www.varonis.com/blog/what-is-a-security-policy Gurr, T. R. (1970). *Why men rebel*. Princeton University Press.

Gurr, T. R. (1993). *Minorities at risk: A global view of ethnopolitical conflicts*. United States Institute of Peace Press.

Haferkamp, H., & Smelser, N. J. (Eds.) (1992). *Social change and modernity*. University of California Press. http://ark.cdlib.org/ark:/13030/ft6000078s/

Hamid, S., & Dar, R. (2016, July 15). Islamism, Salafism, and jihadism: A primer. Brookings. https://www.brookings.edu/articles/islamism-salafism-and-jihadism-a-primer/

Hashemi, N. (2015). The meaning of an Islamic state: A general theory. *Journal of Islamic State Practices in International Law, 11*(2), 24–38.

Hassan, I. (2015). Counterinsurgency from below: The need for local grassroots defenders in curbing the insurgency in north-east Nigeria. *West African Insight, 12*(1), 61–76.

Hendrickson, D., & Karkoszka, A. (2002). The challenges of security sector reform. In *SIPRI Yearbook 2002: Armaments, disarmament and international security* (pp. 176–201). Stockholm International Peace Research Institute. https://www. sipri.org/sites/default/files/04..pdf

Higazi, A. (2013). The origins and transformation of the Boko Haram insurgency in northern Nigeria. *Politique africaine,* No 130(2), 137-164. https://shs. cairn. info/journal-politique-africaine-2013-2-page-137?lang=en. https://doi.org/ 10.3917/polaf.130.0137

Hoffman, F. G. (2011). Neo-classical counterinsurgency? *Parameters, 41*(4). https://press.armywarcollege.edu/cgi/viewcontent.cgi?article=2607&conte xt=parameters

Human Rights Watch. (2023, January 12). Africa: Conflicts, violence threaten rights: Improve civilian protection, accountability for abuses. *Human Rights Watch*. https://www.hrw.org/news/2023/01/12/africa-conflicts-violence-threaten-rights. https://doi.org/10.55540/0031-1723.2607

Ibrahim, J., & Bala, S. (2018). *Civilian-led governance and security in Nigeria after Boko Haram* (Special Report No. 438). United States Institute of Peace. https://www.usip.org/sites/default/files/2018-12/sr_437_civilian_led_governance_and_security_in_nigeria_0.pdf

ICIR Nigeria. (2016, July 22). 250 Civilian-JTF members recruited into Nigerian Army. *News*. https://www.icirnigeria.org/250-civilian-jtf-members-recruited -nigerian-army/

Ide, T. (2023). Climate change and Australia's national security. *Australian Journal of International Affairs, 77*(1), 26–44. https://doi.org/10.1080/10357718.2023. 2170978

Idris, H., Ibrahim, Y., & Sawab, I. (2014, March 25). Who are Borno's "Civilian JTF"? *Nigerian Daily Trust Newspaper*. http://www.dailytrust.com.ng/weekly/ index.php/top-stories/16115-who-are-borno-s-civilian-jtf#xa6RjGs6yGXzx GcW.99

Idu, J. C. (2019). *Human insecurity in Nigeria: A case study of Boko Haram from 2009–2019* [Minor dissertation, Master of Social Science: International Relations]. University of Cape Town. https://open.uct.ac.za/server/api/core/ bitstreams/d7522da3-a7b6-4a6e-8eba-0c2a94445d89/content (Accessed 8 September 2024).

Igbuzor, O. (2011). Peace and security education: A critical factor for sustainable peace and national development. *International Journal of Peace and Development Studies, 2*(1), 1– 7.

Imobighe, T. A. (n.d.). Conflict in Niger Delta: A unique case or a "model" for future conflicts in other oil-producing countries? In *Oil policy in the Gulf of Guinea* (pp. 101–120). Friedrich-Ebert-Stiftung. https://library.fes.de/pdf-files/iez/02115/imobighe.pdf

Internal Displacement Monitoring Centre. (2018). *Global report on internal displacement*. https://www.internal-displacement.org/global-report/grid2018/ downloads/2018-GRID.pdf

Internal Displacement Monitoring Centre. (2019). *Global report on internal displacement 2019*. Internal Displacement Monitoring Centre. https://www. internal- displacement.org/global-report/grid2019/

International Alert. (2016). *Displacement and dispossession in the Middle East and North Africa*. https://www.international-alert.org/sites/default/files/ Displacement-and-Dispossession-in-the-MENA.pdf

International Crisis Group. (2014). *Curbing violence in Nigeria (I): The Jos crisis*. https://www.crisisgroup.org/africa/west-africa/nigeria/219-curbing-violence-nigeria-i-jos- crisis

International Crisis Group. (2017). *Curbing violence in Nigeria (II): The Boko Haram insurgency*. https://www.crisisgroup.org/africa/west-africa/nigeria/ curbing-violence- nigeria-ii-boko-haram-insurgency

International Crisis Group. (2017, February 27). *Niger and Boko Haram: Beyond counter- insurgency* (Report No. 245). https://www.crisisgroup.org/africa/west- africa/niger/245-niger-and-boko-haram-beyond-counter-insurgency

International Crisis Group. (2018). *Understanding and combating Nigeria's Boko Haram.* https://www.crisisgroup.org/africa/west-africa/nigeria/263-understanding-and-combating- nigerias-boko-haram

Javed, A. (2010). Resistance and its progression to insurgency. *Strategic Studies, 30*(1/2), 171–186. https://www.jstor.org/stable/48527670

Johnson, R. (n.d.). *Future trends in insurgency and countering strategies.* NATO COE-DAT. https://www.coedat.nato.int/publication/researches/03-FutureTrends.pdf

Joint Data Center on Forced Displacement. (2024). *Forced displacement: Literature review.* https://www.jointdatacenter.org/wp-content/uploads/2024/05/2024-05-Literature-Review-Clean.pdf

Kaldor, M. (2012). *New and old wars: Organised violence in a global era* (3rd ed.). Polity. Kalyvas, S. N. (2006). *The logic of violence in civil war.* Cambridge University Press.

Kamali, M. H. (2008). The Shari'ah and its implications for modern legislative systems. In R. C. An-Na'im & A. A. H. Mahmood (Eds.), *Law and society in the Muslim world* (pp. 157– 181). Brill.

Kapatika, H. W. (2022). *Epistemicide: A conceptual analysis in African epistemology* [Mini- thesis]. University of the Western Cape. https://etd.uwc.ac.za/bitstream/handle/11394/9191/kapatika_phd_art_2022.pdf

Karbo, T. (2012, October 17). Localising peacebuilding in Sierra Leone. Paper presented at the Peacebuilding Conference. ACCORD. https://www.accord.org.za/publication/localising-peacebuilding-sierra-leone/

Kawachi, I., & Berkman, L. F. (2001). Social ties and mental health. *Journal of Urban Health, 78*(3), 458–467. https://doi.org/10.1093/jurban/78.3.458

Kelling, G. L., & Moore, M. H. (1988). The evolving strategy of policing. *Perspectives on Policing, 4*, 1–27.

Khanyile, M. B. (2003). *Security and co-operation: A conceptual framework* (Chapter 1). University of Pretoria. https://repository.up.ac.za/bitstream/handle/2263/23435/01chapter1.pdf?sequence=2&isA llowed=y

Kilcullen, D. (2005). Countering global insurgency. *Journal of Strategic Studies, 28*(4), 597–617. Kilcullen, D. (2006). *Counterinsurgency.* Oxford University Press. https://doi.org/10.1080/01402390500300956

Kilcullen, D. (2009). *The accidental guerrilla: Fighting small wars in the midst of a big one.* Oxford University Press.

Kilcullen, D. (2010). *Counterinsurgency.* Oxford University Press.

Kindersley, N., & Rolandsen, Ø. H. (2019a). Violence, local orders and statebuilding in peace processes. *Stability: International Journal of Security and Development, 8*(1), 1–12.

Kindersley, N., & Rolandsen, Ø. H. (2019b). Who are the civilians in the wars of South Sudan? *Security Dialogue, 50*(5), 383–397. https://doi.org/10.1177/0967010619863262

Kiras, J. D. (2010). Irregular warfare: Terrorism and insurgency. In J. Baylis, J. J. Wirtz, & C. S. Gray (Eds.), *Strategy in the contemporary world: An introduction to strategic studies* (4th ed., pp. 307–322). Oxford University Press.

Kitson, D. (1971). *Low-intensity operations: Subversion, insurgency, peacekeeping.* Faber & Faber.

Korab-Karpowicz, W. J. (2023). Political realism in international relations. In E. N. Zalta & U. Nodelman (Eds.), *The Stanford encyclopedia of philosophy* (Winter 2023 Edition). https://plato.stanford.edu/archives/win2023/entries/realism-intl-relations/

Krause, L. B., & Nye, J. S. (1975). Reflections on the economics and politics of international economic organizations. *International Organization, 29*(1), 323–342.

Leonardsson, H., & Rudd, G. (2015). The "local turn" in peacebuilding: A literature review of effective and emancipatory local peacebuilding. *Third World Quarterly, 36*(5), 825–839. https://doi.org/10.1080/01436597.2015.1029905

Levi-Faur, D. (2023). The regulatory security state as a risk state. *Journal of European Public Policy, 30*(7), 1458–1471. https://doi.org/10.1080/13501763.2023.2174170

Mac Ginty, R. (2010). Hybrid peace: The interaction between top-down and bottom-up peace. *Security Dialogue, 41*(4), 391–412. https://doi.org/10.1177/0967010610374312

Mac Ginty, R. (2011). *International peacebuilding and local resistance: Hybrid forms of peace.* Palgrave Macmillan. https://doi.org/10.1057/9780230307032

Mac Ginty, R. (2015). *International peacebuilding and local resistance: Hybrid forms of peace.* Palgrave Macmillan.

Mac Ginty, R. (2018). *Counterinsurgency and the elusive enemy: The threat from the Taliban, the IRA, and al-Qaida.* Polity.

Mac Ginty, R., & Richmond, O. P. (2013). The local turn in peace building: A critical agenda for peace. *Third World Quarterly, 34*(5), 763–783. https://doi.org/10.1080/01436597.2013.800750

Macaspac, N. (2020). *Insurgent peace: Healing our violent society* [Video]. TEDx Talks. https://www.youtube.com/watch?v=vdDULpG0V1c&t=9s

Macaspac, V. N. (2019). Insurgent peace: Community-led peacebuilding of indigenous peoples in Sagada, Philippines. *Geopolitics, 24*(4), 839–877. https://doi.org/10.1080/14650045.2018.1521803

Maier, C. S. (1990). *Peace and security for the 1990s.* Unpublished paper for the MacArthur Fellowship Program, Social Science Research Council, 12 June. As quoted in Romm, J.J. (1993). *Title of Romm's work* (p. 5).

Maier, C. S. (1990, June 12). *Peace and security for the 1990s* [Unpublished manuscript]. MacArthur Fellowship Program, Social Science Research Council. As quoted in Romm, J. J. (1993). *Defining security: The changing politics of security.* Council on Foreign Relations Press.

Malešević, S. (2010). *The sociology of war and violence.* Cambridge University Press. Manwaring, M. G. (2005). *Street gangs: The new urban insurgency.* Strategic Studies Institute. https://www.files.ethz.ch/isn/14325/Street%20Gangs_The%20New%20Urban%20Insurgency.pdf

Martin Luther King, Jr. Research and Education Institute. (n.d.). *Nkrumah, Kwame (September 21, 1909 - April 27, 1972)*. Stanford University. https://kinginstitute.stanford.edu/nkrumah-kwame (Accessed 21 September 2024)

Mesjasz, C. (2004). *Security as an analytical concept* (draft version). http://www.afes- press.de/pdf/Hague/Mesjasz_Security_concept.pdf

Migration Data Portal. (2024, June 20). *Forced migration or displacement.* International Organization for Migration (IOM). https://www.migration dataportal.org/themes/forced- migration-or-displacement

Millar, G. (2018). Ethnographic peace research: The underappreciated benefits of long-term fieldwork. *International Peacekeeping, 25*(5), 653–676. https://doi.org/10.1080/13533312.2017.1421860

Misago, J. P. (2019). Linking governance and xenophobic violence in contemporary South Africa. *African Journal on Conflict Resolution (AJCR),* 2019(1). https://www.accord.org.za/ajcr-issues/linking-governance-and-xenophobic-violence-in- contemporary-south-africa/

Mitchell, C., & Hancock, L. E. (2012). Local peacebuilding and national peace: Interaction between grassroots and elite processes.

Mockaitis, T. (2011). Terrorism, insurgency, and organized crime. In P. Shemella (Ed.), *Fighting back: What governments can do about terrorism* (pp. 11–26). Redwood City: Stanford University Press. https://doi.org/10.1515/97808047 78220-004

Mokhoathi, J. (2020). Religious intersections in African Christianity: The conversion dilemma among indigenous converts. *Scriptura, 119,* 1–12. https://dx.doi.org/10.7833/118-1-1686

Møller, B. (2000). *The concept of security: The pros and cons of expansion and contraction.* Copenhagen Peace Research Institute. https://ciaotest.cc. columbia.edu/wps/mob01/

Moore, A. (2013). *Peacebuilding in practice: Local experience in two Bosnian towns.* Cornell University Press. https://doi.org/10.7591/9780801469565

Moore, J. (2007). *Beyond coercion: The durability of military power in the age of the market- military.* Cambridge University Press.

Mudasiru, S., Olushola, B., & Fatai, S. (2019). Conflicts and insurgency: Barriers to global quality health service for internally displaced persons in the North Eastern part of Nigeria. *African Journal of Political Science and International Relations, 13*(4), 40–52. https://doi.org/10.5897/AJPSIR2019.1157

Muhammad, U. M., & Salleh, M. A. (2024). Multi-national Joint Task Force and the fight against Boko-Haram insurgency: A study of Nigeria, Niger, Chad, and Cameroon republics. *African Journal of Politics and Administrative Studies (AJPAS), 17*(1), 733–757. https://doi.org/10.4314/ajpas.v17i1.36

Muzan, A. O. (2014). Insurgency in Nigeria: Addressing the causes as part of the solution. *African Human Rights Law Journal, 14*(2), 217–243. https://www.saflii.org/za/journals/AHRLJ/2014/13.pdf

Nagl, J. A. (2002). *Learning to eat soup with a knife: Counterinsurgency lessons from Malaya and Vietnam.* University of Chicago Press.

Nanda, B. R. (2012). The fight against racialism. In *Gandhi and his critics* (pp. 95–107). Oxford India Paperbacks. https://doi.org/10.1093/acprof:oso/978 195633634.003.0005

Netswera, M. M. (2023). Implications of municipal boundary determination on social integration of diverse communities in South Africa. *African Journal of Governance and Development, 12*(1), 43–61. https://doi.org/10.36369/ajgd.v12i1.40

Njuafac, T. A., & Katman, F. (2023). The socio-economic causes and consequences of Boko Haram terrorism in the 21st century: The case of Nigeria. *Russian Law Journal, 11*(6), 75–86.

Nsirim, O., Clement-Abraham, C., & Ajie, A. (2024). Enhancing national security and combating insurgency in Nigeria: The role of the library. *Southern African Journal of Security.* https://doi.org/10.25159/3005-4222/15742

Nwangwu, C. (2023). Neo-Biafra separatist agitations, state repression, and insecurity in South- East, Nigeria. *Sociology, 60*(1), 40–53. https://doi.org/10.1007/s12115-022-00782-0

Nwankpa, M. (2024). Understanding the role of women in Nigeria's non-state armed groups and security architecture. *Ifri Papers.* Ifri.

Nye, J. S. (2017). *The future of power.* Public Affairs.

Nyumba, T. O., Wilson, K., Derrick, C. J., & Mukherjee, N. (2018). The use of focus group discussion methodology: Insights from two decades of application in conservation. *Methods in Ecology and Evolution, 9*(1). https://besjournals.onlinelibrary.wiley.com/doi/full/10.1111/2041-210X.12860. https://doi.org/10.1111/2041-210X.12860

Odusola, A., Bandara, A., Dhliwayo, R., & Diarra, B. (n.d.). Inequalities and conflict in Africa: An empirical investigation. In *Income inequality trends in sub-Saharan Africa: Divergence, determinants, and consequences* (pp. 220–241). United Nations Development Programme (UNDP). https://www.undp.org/sites/g/files/zskgke326/files/migration/africa/undp-rba_Income-Inequality-in-SSA_Chapter-10.pdf

Okoli, A. C. (2019). Boko Haram insurgency and the necessity for trans-territorial forestland governance in the Lower Lake Chad Basin. *African Journal on Conflict Resolution, 2019*(1). https://www.accord.org.za/ajcr-issues/boko-haram-insurgency-and-the-necessity-for-trans-territorial-forestland-governance-in-the-lower-lake-chad-basin/

Oladeji, S. I., & Folorunso, B. A. (2006). The imperative of national security and stability for development process in contemporary Nigeria. *European Journal of Social Sciences, 2*(2), 290–303.

Olonisakin, A. G. (2016). Counterinsurgency: Is the quest for human rights a distraction or sine qua non? Paper presented at the 55th session of Nigerian Bar Association Conference, Abuja.

Omeni, A. (2017). *Counterinsurgency in Nigeria: The military and operations against Boko Haram, 2011–2017.* Routledge. https://doi.org/10.4324/9781315104287

Onapajo, H., & Ozden, K. (2020). Non-military approach against terrorism in Nigeria: Deradicalization strategies and challenges in countering Boko Haram. *Security Journal, 33*, 476–492. https://doi.org/10.1057/s41284-020-00238-2

Onuoha, F. C., & Ugwueze, M. I. (2020). Special operations forces, counter terrorism and counter insurgency operations in the Lake Chad area: The Nigerian experience. In U. A. Tar & B. Bashir (Eds.), *New architecture of regional security in Africa: Perspectives on counter-terrorism and counterin surgency in the Lake Chad Basin* (pp. 267–294). Lexington Books. https://doi.org/10.1057/s41284-020-00234-6

Onuoha, F. C., Nwangwu, C., & Ugwueze, M. I. (2020). Counterinsurgency operations of the Nigerian military and Boko Haram insurgency: Expounding the viscid manacle. *Security Journal, 33*, 401–426.

Onuoha, F. C., Oluwole, O., & Akogwu, C. J. (2023). Climate change and natural resource conflict in ECOWAS and ECCAS regions: Implications for state security forces. *African Journal on Conflict Resolution, 23*(2). https://www.accord.org.za/ajcr-issues/climate-change-and-natural-resource-conflict-in-ecowas-and-eccas-regions-implications-for-state-security-forces/. https://doi.org/10.17159/ajcr.v23i2.17636

Ordu, G. E.-O., & Nnam, M. U. (2017). Community policing in Nigeria: A critical analysis of current developments. *International Journal of Criminal Justice Sciences, 12*(1), 83–97. https://doi.org/10.5281/zenodo.345716

Osumah, O. (2013). Boko Haram insurgency in Northern Nigeria and the vicious cycle of internal insecurity. *Small Wars and Insurgencies, 24*(3), 536–560. https://doi.org/10.1080/09592318.2013.802605

Otto, G., & Ukpere, W. I. (2012). National security and development in Nigeria. *African Journal of Business Management, 6*(23), 6765–6770. http://www.academicjournals.org/AJBM. https://doi.org/10.5897/AJBM12.155

Owonikoko, B. S., & Onuoha, F. C. (2019). *Child of necessity: (AB) uses of the Civilian Joint Task Force in Borno State, Nigeria. Journal of African-Centred Solutions in Peace and Security, 3*(1), 27–108.

Paffenholz, T. (2015). Unpacking the local turn in peacebuilding: A critical assessment towards an agenda for future research. *Third World Quarterly, 36*(5), 857–874. https://doi.org/10.1080/01436597.2015.1029908

Paffenholz, T. (2021). Perpetual peacebuilding: A new paradigm to move beyond the linearity of liberal peacebuilding. *Journal of Intervention and Statebuilding, 15*(3), 367–385. https://doi.org/10.1080/17502977.2021.1925423

Paleri, P. (2008). *National security: Imperatives and challenges.* Tata McGraw-Hill. Paleri, P. (2008). *National security: Imperatives and challenges.* Tata McGraw-Hill.

Paterson, T. (2023). Unmasking ecological warfare – Shell-BP, Nigeria, and the movement for the survival of the Ogoni people [Thesis, Georgia State University]. https://doi.org/10.57709/2c7v-7f31

Pérouse de Montclos, M.-A. (Ed.). (2014). *Boko Haram: Islamism, politics, security and the state in Nigeria* (Vol. 2). African Studies Centre. https://horizon.documentation.ird.fr/exl-doc/pleins_textes/divers15-04/010064362.pdf. https://doi.org/10.4000/books.ifra.1703

Peters, R. (2007). Progress and peril: New counterinsurgency manual cheats on the history exam. *Armed Forces Journal International, 144*(1), 34–39.

Petraeus, D. H. (2010). Beyond the big war: Toward a new military strategy. *Foreign Affairs, 89*(1), 32–48.

Pew Research Center. (2015). *Religious composition of Nigeria.* https://www.pewresearch.org Philipsen, L. (2022). Three locals of peace: A typology of local capacities for peace. *Third World Quarterly, 43*(8), 1932–1949.

Piazza, J. A. (2007). Draining the swamp: Democracy promotion, state failure, and terrorism in 19 Middle Eastern countries. *Studies in Conflict and Terrorism, 30*(4), 521–539. http://www.tandfonline.com/doi/abs/10.1080/10576100701 329576. https://doi.org/10.1080/10576100701329576

Pringle, C. M. (2010). The risk of humanitarianism: Industry-specific political-security risk analysis for international agencies in conflict zones [Master's thesis, University of Stellenbosch]. Stellenbosch University. https://scholar. sun.ac.za/server/api/core/bitstreams/9d58b550-e2ad-4a09-819c-053428e5 a53e/content

Putnam, R. D. (2000). *Bowling alone: The collapse and revival of American community.* Simon and Schuster. https://doi.org/10.1145/358916.361990

Raffoul, A. W. (2019). Tackling the power-sharing dilemma? The role of mediation [Report]. Swisspeace. https://www.swisspeace.ch/assets/publications/ downloads/Reports/7df2350452/Power- sharing-and-mediation.pdf

Rafliana, I., Jalayer, F., Cerase, A., Cugliari, L., Baiguera, M., Salmanidou, D., ... & Hancilar, U. (2022). Tsunami risk communication and management: Contemporary gaps and challenges. *International Journal of Disaster Risk Reduction, 70*, 102771. https://doi.org/10.1016/j.ijdrr.2021.102771

Rahman, M. F., Falzon, D., Robinson, S. A., Kuhl, L., Westoby, R., Omukuti, J., ... & Nadiruzzaman, M. (2023). Locally led adaptation: Promise, pitfalls, and possibilities. *Ambio, 52*(10), 1543–1557. https://doi.org/10.1007/s13280-023-01884-7

Rakoto, A. D., & Rauchfuss, G. (Eds.). (2017). *Counterinsurgency: A generic reference curriculum.* NATO. https://www.nato.int/nato_static_fl2014/assets/pdf/pdf _2017_09/20170904_1709- counterinsurgency-rc.pdf

Rincón Barajas, J. A., Kubitza, C., & Lay, J. (2024). Large-scale acquisitions of communal land in the Global South: Assessing the risks and formulating policy recommendations. *Land Use Policy, 139*, 107054. https://doi.org/10. 1016/j.landusepol.2024.107054

Robinson, K. (2021, December 17). Understanding Sharia: The intersection of Islam and the law. *Council on Foreign Relations.* https://www.cfr.org/back grounder/understanding-sharia-intersection-islam-and-law

Rosenbaum, D. P., & Lurigio, A. J. (1994). Community policing: A promising practice in need of improved evaluation. *Criminology & Public Policy, 4*(1), 43–62.

Ruppel, S., & Leib, J. (2022). Same but different: The role of local leaders in the peace processes in Liberia and Sierra Leone. *Peacebuilding, 10*(4), 470–505. https://doi.org/10.1080/21647259.2022.2027152

Russo, J. (2022). Protecting peace? How the protection of civilians contributes to peace processes. *The Global Observatory.* https://theglobalobservatory. org/2022/05/protection-of-civilians-peace-processes

Sartori, G. (1984). *Social science concepts: A systematic analysis.* SAGE Publications.

Sedra, M. (Ed.). (2010). *The future of security sector reform.* The Centre for International Governance Innovation. https://www.cigionline.org/sites/default/ files/the_future_of_security_sector_reform.pdf

Seekings, J. (2003). Social stratification and inequality in South Africa at the end of apartheid (CSSR Working Paper No. 31). Centre for Social Science

Research, University of Cape Town. https://open.uct.ac.za/server/api/core/ bitstreams/a7c4bdf6-3fff-44bb-86fe- 5f36ca4e54ab/content

Sheldon, R. M. (2020). Introduction. *Small Wars & Insurgencies, 31*(5), 931– 955. https://doi.org/10.1080/09592318.2020.1764713

Simmel, G. (2021). *Sociology: Inquiries into the construction of social forms* (A. J. Blasi, A. K. Jacobs, & M. Kanjirathinkal, Trans. & Ed.; H. J. Helle, Intro.). Brill. (Original work published 1908)

Skjelderup, M. W., & Ainashe, M. (2023). Counterinsurgency as order-making: Refining the concepts of insurgency and counterinsurgency in light of the Somali civil war. *Small Wars & Insurgencies, 34*(6), 1180–1203. https://doi. org/10.1080/09592318.2023.2231203

Slaughter, A.-M. (2017, February 13). 3 responsibilities every government has towards its citizens. *World Economic Forum.* https://www.weforum.org/ agenda/2017/02/government-responsibility-to-citizens-anne-marie-slaughter/

Smith, M. G., & Whelan, J. (2008). Advancing human security: New strategic thinking for Australia. *Security Challenges, 4*(2), 1–22. http://www.jstor.org/ stable/26459139

Soomro, Z. A., Shah, M. H., & Ahmed, J. (2016). Information security management needs more holistic approach: A literature review. *International Journal of Information Management, 36*(2), 215–225. https://doi.org/10.1016/j.ijinfomgt. 2015.11.009

Stewart, F. (2005). Horizontal inequalities: A neglected dimension of development. In *Wider Perspectives on Global Development. Studies in Development Economics and Policy.* Palgrave Macmillan. https://doi.org/10.1057/9780230501850_5

Stringham, N., & Forney, J. (2017). It takes a village to raise a militia: Local politics, the Nuer White Army, and South Sudan's civil wars. *Journal of Modern African Studies, 55*(2), 177–199. https://doi.org/10.1017/S0022278X1 7000064

Terre des Hommes Switzerland. (2024, June 27). A holistic approach to security. https://www.terredeshommesschweiz.ch/en/security-with-a-holistic-approach/

Thompson, R. W. (1967). *Defeating Communist insurgency: The lessons of Malaya and Vietnam.* Chatto & Windus.

U.S. Department of State. (2009). *U.S. government counterinsurgency guide.* Bureau of Political-Military Affairs. https://2009-2017.state.gov/documents/ organization/119629.pdf

U.S. Department of State. (2022). *2022 report on international religious freedom: Nigeria.* https://www.state.gov/reports/2022-report-on-international-religious -freedom/nigeria/

Ulusoy, H. (2003). Revisiting security communities after the Cold War: The constructivist perspective. *Perceptions: Journal of International Affairs, 8*(3), 1–22. https://doi.org/10.1515/9780773571549-003

UNHCR. (2019). *Global trends: Forced displacement in 2019.* United Nations High Commissioner for Refugees. https://www.unhcr.org/flagship-reports/global trends/globaltrends2019/

United Nations. (2012). *The corporate responsibility to respect human rights: An interpretive guide* (HR/PUB/12/02). https://www.ohchr.org/sites/default/ files/Documents/publications/hr.puB.12.2_en.pdf

Usman, S. A. (2015). Unemployment and poverty as sources and consequences of insecurity in Nigeria: The Boko Haram insurgency revisited. *African Journal of Political Science and International Relations, 9*(3), 90–99. https://doi.org/10.5897/AJPSIR2014.0719

van Aarde, T. A. (2018). The relation between religion and state in Islam and Christianity in the rise of ISIS. *In die Skriflig, 52*(1), 1–11. https://dx.doi.org/10.4102/ids.v52i1.2244

Von Boemcken, M., & Schetter, C. (2016). Think Piece 09: Security – What is it? What does it do? https://www.fes.de/e/think-piece-09-security-what-is-it-what-does-it-do

Walker, A. (2012). *What is Boko Haram?* (Special Report 308). United States Institute of Peace. https://www.usip.org/sites/default/files/SR308.pdf

Watson, D. C. (2023). Rethinking inter-communal violence in Africa. *Civil Wars*, 1–30. https://doi.org/10.1080/13698249.2023.2180924

Weiner, A. S. (2006). The use of force and contemporary security threats: Old medicine for new ills? *Stanford Law Review, 59*(2), 415–504. http://www.jstor.org/stable/40040302

Wivel, A. (2019, January 7). Security dilemma. *Encyclopedia Britannica.* https://www.britannica.com/topic/security-dilemma

Wolff, J. (2022, March). The local turn and the Global South in critical peacebuilding studies (PRIF Working Paper No. 57). Peace Research Institute Frankfurt (PRIF). https://www.prif.org/fileadmin/user_upload/PRIF_WP_57.pdf

Wright, H. (2022, December 29). Critical ethnography in national security institutions: Methodological and ethical reflections. *PS: Political Science and Politics.* https://politicalsciencenow.com/critical-ethnography-in-national-security-institutions-methodological-and-ethical-reflections/. https://doi.org/10.1017/S1049096522000762

Yin, R. (2014). *Case study research: Design and methods* (5th ed.). Sage Publications.

Yusuf, A., & Mohd, S. (2022). Growth and fiscal effects of insecurity on the Nigerian economy. *The European Journal of Development Research.* Advance online publication. https://doi.org/10.1057/s41287-022-00531-3

Zambernardi, L. (2010). Counterinsurgency's impossible trilemma. *The Washington Quarterly, 33*(3), 21–34. https://doi.org/10.1080/0163660X.2010.492722

www.ingramcontent.com/pod-product-compliance
Lightning Source LLC
Chambersburg PA
CBHW072122020426
42334CB00018B/1681